The Call of Memory

The Call of Memory:
Learning About the Holocaust Through Narrative
An Anthology

Karen Shawn and Keren Goldfrad, Editors
William Younglove, Associate Editor

Ben Yehuda Press

Published by Ben Yehuda Press
430 Kensington Road
Teaneck, NJ 07666

http://www.BenYehudaPress.com

Ben Yehuda Press books may be purchased for educational, business or sales promotional use. For information, please contact:
Special Markets, Ben Yehuda Press
430 Kensington Road, Teaneck, NJ 07666.
markets@BenYehudaPress.com.

ISBN13 978-0-9789980-0-4
ISBN 0-9789980-0-6

Cover illustration: "Transports" © 1985 Netty Vanderpol

07 08 09 / 10 9 8 7 6 5 4 3 2 1

Acknowledgments

This work was made possible, in part, by generous grants from

- The Sara, Shulamit, and Joseph Lapidus Fund
- The Sarna Family Holocaust Education Fund
- The Estate of Dr. Kenneth H. Wickwire

This book would never have come to be had it not been for the contributions of the following people:

Mark and Anita Sarna, whose great generosity and belief in this work have always been a source of strength and inspiration.

Debbie Nahshon, whose support has been crucial and unwavering; we thank her for awarding the book the Lapidus Fund Grant.

Lolle Boettcher, whose friendship and support came exactly when it was needed most.

The fall 2005 class in Holocaust literature at Yeshiva College, whose young undergraduates were extraordinary readers and thinkers, and the spring 2007 class at Yeshiva University's Azrieli Graduate School of Jewish Education and Administration, whose students' keen eyes helped to perfect these pages.

Bernard Gotfryd and Susan Prinz Shear, survivor and child of survivors respectively, who contributed their friendship along with their memorable and personal stories.

Netty Vanderpol, whose cover needlepoint memorial urges readers to learn this history.

Eve Yudelson and Larry Yudelson, our publishers at Ben Yehuda Press.

Karen Shawn, Keren Goldfrad, and William Younglove
October 2007

"No cry of distress can be greater than that of one person ...
The whole world cannot be in more distress than one soul."

—Ludwig Wittgenstein

Contents

Acknowledgments   vii
Preface   *Keren Goldfrad*   xiii
Introduction   *Karen Shawn*   xviii

In the Beginning

The Hunt   *Aharon Appelfeld*   3
No Way Out:
Letters from the Holocaust *Susan Prinz Shear*   14
Prelude   *Albert Halper*   44

The Gathering Storm

The End   *Ida Fink*   57
The Threshold   *Ida Fink*   61
An Evening Guest   *Elie Wiesel*   67

Under Occupation

Fear of Fear   *Ilse Aichinger*   77
A Chicken for the Holidays *Bernard Gotfryd*   96
Grandson   *Clara Asscher-Pinkhof*   104
White Lie   *Clara Asscher-Pinkhof*   107

Daily Life in the Ghetto

A Cupboard in the Ghetto   *Rachmil Bryks*   113
Bread   *Isaiah Spiegel*   121
The Last Morning   *Bernard Gotfryd*   131
On Guilt   *Bernard Gotfryd*   139

Choiceless Choices

A Conversation   *Ida Fink*   151
Aryan Papers   *Ida Fink*   155

The Gray Zone

Kurt   *Bernard Gotfryd*   163
Helmut Reiner   *Bernard Gotfryd*   170
By the Railway Track   *Zofia Nalkowska*   181

The Abyss

Yom Kippur: The Day
Without Forgiveness   *Elie Wiesel*   189
The Shawl   *Cynthia Ozick*   196

Sparks of Humanity

The Camp Blanket   *Sara Nomberg-Przytyk*   205

Trying to Start Anew

An Encounter in Linz   *Bernard Gotfryd*   213
The Watch   *Elie Wiesel*   220
An Old Acquaintance   *Elie Wiesel*   225

The Second Generation and Beyond

Adam   *Kurt Vonnegut, Jr.*   241
The Name   *Aharon Megged*   250

About the Authors   267
About the Cover   275

Echoes: A Preface
Keren Goldfrad

Every night she prayed:

Dear God,

Help my father sleep peacefully tonight. Help him
get through the night without waking up from
his anguished nightmares. Help him, for I cannot
bear to hear his frightful screams.

Day after day I air out my parents' room and fluff
up their pillows before they come back from work,
in the hope that my father will be lulled into a
cozy and tranquil sleep. I pray that tonight he
will not relive his past and think about his children, wife and other family members who were
murdered during the war. Help him sleep, so that
I may sleep as well and be able to focus tomorrow
in school.

Please God, don't forget my mother. Help her
get up in the morning without passing out. Every
morning she walks to the bathroom and then we
hear her body slump to the floor. It is because of
the war, the doctors say, that dreadful war...

She was not able to discuss her distress with any family member, for there was an unspoken taboo forbidding the mention of

anything that would bring up the past. The Holocaust was over, so her parents thought, and the tendency was to try and save their sanity by disconnecting themselves from that excruciatingly painful past. They had married in a Displaced Persons' camp in Litomerice, Czechoslovakia, became parents of two daughters, and came to Israel on a ship, determined to bury their past in Europe and create a new life for themselves and their two baby daughters. Years later, my mother, the younger of the two, is still haunted by her father's grief-stricken screams and her mother's difficult mornings.

My father and his twin brother were also born in a DP camp in Bayreuth, Germany, to two Holocaust survivors. Despite the fact that my grandparents found a comfortable house to live in after the war, they decided to leave that cursed and treacherous land and waited for certifications that would grant them an entrance to the Land of Israel. Throughout the years, neither of my parents dared to bring up the subject of the Holocaust with their parents, and they both recall that silent agreement. They felt a responsibility to protect their parents and shelter them, for they had suffered more than conceivably possible for one lifetime. The common tendency in Israel at the time that my parents were growing up was to start a new life in this newfound country and repress past experiences, as Dalia Ofer (1996) explains in her article "Israel Reacts to the Holocaust":

> The general atmosphere in the country did not encourage discussion about the past, for it was considered a hindrance to the survivors' rehabilitation. The future was what counted, with new assignments and hopes and a strong denial of bonds with the Diaspora ... the formal policy for counselors was specifically not to provide a time or place for a discussion of the past. As far as they were concerned, the beginning of the survivors' new lives was the date of their immigration (p. 864).

So strong was this communal decision to begin a new epoch that when my father was recruited into the army, he was commanded to change his foreign-sounding name to an Israeli name within 24 hours. He hurriedly consulted his twin brother and they decided on the Israeli-sounding name Shachar, which resembles their Polish name Shtrochlitz. In addition to its phonological semblance, the Hebrew word shachar means "dawn" and therefore symbolizes a new and bright beginning. "For many survivors, though, their names were the only remembrance they might have of their lost families" (p. 865). Retaining this inner conflict of starting anew and at the same time remembering their lost family members, the twins continue to use the Israeli-sounding name, Shachar, whereas their younger brother, who was born in Israel, kept the paternal family name, Shtrochlitz. It is quite apparent, therefore, that despite the unspoken taboo, the distancing of the past, and the willingness to start anew, the echo of the past reverberated loudly throughout my parents' childhood and adulthood.

That same echo silently crept into our childhood. My siblings and I grew up in the shadows of the Holocaust. All four of our grandparents went through the concentration camps, where their mothers and fathers, aunts and uncles, sisters and brothers, wife, husband, daughter, son, and infant baby were murdered by the Nazis. We knew that we had to finish the food on our plates, for food should not be thrown out nor complained about. We knew too well that many people during the Holocaust would have given their lives for another piece of dry bread. We knew that we have very few relatives in this world because they were all killed somewhere in Europe. We knew, and yet there was so much we did not know, still do not know, and will never fully know or understand.

The Holocaust is historically over, but the mental, physical, and spiritual devastation that these people suffered is not over. Many do not perceive that even today, the "repercussions and consequences [of the Holocaust] are still actively evolving" (Felman

& Laub, 1992, p. xiv). The implications of the Holocaust are not limited only to their direct impact on the surviving victims and their immediate descendants. Rather, the Holocaust has much wider and broader implications and "should be recognized as a turning point in world history, a catastrophe that altered fundamental assumptions about the human condition" (Kremer, 1989, p. 7). The catastrophic effects of the Holocaust shook the seemingly fortified, intellectual, and ethical culture of the 20th Century. As Donald Schwartz (1990) writes: "The Holocaust is an unsettling subject, one that seriously questions basic assumptions about our society and its values" (p. 101). Indeed, many philosophers and researchers are reevaluating fundamental cultural issues in every sphere of life, for the disaster that befell the Jewish people is the disaster of the entire civilized world.

There is a famous Hassidic legend about the Ba'al Shem Tov, who was the founder of the Hassidic movement. According to the legend, the Ba'al Shem Tov knew a prayer that was to be recited at a specific time and place on a flame that was lit in the heart of a forest; a prayer that would be heard by G-d and had the power to prevent a disaster. After the Ba'al Shem Tov passed away, his student was asked to follow in his footsteps. The student knew the timing and the place of the prayer and even knew how to kindle the fire, but, alas, he did not know the prayer itself; nevertheless, this sufficed. His prayer was heard and answered by G-d, and a disaster was averted. When this student passed away, the student's student had to carry out the task. He did not know the exact place in the forest, nor the timing of the prayer. He did not know the prayer itself, but he did have the right intention. This pure intention, which relied on the teachings of his predecessors, helped him devise his own prayer, and this sufficed for the prayer to be heard and the disaster was once again prevented.

Testimonies and narratives of Holocaust survivors, born of personal tribulations, serve historians' records by providing primary sources for documentation, as well as by assisting in the reconstruction of particular events. Some witnesses did manage to gather enough strength after the war to produce a testimony that could somehow ford the unbridgeable chasm between the dead and the living. The narratives in this volume offer an individual perspective and dimension to the existing historical data. Yehuda Bauer (1983) says that people who did not experience the horrors of the Shoah cannot be "in the heart of the forest" and can never be able to fully comprehend the extent of those horrors. Nevertheless, we can learn from the narratives of those who were there, even though their words are merely echoes of the Holocaust reality.

In this anthology you will read short narratives of survivors who were "in the heart of the forest," and narratives of survivors' descendants who "do not know the prayer itself" but heard first-hand testimonies from their parents of those traumatic events. In addition, you will read narratives of people who do not have a direct relation to the Holocaust, but who have the "pure intention" of writing about it while relying on survivors' testimonies and historical data with the goal of enabling future generations to carry through the ages the memory of what was, so that it will never be forgotten.

References

Bauer, Y. (1983). Against mystification—The Holocaust as a historical period. Appeared in Hebrew in Biymay Shoah Upkuda. Unit 1–2. Tel Aviv: Open University Press.

Felman, S. & Laub, D. (1992). Testimony: Crises of witnessing in literature psychoanalysis, and history. New York: Routledge.

Kremer, L. S. (1989). Witness through the imagination. MI: Wayne State University Press.

Ofer, D. (1996). "Israel reacts to the Holocaust." In Wyman, D. S., (Ed.). The world reacts to the Holocaust, pp. 836–923. Baltimore, MD: The Johns Hopkins University Press.

Schwartz, D. (1990). "Who will tell them after we're gone?" Reflections on teaching the Holocaust. The History Teacher 23:2, pp. 95-110.

Introduction
Karen Shawn

In the literature of the Holocaust, there is conveyed that
which cannot be transmitted by a thousand facts and figures.
—Albert H. Friedlander

Gideon Hausner (1966), attorney general of Israel and prosecutor in the trial of Adolf Eichmann, was convinced, as he constructed his case and later wrote, that

> the story of a particular set of events, told by a single witness, is still tangible enough to be visualized. Put together, the various narratives of different people about diverse experiences would be concrete enough to be apprehended. In this way I hoped to superimpose on a phantom a dimension of reality (p. 292).

Hausner was an early proponent of the idea "that, for those who did not experience it firsthand, fullest comprehension of the Holocaust might come not through study of its immensity, but by ... the recollected and reconstructed experience of individual survivors" (Farrant, 1989, p. 25).

For this literature anthology, the only one of its kind specifically developed for use in high school, college, and graduate studies, we chose 23 such survivor narratives as well as four other stories by authors whose creative ability to render precisely the "reconstructed experience" of those who were there further enrich our understanding of survivors, their children, and future generations that will live in the wake of the Holocaust. A brief biographical note about each author is included.

What Is Narrative?

Narrative may be defined as "a story of events, experiences, or the like, whether true or fictitious; it is the general term for a story long or short; of past, present, or future; factual or imagined; told for any purpose, and with or without much detail" (Stein, 1981, p. 951). Broader and more inclusive than such synonyms as chronicle, tale, memoir, or story, narrative precisely describes the literature of the Holocaust presented here, a collection of testimonial memoirs, recollected experiences, creative nonfiction, and individual, experienced truths.

Why Narrative?

Libowitz (1988) defines the initial task of Holocaust education as raising the consciousness of students, leading them "to a realization of the enormity of the event itself" (p. 63). To achieve this, we believe, as Hausner (1961) concluded, that we cannot "let [only] the archives speak," because "the whole extent of the Jewish catastrophe surpasses human comprehension"; we also need "a living record," witnesses "who could tell a tiny fragment of what [they] had seen and experienced" (pp. 291-292). In 1961, Hausner invited survivors to come to the trial in person to tell their stories; almost a half-century later, we must depend on their stories one step removed—on paper in the form of literature, its artistic expression and structure allowing us, the readers, to recognize the humanity "behind the mounting totals of victims" (p. 292).

It is "the unique significance of literature that enables us to 'live through' an experience that is not our own but that ... we make our own. ... This 'living through'... is capable of altering the very grain of our being. ... Literature is a supremely potent mode of significant experience" (Thomson, 1987, p. 65). We recognize, however, that teaching the Holocaust in the United States and in Israel more typically falls to the social scientist—the historian, the teacher of history—than to the teacher of literature, and that an offering in that context may well be a survey course replete with requisite research papers, essays, data, examinations, but absent any literature at all. Yet more than 30 years ago, Rosenblatt (1976) affirmed the complementary relationship between literature and the social sciences, noting the immediate, personal impact of the former and the objective, analytic experience of the latter. She asked,

> Will the history of the Great Depression impress [the student] as much as will Steinbeck's *The Grapes of Wrath*? ... Obviously, the analytic approach needs no defense. But may not literary materials contribute powerfully to the student's images of the world, himself, and the human condition? (p. 8).

Like Rosenblatt, whose seminal text *Literature as Exploration* (1938) has influenced teachers for almost seven decades, we believe that literature, in addition to its intrinsic value, is a necessary complement to the history text. Literature humanizes, concretizes, and specifies the general and the abstract; it enhances the study of history by adding both immediacy and lasting value as students come to recognize the reciprocity between broad implications and their particulars, between generalizations about civilization, government, and conflict and the conduct of real people. It is instructive, then, that Hausner decided that the case against Eichmann "would rest on two main pillars ... documents and oral evidence" (p. 291).

We believe that teaching the Holocaust without literature is insufficient for at least three reasons. First, "rational and factual analysis cannot, by its very nature, serve as an exclusive instrument in grasping and understanding those processes in which the irrational exceeds the rational" (Schatzker, 1980, p. 224).

Second, such teaching does not take into account the phenomenon that students, confronted by facts and figures only, may, ironically, use these facts and figures to avoid knowing about the reality of the event. Revelation, sensitization, reflection, evaluation, and the desire to learn more, if those are among our goals, are "rarely achieved through the memorization of place names, dates, or numbers; in the case of the Holocaust, those are the 'trivial' details ... which will actually impede attainment of the educational desiderata" (Libowitz, 1988, p. 63).

Third, as Hausner understood,

> Our perceptions and our senses are geared to limited experiences. ... There is a limited intensity of horrors that our minds can grasp; any further piling up of shocks fails to register—it makes us recoil and leaves us blank. We stop perceiving living creatures ... they turn into incomprehensible statistics (p. 292).

Stories neither replace nor conflict with history; instead, they help us to understand it more fully, making the complex ideas and events of the Holocaust personally significant. "History records the events and compiles the statistics, and literature translates the events and statistics into real things happening to real people. Each without the other is inadequate; together, they provide a window into the truth" (Drew, 2001, p. 23).

Thus, we offer these literary narratives to help readers enter what Elie Wiesel has called "the kingdom of fire and ashes," to help them explore this event that has forever altered human sensibilities, and to help them listen as each story speaks of the one within the 6 million, of the Jews as vital and vibrant individuals even as they were nameless victims, of particular acts of dignity, resistance, courage, and righteousness. We offer these narratives because we agree that

ultimately, it will most probably be literature that
will give us the most faithful picture of the Jewish catastrophe in Europe, thanks to the quali-
ties and attributes that exist only in literature and
that have secured for literature its place in human
culture and civilization, where it can never be replaced. Aristotle was wise when he gave priority
to poets over historians in the effort to find the
truth (Lustig, 1979, p. 312).

Why Short Story Narratives?

The short story lends itself "to better techniques of reading
through sensitivity to diction, tone, structure, image, symbol,
narrative movement ... to make the more refined responses that
are ultimately the source of human understanding and sensitivity to human values" (Rosenblatt, 1995, p. 276). Master teachers
and professors from the United States, Israel, and Australia chose
stories that they know from classroom experience will engage
readers; when students are involved, their sensitivity to the story
structure enhances their understanding of the story's implications. "A reciprocal process emerges, in which growth in human
understanding and literary sophistication sustain and nourish
one another" (p. 52).

Why These Short Stories?

Our goal was to design an anthology of unsurpassed literary
merit, of "extraordinary work[s] of witness and of art" (Prose,
2006, p. 6) that educators would find engrossing, historically ac-
curate, immediately teachable, and appropriate for a wide range of
students. We wanted stories that, through their power, imagery,
and brevity, would "put before the reader life's harshest enigmas
with clarity and compassion" (Siegel, 2007, p. 12), capturing and
holding the interest of students and provoking them to want to
read more. We identified nine criteria guiding our selection of

narratives; each principle was determined with our audience and objectives in mind (Shawn, 1994, 2001).

First, we chose stories that help those who were not there enter imaginatively and vicariously into the experiences of those who were. Stories narrated by a survivor and told in the first person are intimate, immediate, and authentic; they engage and enfold the listener/reader in the reconstructed telling. We chose six of survivor Bernard Gotfryd's stories, for example, because they are the next best thing to having him come in person into our classrooms.

Next, we chose stories that are developmentally appropriate, presenting the truth without unduly traumatizing the adolescent and young adult reader. Thus, four selections can be comfortably taught to students in most eighth-grade classrooms: Albert Halper's "Prelude," Clara Asscher-Pinkhof's "Grandson" and "White Lie," and Bernard Gotfryd's "A Chicken for the Holidays," while the others are suitable only for older readers.

Unduly, of course, is a subjective term; we struggled with the concern expressed by Chaim Schatzker (1980):

> Careful attention should be paid to the proper age of the students and to the content with which [they] can be confronted without causing harm and without leading to a total rejection of the entire subject. The problem is how to present the truth without causing dangerous mental consequences—how to impress without traumatizing (p. 222).

Lest his and our concerns seem old-fashioned for today's know-all generation, psychologist Daniel Goleman (2006) offers scientific support for them:

> The emotional centers of the brain are intricately interwoven with the neurocortical areas involved in cognitive learning. When

a child trying to learn is caught up in a distressing emotion, the centers for learning are temporarily hampered. The child's attention becomes preoccupied with whatever may be the source of the trouble. Because attention is itself a limited capacity, the child has that much less ability to hear, understand, or remember what a teacher or a book is saying. In short, there is a direct link between emotions and learning (http://www.danielgoleman.info/sel/index.html).

Thus, the stories that are most graphic, such as Cynthia Ozick's "The Shawl"; that deal with particularly sensitive moral dilemmas, such as Ida Fink's "A Conversation" and "Aryan Papers"; and those that deal with especially difficult concepts, such as Aharon Appelfeld's "The Hunt" and Ilse Aichinger's "Fear of Fear" should be used judiciously, if at all, with students below 12th grade. Age-appropriate options represent a modified "spiral curriculum" and reflect the thinking of Jerome Bruner (1960), who reasoned,

> If it is granted ... that it is desirable to give children an awareness of the meaning of human tragedy and a sense of compassion for it, is it not possible at the earliest appropriate age to teach the literature of tragedy in a manner that illuminates but does not threaten? ... In time, one goes beyond to more complex versions of the same literature. ... What matters is that later teaching builds upon earlier reactions to literature, that it seeks to create an ever more explicit and mature understanding of the literature of tragedy (pp. 52–53).

Third, we chose stories that are rooted in a historical context and reflect a historical reality, and we organized them chronologically. Susan Prinz Shear's "No Way Out: Letters from the Holocaust" is epistolary literature, a story told through the letters sent among members of her family between the years 1938–1947.

Ilse Aichinger's "Fear of Fear" is a fictionalized account of aspects of her childhood as a *Mischling*, while Bernard Gotfryd's "A Chicken for the Holidays," "The Last Morning," "On Guilt," "Kurt," "Helmut Reiner," and "An Encounter in Linz" are virtual testimonies written with an artist's sensibility.

While fiction about the Holocaust must be used with great caution, we recognize, as Francine Prose (2006) notes, that

> the liberties and devices of fiction (dialogue, voice, characterization, and so forth) enable the writer to take us into the mind and heart of a person not unlike ourselves who talks to us from a distant period and place, and so becomes our guide to its sights and sounds ... [and] sorrows (p. 6).

The four pieces of fiction we included are wide-ranging in their distant period and place. Albert Halper's "Prelude" is set in 1938 Chicago; Cynthia Ozick's "The Shawl" drags us into Auschwitz; Kurt Vonnegut's "Adam" brings us again to Chicago in the early post-Holocaust years, while Aharon Megged's "The Name" unfolds in Israel, helping us to understand the perspective of survivors and their Israeli children and grandchildren. Each depicts the truth of those times and places with the highest degree of accuracy, reflecting authentic dialogue, dilemmas, feelings, and experiences.

Fourth, we chose stories that personalize the statistics and foster compassion and involvement, that prompt readers to want to sense the feelings and understand the experiences of another person. We recognize that we are, of course, outsiders to the suffering, but as Baum (1996) points out, "We cannot simply stand away from Holocaust victims and feel sorry for them"; we should instead "try to understand more fully their emotions and actions, through empathy" (p. 48). "Empathy," Baum continues, "holds out the promise that the distance that separates individual experiences can be bridged, that memory might be used in building compassion towards others." According to Goleman (2007), empathy is "the prime inhibitor of human cruelty" (cited in Matousek, p. 38). Thus the narratives speak of one particular person, family, theme, situation, event, or country in a language that faithfully portrays the feelings of the victim. Clara Asscher-Pinkhof's "Grandson" and "White Lie," for example, detail unforgettable moments of daily life for two children in Amsterdam through the voice and sensibility of each child, while Albert Halper's "Prelude" captures, in its distinctly American idiom, the frustration and fear of American Jewish teens in 1938, bullied by thugs and ignored by bystanders. The stories engage and affect students through the quality of the writing, the age and appeal of the characters, the poignancy of the plot, and the power of the theme. They "carry both literal truthfulness and a larger Truth, told with a clear voice, with grace" (Gerard, 1996, p. 208).

Fifth, we selected stories that feature, rather than marginalize, the Jewish experience during the Holocaust. They highlight particular Jewish responses, as in, for example, Elie Wiesel's "An Evening Guest" and "Yom Kippur: The Day Without Forgiveness"; Bernard Gotfryd's "A Chicken for the Holidays"; and Rachmil Bryks's "A Cupboard in the Ghetto," rather than such other aspects as the actions of the perpetrators. The predominant focus is on Jews *as they lived*, rather than as they died. Narratives such as these help students understand the concept of religious and spiritual resistance and address the question "How did people summon the will to live?"

Sixth, we chose stories that have the potential to motivate students to examine their own lives and behavior and effect change where possible, "to make their emotions" evoked by these readings "useful in their present lives" Baum, 1996, p. 2). Pierre Sauvage (1988) asserts,

> One can never be the same after ... realiz[ing] that it is possible for man to hate that much ... to love that little. What one *does* with that know-

> ledge, what lessons one derives ... has the power
> to shape how we live, perhaps to determine our
> very ability to live (p. 526).

Rosenberg (1988) elaborates, positing that understanding the Holocaust should, theoretically, "radically change how one experiences and acts in the world" and that students would come to evaluate both their "own behavior and that of one's society" through the lens of the Holocaust. "Those who integrate the Holocaust into consciousness," he says, "find that their world becomes a different world and that they must generate a new way to be in the new world" (p. 380).

Thus, our collection includes Bernard Gotfryd's "Kurt" and Sara Nomberg-Przytyk's "The Camp Blanket," which present the possibility of noble actions even in the heart of evil. As Hausner (1966) wrote, "There were, after all, sparks of humanity even in Nazi Germany [;] it was all-important to know it, to sustain a belief in the morality of man" (p. 297). We include Elie Wiesel's "The Watch" and "An Old Acquaintance," which, by their haunting portrayal of the aftermath of Holocaust trauma, promote opportunities to explore universal issues and themes inherent in the recognition of this century's ongoing genocides. We include Kurt Vonnegut's "Adam" and Aharon Megged's "The Name," stories that provide a bridge from the world of the Holocaust to the second, third, and fourth generations beyond.

Seventh, we chose stories by authors forever linked to Holocaust literature, such as Elie Wiesel, and by those never linked, such as Kurt Vonnegut; stories by victims, such as Isaiah Spiegel and Rachmil Bryks, and by horrified witnesses, such as the Polish writer Zofia Nalkowska; and stories written during the catastrophe and those written decades after, to ensure a broad perspective on the experience. As Aaron (1990) notes, literature created during the Holocaust "lays bare insiders' perspectives on the events in the very process of their unfolding. ... [I]t shows how the condemned people felt and what they thought, how they responded to life and death" (p. 14). Literature written as events occur is different from the literature of memoirs, since memory selects and thus reshapes to some extent the details of the past. Those written during and immediately after the catastrophe include Susan Prinz Shear's "No Way Out: Letters from the Holocaust," "Albert Halper's "Prelude," Clara Asscher-Pinkhof's "Grandson" and "White Lie," Isaiah Spiegel's "Bread," Rachmil Bryks's "A Cupboard in the Ghetto," and Zofia Nalkowska's "By the Railroad Track." By these inclusions, we honor the mission of such writers, which "was, among other things, to have an audience in generations to come" (p. 2).

Eighth, we chose stories that offer great flexibility and opportunity in the classroom. Each is short, relatively easy to read and discuss, and stands on its own merits as fine literature; none requires unreasonable preparation on the part of a teacher beyond a basic knowledge of Holocaust history and familiarity with the references offered in the companion *Teacher's Guide* (Shawn & Goldfrad, 2007); yet each lays the groundwork for subsequent additional learning of that history. These stories and their guides, arranged thematically within their chronological framework, provide the means for engagement that may encourage students to explore and analyze the social, political, and historical issues that underlie the narrative, to leave their "experience of the literary work eager to learn what the ... historian [has] to offer" (Rosenblatt, 1995, pp. 114–115).

Hausner (1966) wrote, "Human nature finds it painful to look unflinchingly at the horrors of the past; it is very quick to forget them" (p. 447). Finally, then, we chose works by and about survivors who we believe would, if they could, "compel the world to confront its yesterdays anew" by telling their stories directly to you, the teachers and students who will read this book. Valentino Achak Deng, a Sudanese refugee and character in *What Is the What: The Autobiography of Valentino Achak Deng: A Novel* (Eggers, as cited in Prose, 2006), gives voice to the determination of such survivors when his own story of survival of a much more recent "yesterday" concludes,

> Whatever I do ... I will tell these stories. ... I speak to you because I cannot help it. ... I will tell stories to people who will listen and to people who don't want to listen, to people who seek me out and to those who run. All the while I will know that you are there. How can I pretend that you do not exist? It would be almost as impossible as you pretending that I do not exist (p. 6).

You exist; survivors exist. Come and read their stories.

References

Aaron, F. W. (1990). *Bearing the unbearable: Yiddish and Polish poetry in the ghettos and concentration camps.* Albany: State University of New York Press.

Baum, R. N. (1996). "What I have learned to feel": The pedagogical emotions of Holocaust education. *College literature,* 23 (3): 44–57.

Bruner, J. (1960). *The process of education.* Cambridge: Harvard University Press.

Drew, M. A. (2001). Teaching Holocaust literature: Issues, caveats, and suggestions. In S. Totten (Ed.), *Teaching _Holocaust literature* (pp. 11–23). Boston: Allyn and Bacon.

Farrant, Patricia A. (1989, April). On the necessity of reading Holocaust literature. In *Peace/Shalom after atrocity* (pp. 23–29). Greensburg, PA: The National Catholic Center for Holocaust Education, Seton Hill College.

Friedlander, A. H. (1968). *Out of the whirlwind: A reader of Holocaust literature.* New York: Union of American Hebrew Congregations.

Gerard, P. (1996). *Creative nonfiction: Researching and crafting stories of real life.* Cincinnati: Story Press.

Goleman, D. (2006). Social and emotional learning. Article on D. Goleman's Web site and blog retrieved December 20, 2006, from http://www.danielgoleman.info/sel/index.html.

Hausner, G. (1966). *Justice in Jerusalem.* New York: Holocaust Library.

Libowitz, R. (1988). Asking the questions: Background and recommendations for Holocaust study. In Z. Garber (Ed.), *Methodology in the academic teaching of the Holocaust* (pp. 57–73). New York: University Press of America.

Lustig, A. (1979). Appendix to J. Knopp, Holocaust literature II: Novels and short stories. In S. L. Sherwin & S. G. Ament (Eds.), *Encountering the Holocaust: An interdisciplinary survey* (p. 312). Chicago: Impact Press.

Matousek, M. (2007, January & February). We're wired to connect. In *AARP The Magazine,* 36–38.

Prose, F. (2006, December 24). The lost boy. [Review of the book *What is the what: The autobiography of Valentino Achak Deng: A novel.*] *The New York Times Book Review,* 1, 6.

Rosenberg, A. (1988). The crisis in knowing and understanding the Holocaust. In A. Rosenberg & G. E. Meyers (Eds.), *Echoes from the Holocaust: Philosophical reflections on a dark time* (pp. 379–395). Philadelphia: Temple University Press.

Rosenblatt, Louise M. (1938). *Literature as exploration* (1st ed.). New York: Appleton-Century.

_____ (1976). (3rd ed.). New York: Noble and Noble.

_____ (1995). (5th ed.). New York: The Modern Language Association of America.

Sauvage, P. (1988, July). Learning hope from the Holocaust. *Remembering for the future: Jews and Christians during and after the Holocaust*, International Scholars' Conference, Oxford University, United Kingdom (pp. 526–540). Oxford: Pergamon Press.

Schatzker, C. (1980, July). The teaching of the Holocaust: Dilemmas and considerations. *The annals of the American academy of political and social science*. 450, 219–226.

Shawn, K. (2001) Choosing Holocaust literature for early adolescents. In S. Totten & S. Feinberg (Eds.), *Teaching and studying the Holocaust*. Boston: Allyn and Bacon.

_____ (1994). "What should they read and when should they read it?" A selective review of Holocaust literature for students in grades two through twelve. *Dimensions: A journal of Holocaust studies*, 8 (2): G1–16.

Shawn, K. & Goldfrad, K. (2007). *The call of memory: Learning about the Holocaust through narrative: A teacher's guide*. Teaneck, NJ: Ben Yehuda Press.

Siegel, L. (2007, January 21). Maestro of the human ego. [Review of the book *The castle in the forest*.] *The New York Times Book Review*, 12.

Stein, J. (Ed.). (1981). *The Random House dictionary of the English language: The unabridged edition*. New York: Random House.

Thomson, J. (1987). *Understanding teenagers' reading: Reading processes and the teaching of literature*. New York: Nichols Publishing Company.

In the Beginning

The Hunt

Aharon Appelfeld

Translated from the Hebrew by Nicholas de Lang

The song of the oars was gradually broken up and silenced. Stray voices still continued to sing to themselves like echoes; fire glided on the surface of the water. The boats were drawn into the ever-narrowing channel: and the rhythmic singing, remembered through generations, left silence behind it.

It was a slack season, but the departure was conducted with the habitual ceremony. Women and children lined the shore, and waved for a long time. Eventually there remained the sun, the wind and the water, as they always do in this enclave, and only a solitary cow continued to scan with her stammering eyes the silence that had fallen all around.

A single boat circled as though lost at the entrance to the strait, as though afraid to enter the channel: finally it too was caught and swept downstream into the faint darkness. "Like it or not," said the fisherman, "there's no point in lingering. It's a rule. At this season you have to go a long way off." He steadied the oars and positioned the boat in the vein of current which was growing slacker the further they went. "There are no fish here; for a modest catch a man must row to the home of the Devil himself."

The boat floated with the stream. The green water yielded to the bows and splashed against the sloping sides. Heavy branches wove a cold canopy overhead. Janek was not listening to the fisherman's prattle. For many days he had been battered by the mountain winds and the damp darkness, the smell of sacking, his body was plunged into a torpor. He sensed the pull of the current, the weight of his body being dragged to the bottom of the boat like a wet, full sack.

The fisherman cursed, sang, as though he were not carrying a man among his tackle. He had known this route for years. Generations of his forebears had passed here on their way to the lakes. There were many tales about this deep narrow channel which had swallowed up not a few fishermen. A dislodged rock, a loose branch, or sometimes the deep itself.

"Where to," asked the fisherman as though looking for someone to talk to, "where are you headed?" Janek tried to raise his body. The fisherman's voice seemed to sound in his sleep. "I'll pay, to the lakes," he answered. The fisherman laughed to hear Janek's reply and carried on with his chatter. The water became shallower, and the vista stretched open before them, splashed with summer sunshine. The fisherman brought the boat to a stop.

For a while the fisherman sat lifeless in the cramped silence. Now Janek could feel the damp in his shirt, the faint freezing in his limbs. The late summer sun gilded the shorn meadows, and the trees, their branches stained with gold, seemed stark and insubstantial, as though they had risen disjointed from the ground. He was uncertain where he was, or who was this fisherman who had agreed to take him to the lakes in his boat.

"And what will you do when you get there," said the fisherman, and he tore a piece of smoked fish. He sat foursquare in the boat as if he were a part of it. The bristles ringed his jowl like peeling birch-bark. "Don't know yet," he said, and sensed that this was not what he should have answered. The fact of the horse's death became palpable, as though the last traces of life still steamed from the thick damp coat. He could see now the horse's dead eyes looking at him with a final comprehension. It seemed to him that this was no more than a light sleep which had overtaken him and also felled the horse. He strained his ears and the silence that rocked on the water brought to his nostrils a smell of rotting hay.

"The horse is dead," said Janek.

"Your horse."

"Yes, I inherited him."

Janek took some bread out of his bag and the fisherman offered him a piece of fish.

While the silence still rocked on the water there appeared, as though they had come down from the trees, a flock of black men. They were twittering to each other, but when they sensed the fisherman's look they folded into a huddle. The feelers that were above them folded with them. They had not been expecting, apparently, to find anyone here.

The fisherman's eyes sharpened and his eyebrows stiffened. A network of red blood vessels stood out in whites of his eyes. He measured the distance. They opened their eyes wide, their eyes filled their foreheads. They too measured the distance. "Damn 'em, they're out of range," the fisherman said, and cast his eyes downwards as though looking for something he could cast. For an instant the summer turned to blue. Bundles of flax stirred in the breeze, and the trees in their shadow. And Janek had the impression that even the faint shadows that moved at the foot of the trees were digging themselves in. Smoke came from the village and stood for a moment in a certain clarity, thought better of it and fled.

"They've sat down," said the fisherman, not taking his eyes off them.

For a long while the fisherman sat without moving. His whole being was concentrated. The skin around his eyes turned blue. Attention and watchfulness gnawed at his face, and an involuntary muscle under his jaw stirred of its own accord, a hint of gathering force. There was a pathetic transparency about their bodies, like stretched skin throbbing with a network of pink blood vessels. Neither ugly nor beautiful, like hens whose neck-feathers have been plucked out by the summer, and whose long bare necks somehow conjure up the image of a sharp knife.

In front of Janek's watching eyes this transparency seemed to cloud over and their bodies took on a coat of gleaming armour. They suddenly looked short and heavy.

The fisherman's eyes became more businesslike, as though he was about to buy them. He eyed them like a peasant at market with his hands clasped behind his back. It did not occur to Janek that these were hunting thoughts being woven in secret, gradually concentrating to the point, where there is no further need of thought. The fisherman once more encompassed them with his gaze. It was not a look of hatred. He was calm as though in anticipation.

"I can't abide them," said Janek.

"Why," said the fisherman.

"No reason."

"I can watch them sometimes."

"I can't."

"When I was young I used to practise Jewhunting. For every Jew you bagged you got a modest bounty. When I was young I was crazy for money."

The fisherman watched them again, like peasants who keep livestock and feel an affection for the beasts, so long as they are alive.

"I can't abide them," said Janek again.

The fisherman did not reply. A silence stood between them. They moved and arranged themselves under a tree. Janek followed their movements closely now. There were a lot of them. The shadows of the branches dappled their whiteness. They looked like creatures who have arrived from a long journey, and the journey is still ahead of them.

"They're tired now," said fisherman. "If only they were closer I'd have a go at hunting them." He smiled, the smile of an old man who still has a few tricks up his sleeve to surprise youngsters with. The age-old curiosity of the peasant smiled from his sidelong glance. The thrill of the hunt had almost faded from his eyes, and the caressing look, focussing on small details, knitted in his eyebrows, as if he were on the point of assessing their age; but he said: "They have long legs hidden under their clothes, that's how they manage to leap like grasshoppers." Then this look too dissolved, and the curiosity which studies nature with the senses reappeared in his eyes, as though he were about to feel their clothes, their legs, like a peasant feeling a beast.

"Have you noticed how they raise their eyes up on their feelers. That's how they listen."

Now they looked thin and their stare had grown with them as though all their being was in it. They did not look at anything in particular, but their stare was all-encompassing, all-absorbing. And then it seemed as though if they went on like this they would be obliterated entirely, and their stare would continue to function without them, without their eyes. Even the fisherman was overcome. It was plain to see: in a moment he would call to them with a chirruping sound, as one calls to a domestic animal.

The sun stood fixed in the sky, giving no heat. The water rippled gently in the river, and the clear bottom was visible. The fisherman watched them calmly, with a faint affection.

The thought that some of their blood flowed in his veins frightened Janek more than ever now, as though he had discovered the secret of death. He recalled now as though through thick but still transparent glass that his mother used to whisper to him that they were wonderful people, that she missed them, that they were not like the peasants. In her last years she hardly mentioned them. The father gave orders that they were not to be mentioned in his house, and the mother, who was obedient, repressed her thoughts.

"It would be interesting to know," said the fisherman, "how they mate."

He had finished eating. His slackness had abandoned him. A secretive mockery stirred round his mouth.

"It's been years since I've tried my hand at Jewhunting. I used to lie in wait for them in the winter, but in recent years they've managed to become so agile, they slip between your fingers like fish."

The fisherman gave no hint of anger. He resembled a craftsman who is able when he wishes to appreciate the work of a rival.

They stretched themselves out under the tree and opened their cases. Some of them removed their black coats and the white of their shirts shone in the sunlight. It was plain to see: they were no longer frightened. They spoke among themselves in raised voices as though they were on their own.

He was perhaps further from wonderment at the life of those who now lay sprawled under the trees than was the fisherman. From them he now grasped the secret of his own death. All who have this blood flowing in their veins are doomed to die an unnatural death: that is their destiny. He now understood differently his father's hatred of them. His father was fighting against the death that dwelt within himself.

He raised his eyes from within himself and looked at them. Sadness overflowed from their eyes. Janek's eyes clung for a moment to their sad stare. He knew that such sadness could dwell only in them, for this was a final sadness. He craved their sadness as one craves for water, but they were remote from him and their sadness slipped past him without touching him.

"When I was a little boy," said the fisherman, "they used to descend in flocks and invade the village to buy things. We used to run after them and throw stones at them. They accepted the stones and repressed their cries. Once we chased them as far as the bridge. When they got to the bridge they screamed. Apparently they can't swim. A strange breed of human beings."

The sun began to move southwards over the trees. They rose and shook their black clothes. They stretched to their full height on their long legs. They sought the right direction and when they found it they held fast to it like birds. For an instant it looked as though they were about to take to the air, but they stood there and settled in a standing position.

"Apparently they have a highly developed sense of smell," said the fisherman.

The thought that his father and mother belonged to their ranks had still not abandoned him. He imagined to himself how they had cut themselves off, how they had been pursued; and the picture gradually etched itself with a certain clarity.

"And are they not able to change."

The fisherman took in the question and said: "At any rate around here they can't camouflage themselves. We know them. Sometimes they try but we know them, from way back."

And suddenly something changed in the expression on his old face and he said: "Be careful of them, son, they're crafty, they're human foxes. If you close the net on a runaway bear, he'll growl but eventually he'll be caught—but a fox, son, you have to watch out for him."

The thought that it was his father who had saved him from this fate momentarily stirred his slight egotism. But his enjoyment was short-lived. He was reminded that the peasants among themselves would say that the Yids had provoked their God and would have to pay the penalty. He was sad, because he sensed that the judgment must still stand and that this air poised in its twilight would not last many hours. Damned darkness or a pack of wolves or a nameless affliction would overtake him. No one who provoked his fathers' God could hope for pardon; and even if the words had been spoken by stupid peasants, contemptible fishermen, they sounded to him now like a prophecy. For a moment it seemed to him that this boat, this twilight, was a palace to which he had been led by the anger of his fathers' God.

"You're no fisherman," said the fisherman.

"How can you tell?" He was shaken out of his thoughts.

"From the hands. If a fisherman puts out his hand in the night in the dark, we can tell that he is a fisherman. Fishermen have clenched hands. So where do you work, as a clerk in the forest or in the stores?"

"In the stores."

"I knew you weren't one of us."

And after a pause he added like a man talking to himself: "If a fisherman travels to the other side of the lakes and comes back after many years we know he's one of us. The fishermen who crossed the lakes and went to work in factories died of homesickness."

Janek sensed now that their stares were turned towards him. They were remote, wondering stares, that caught in him as in a thicket. He tried to disentangle himself from them. If the fisherman had said: Come on, let's chase them away, he would have done it. But the fisherman continued to stare at them; apparently detecting a change in their stance he said: "They're praying."

He too hated them, like his father. But this inherited hatred lacked force, and consequently it contained a certain sadness.

The fisherman did not take his eyes off them; no doubt this was the way he tracked a shoal of fish, curiosity mingled with the thrill of the hunt.

The day was drawing to a close and the fisherman's chatter ceased. He prepared his nets for the night. His gaze was as watchful as ever. Skillfully he spliced torn ropes, unravelled snags. For a week now he had brought nothing up. Fish were getting scarce, there was a rumour in the village that the salinity of the lake had risen since the spring.

Now Janek was left exposed to their stares. They stopped praying and simply stood. Sadness floated on their stare, as though they had reached the limit of hopelessness. The day has tired them, apparently, Janek thought. If the horsemen come, they will not be able to fly away. Now he understood that he too was due to suffer a transformation. His clothes would turn black, his face would lose its tan. He would wander over the face of the earth, the peasants would pursue him; and they, whose blood flowed in his veins, would not admit him to their throngs.

He would have liked to approach them but he knew that if he did they would take wing and escape like night birds among the trees.

The day dragged on in twilight. The fisherman was entrenched in his nets, unravelling, splicing, and whatever flowed in the silence did not interest him, he did not hear.

"What do they do at night," Janek asked.

"They return."

"They have the power of flight."

"Occasionally," said the fisherman in an authoritative tone. "My father told me he once saw two little Jews frozen in a tree. You're a strange chap, haven't you ever seen Jews before, or didn't your ancestors tell you about them."

"Yes, they did," said Janek, "but not much."

Evening drew near and the trees filled with pale crimson. A sharp smell of frost flowed from the mountains. The sorrow left their eyes, they shook themselves like heavy beetles trying to slough off their armour, but they remained heavy and stuck to the ground. An opacity began to cloud their eyes, as though they were about to lose their sight.

"I have an urge to hunt them," the fisherman sat up.

"Why," said Janek without knowing what he was saying.

"Have you never seen a Jewhunt."

The fisherman's gaze became concentrated once more in his eyebrows. It was a concentration accompanied by an inner smile.

"Come here," the fisherman called out in a voice of thunder, "I want to buy some salt from you."

The fisherman's voice shook the silence. They froze for a moment under the blow, and huddled into a tight black mass. Their eyes quivered in alarm on top of the feelers.

"Come here, I want to buy some salt from you. I have cash."

At first it seemed that they were going to come all together in a body, but it transpired that one of them was willing to go. Still they held him back. Others rummaged in their cases, either hiding or searching.

"Are you coming, if not I'm going."

A tall one detached himself from the mass and came closer. He approached slowly and his white face came closer too.

"How much do you want," he called out.

"A pood," said the fisherman.

"We haven't got that much."

"Well how much have you got then."

"A quarter."

"Pity, I wanted more."

"We haven't got more," he said.

"Why didn't you think to bring more, and where is the salt you're talking about."

"I've got it here."

"In that case, why don't you come closer."

"Throw the money and I'll throw it to you."

"Don't you trust an old fisherman."

He drew a little closer, the fisherman fiddled in his back pocket as though feeling for coins.

"Throw," he said.

"You throw first."

"How much."

"One silver coin."

And the fisherman, who while he was bent over had tensed himself, drew a knife and threw it. The knife did not miss. The man collapsed in a heap. His brothers hurried to him. He howled, but they like a trained team quickly dragged him away. The fisherman leapt from the boat. They retreated, and their retreat was more organised the closer the fisherman approached. At first the howls of the wounded man could still be heard, but they were gradually halted. The fisherman did not relent.

A smell of fresh blood mingled with a smell of plucked feathers filled the air, and the final silence absorbed within itself the howls of the wounded man. The silence did not last long. Nocturnal birds of prey roused themselves from their sleep and came down as though after a kill, to be witnesses and accomplices; but since there was nothing there they wheeled and wheeled again, and their shrieking filled the space with another smell, a cold smell of cruel rage, as though they were about to plunge their beaks in the ground.

"You see," he said when he returned. "If you don't take them by surprise, like fish they slip through your fingers. We should have rounded them up, the two of us."

The evening came down and now bells were ringing in Janek's brain. And as in a dream the shadows returned and redoubled themselves. The howls of the wounded blended with the sound of the bells. The gloom was complete. The fisherman plunged his oars deep in the water, as though he knew that his bad luck would dog him this night too in the lakes. They had not left a single case behind them. In future he would treat them to the only form of hunting they deserved, the ambush.

The water turned black. The boat advanced without a splash, gliding. There was no more need for oars. Janek knew now that this faint darkness which was spreading its nets was the gateway to another darkness; and even when they were inside, in the channel, in the current that would carry them to the lakes, he could still see their roaming eyes on top of the feelers and them themselves, too thin to be substantial, and then only the stares, as though their whole being was in those radiant stares.

No Way Out:
Letters from the Holocaust
Susan Prinz Shear

Translated from the German by Erwin Deutsch, Martin Deutsch, and Margot Deutsch Prinz

Background

In 1790, Gerson Guttman was officially granted status as a "Protected Jew" and permitted to live in the Prussian city of Breslau, as described in the prologue.

A century and a half later, the former Kingdom of Prussia was part of the German Third Reich. Among Guttman's descendants still residing in Breslau as the Nazis came to power were the Deutsch family: Stefan and Frieda Deutsch, and their children, Margot, Gerda, Martin, and Erwin.

By 1938, the children are all in their 20s. Margot Deutsch and her husband, Kurt Prinz, are on their way to Holland and will emigrate to America. Martin is unmarried and has already emigrated to America. Erwin is married to Steffie Buch. Gerda is married to Heinz Schottlaender. Heinz comes from a wealthy, influential family who has lived in Germany for three generations. Gerda and Heinz are living in Breslau, Germany.

When the letters begin, Stefan and his son Erwin are imprisoned in a concentration camp following the November 1938 Kristallnacht pogrom.

This true story, told through letters, is theirs.

Prologue

November 20, 1790
From: Royal Majesty of Prussia
To: Gerson Guttman

Whereas our Royal Majesty of Prussia ... has decreed:

What to do about the Jewish situation at Breslau and ... has ordered that the total Jewish community, excluding those residing there under General Privilege, shall consist of 160 family heads, to be called "Protected Jews of Breslau," to each of whom shall be issued a number; now, therefore, since these have to be selected, and one Gerson Loebel Lisner Guttman has been proposed as a subject qualifying for the status of Protected Breslau Jew, the said party is hereby accepted and made the Protected Jew bearing the Number one, provided he always strive to live decently, that he be faithful and honest, that he pay all his taxes as soon as his name is entered on the tax rolls, that he not give shelter to other Jews without advice from the Jewish Commission and Elders. Under these conditions, he is permitted to engage in commerce as provided in Paragraph 15 of the Royal Decree ... He is allowed to study, engage in various mechanical arts, deal in domestic manufactured goods such as jewels, gold, silver, old clothes, horses and generally anything not forbidden to Jews or any commerce reserved to a Guild by special privilege; he can work for daily wages, [and] learn a craft, if the Gentile craftsman will accept him. If he enters such a business, he shall register as required. Thus, he is assured, to the extent he complies with the terms of this Letter of Protection and fulfills his obligations, he shall be powerfully protected against any disturbances of his rights granted herein.

Signed by Special Order of His Graciousness Royal Majesty

Correspondence, 1938-1947

November 18, 1938
Postcard from Buchenwald Concentration Camp
From: Stefan and Erwin Deutsch

Dear Mother, dear Steffi,

Father and I are here and all right. At the moment, there is a mail blockade. Inquiries to the Commander of this place are useless. Please send us 20 *Reichsmark*. Please mark number and block. Also send warm underwear, socks, and high boots, but do <u>not</u> enclose letter. Continue to work on emigration.

Father and Erwin

November 23, 1938
From: Frieda Deutsch, Breslau, Germany
To: The Jewish Committee in Amsterdam

Respectfully, I ask permission to enter Holland for a short stay. My husband, Stefan Deutsch, is a merchant, and, until a short while ago, the owner of a third generation business. We are German citizens and members of the Jewish community. We are forced to leave Germany since my husband has been imprisoned in a concentration camp since November 10, 1938. Our son, Martin Deutsch, who is in excellent financial standing, and lives in Chattanooga, Tennessee, in America, has sent us an affidavit. We have asked the American Consul in Berlin to issue us a visa. I ask you to give us permission to come to Holland until we get our visas for America.

Many thanks in advance.
Sincerely,
Frieda Deutsch

November 29, 1938
From: Martin Deutsch, Chattanooga, Tennessee
To: Kurt Prinz, Amsterdam, Holland

Dear Kurt,

You can imagine how terrible we are feeling here, since November 9. We are 3000 miles away, and only through telegrams do we find out about all this trouble. I won't go into details of what they are doing to the Jews. You know yourself what happened. It's terrible that those people have such power over people who didn't do anything to them. You predicted this. You were right. I did not want to believe you.

Now to the family problems: I received a telegram from Gerda and Heinz that Father and Erwin have been arrested and who knows where they are. Above all, I don't know what happened to Mother. I am really worried about her.

Yours, Martin

November 30, 1938
From: Heinz Schottlaender, Breslau, Germany
To: Margot Deutsch Prinz, Amsterdam, Holland

Dear Margot,

Father is still not back but seems to be okay. Until now it's been impossible to talk to anyone at the American Consulate to get the quota numbers for our parents. The borders to Holland are closed!! We are also making inquiries regarding Uruguay or anything possible. Today, Erwin will find out from the Consulate in Breslau about immigration possibilities for Cuba. We are trying to get information regarding *our* immigration to any of the British colonies.

Best regards, Your Heinz

December 2, 1938
From: Frieda Deutsch, Breslau, Germany
To: Margot Deutsch Prinz, Amsterdam, Holland

Dear Margot,

I hope Father will be home soon; I can't sleep and think of him all the time. It would be horrible if Erwin and Steffi had to leave before he gets out and could not say goodbye. Regarding *our* taxes, all is straightened out; Heinz took care of it. You have no idea how complicated everything is. One must run from one place to the other with a tremendous amount of patience and steady nerves. Heinz and Gerda told us that it is impossible to get an answer from the American Consulate. Therefore, Cuba is the only way out. All other possibilities are hopeless.

Warmest greetings and lots of kisses, Mother

December 6, 1938
From: Heinz Schottlaender, Breslau, Germany
To: Margot Deutsch Prinz, Amsterdam, Holland

Dear Margot,

Your father is as before, but we hope to see him soon. It's *impossible* to find an interim country for your parents. No one wants to issue a visa, since there is no guarantee that they can support themselves. Cuba might be our only hope, since a booking to Shanghai cost 150 English pounds.

Yours, Heinz

December 9, 1938
From: Martin Deutsch, Chattanooga, Tennessee
To: Margot Deutsch Prinz, Amsterdam, Holland

Dear Margot,

I don't know what to do. Everywhere I get denials. I am going crazy. You can imagine how I feel knowing Father is incarcerated and his only chance to get out is a visa. I hope within the next few days I will accomplish something. Heinz writes that he and Gerda are trying to go to Bolivia, even though Heinz is "not very fond of that country." I am afraid he has not learned yet. What does "not fond" mean? When it is a matter of life or death, one cannot be choosy. I wonder how they are treating Father. Is he suffering? Is he hopeful or giving up? When I got a few letters this morning, I was almost afraid to open them. I can see that you are trying everything to get Father released. Keep me posted.

Martin

December 20, 1938
From: Frieda Deutsch, Breslau, Germany
To: Margot Deutsch Prinz, Amsterdam, Holland

Dear Margot,

We are thrilled to have Father home, although it will take days until he is himself. All in all, his health seems to be fine. Warmest greetings and kisses,

Your Mother

December 29, 1938
From: Stefan & Frieda Deutsch, Breslau, Germany
To: Margot & Kurt Prinz, Amsterdam, Holland

My Dear Children!

I am doing fairly well. I am still weak, but with Mother's good care, I hope to be well soon, so do not worry. I was so glad that I could write you. Unfortunately, many of my friends will not be able to do that any more. Also, many of those who did come back are in bad shape. So I am thankful that this trip was all right for me. The saddest fact was that I could not see you, but it was better for you to leave earlier and I only pray to God that we will meet again.

Your Father

December 29, 1938
From: Gerda Deutsch Schottlaender, Breslau, Germany
To: Margot Deutsch Prinz, Amsterdam, Holland

My Dear Margot,

Heinz and I are working on going to Brazil but have little hope. Since we can't think of getting out before March, due to our tax problems, things don't look good. Right now, our parents are the most important problem. I don't see any possibility for them to go to Cuba. Do all in your power to help them. It is urgent!

We will *not* leave until we know they are able to get out.

Father is doing okay. Mother looks very bad; you have no idea! She is re-living the last few weeks and it's catching up with her. Margot, please don't forget me.

As always, Your Gerda

December 29, 1938
From: Stefan Deutsch, Breslau, Germany
To: Erwin & Steffi Deutsch, Martin Deutsch, Kurt & Margot Prinz, Bolivia, USA, Holland

My Dear Children:

The only possibility for us is Bolivia, where Erwin and Steffi are fortunate enough to be. We must leave as soon as possible. I am sure that Gerda and Heinz will write you regarding *their* immigration. Nothing is working out for them and they have no idea what's going to happen. I hesitate to leave Germany before they do. I would never find peace. I am convinced that you are doing everything possible to help us.

Erwin: Keep your chin high and be glad that you are out. Lots of people would give anything for it.

Your Father

January 5, 1939
From: Gerda Deutsch Schottlaender, Breslau, Germany
To: Martin Deutsch, Chattanooga, Tennessee

Dear Martin,

Erwin went to the American Consulate and found out that you can do the following for our parents: Send a copy of your affidavit to Washington, DC, Form 575, to the Immigration Department of Labor. If you have applied for citizenship, which I hope you have, our parents will come under the "second preferred quota." The Department of Labor will then, after you fill out forms, inform the Consulate; the same man who helped you thinks that their numbers will come up by July. Erwin received his transit visa for America. I hope we can proceed the same way with our parents. We have our visa for Kenya and will be going there, but only if Brazil does not work out. Many thanks for sending us the affidavit for America. Father and Mutti are doing well again and look better. Soon you will see Margot, Kurt, Erwin, and Steffi. I can imagine how thrilled you must be to know that you are together again. I only hope that we, too, will see all of you again very soon.

Warmest greetings and lots of kisses, Your Gerda

January 30, 1939
From: District Court, 63 HR. 14190, Breslau, Germany
To: Stefan Deutsch, Breslau, Germany

Into the register of the Board of Trade, Division A, under the firm of Joseph Deutsch, father of Stefan Deutsch, Breslau, (Nr.14190), on January 30th, 1939, the following was entered: The firm has been extinguished.

Signed: Ulrich, Court Employee, Official of the District Court

March 4, 1939
From: Heinz Schottlaender, Breslau, Germany
To: Erwin and Steffi Deutsch, La Paz, Bolivia

Dear Erwin and Steffi,

We were thrilled that you arrived safely in Bolivia. I know you will be working to try to get your parents there. I received your telegram telling me to send you all testimonies and documents, but the certificate you request will be hard to fabricate because I am not a chemical/mining engineer. I will try, but it won't be easy for me to get the documents. Anyhow, many thanks for your efforts.

Your parents are in good health. They will rent their apartment and move in with us by April 30. My sales of properties from January 4 still have not been approved. I hope this will happen soon, because only then can I settle the estate. It does not look good for us to get visas to Bolivia or anywhere else. I don't have the security money for Kenya and nothing is happening in regards to Brazil. I will try to get a visa application for Chile. I wish both of you the best. We think of you a lot.

Your Heinz

March 17, 1939
From: Heinz Schottlaender, Breslau, Germany
To: Erwin and Steffi Deutsch, La Paz, Bolivia

Dear Erwin and Steffi,

I think back to a few months ago, how we ruled out going to Bolivia when it would have been relatively easy. Now we are trying so hard with little success. The rush to go is great and one can understand why they closed the borders, at least for now. Since we can no longer be selective as to where we would like to go, please try your best so we can immigrate to Bolivia. I am a certified electrical engineer in research and development with specialties in telephone, telegraph, and television.

Your Heinz

May 25, 1939
From: Heinz Schottlaender, Breslau, Germany
To: Kurt and Margot Deutsch Prinz, St. Louis, Missouri

Dear Margot,

Our parents booked passage on the "Patria" for June 17, 1939. Their passports and visas are in perfect order. But we are having problems with various lists one has to furnish, since they issued new forms and now we have to fill them out all over again. We had them submitted, and then they changed it in the last moment. One has to furnish proof as to the original purchase date of each item! We are racing to complete all three lists because there is so little time left. I got a bit further settling my estate. But it will probably be July until I get the exit permit and passport. I received an unreasonable immigration number from the Consulate: #67, 927 on the American waiting list.

Your Heinz

May 25, 1939
From Gerda Deutsch Schottlaender, Breslau, Germany
To Erwin Deutsch, La Paz, Bolivia

Dear Erwin,

We won't be able to come to Bolivia; they won't let us in. At least it is okay for our parents and Steffi's father; all three are able to leave Germany. It is important for us to leave, but not so urgent as for the parents. I am trying my best to go to Chile but not sure it will work out.

As always, Gerda

June 5, 1939
From: Gerda Schottlaender, Breslau, Germany
To: Margot Deutsch Prinz, St. Louis, Missouri

Dear Margot,

I wish you the best for your birthday. I wish you and Kurt good health, success in business, and a peaceful life, a life without fear for the next day, without nervousness; a feeling that you are equal, a free person. That is what we are not allowed to have. Everything looks good regarding our parents leaving. We only wait for how much we have to pay. But it does not look good for Steffi's father. He will not be able to leave as planned since he is over 60. We will not be able to leave for another two or three months, since Heinz won't get his exit permit earlier. It looks bad regarding a visa. I think of you often and long for you.

Lots of kisses, Your Gerda

June 14, 1939
From: Heinz Schottlaender, Breslau, Germany
To: Margot Deutsch Prinz, St. Louis, Missouri

Dear Margot,

I want to send you a report before we leave with the parents for the ship. We managed everything but you have no idea how everything hinged on a thin thread. There were so many problems! It took two or three weeks to get your parents ready so our own immigration affairs came to a standstill. There is an application pending for Chile, and a friend, the former ambassador to Spain, intervened on our behalf. But I have my doubts!

Your Heinz

June 15, 1939
From: Gerda Deutsch Schottlaender, Breslau, Germany
To: Margot Deutsch Prinz, St. Louis, Missouri

Dear Margot,

Just a postcard to tell you we are spending the last day with our parents and thinking of you. All needed papers are in order and we feel good about it. Even so, the last few hours will be emotionally very hard. But we are happy they are leaving under good conditions.

All my love, Gerda

June 23, 1939
From: Gerda Deutsch Schottlaender, Breslau, Germany
To: Margot Deutsch Prinz, St. Louis, Missouri

Dear Margot,

Today we received a letter from Erwin telling us that our immigration is 80% guaranteed. That would be fantastic. Still, I will believe it when I have the immigration numbers in hand. Hopefully, we will be reunited sooner than we thought. Many thanks for your good wishes on our wedding anniversary. I hope that I will always be as happy with Heinz as I am now.

Stay well, much love, Gerda

July 12, 1939
From: Gerda Deutsch Schottlaender, Breslau, Germany
To: Margot Deutsch Prinz, St. Louis, Missouri

Dear Margot,

We have a restriction on the use of our money now, and although we had to pay expenses related to Father's and Mother's emigration, the Finance Department reduced, by a tremendous amount, our monthly allotment. Please continue to write to anyone you can think of to sponsor us for a visa. We can't go to England and are working on Australia and Chile and the terribly high immigration number to America. All the best to you.

Gerda

July 24, 1939
From: Erwin Deutsch, La Paz, Bolivia
To: Heinz and Gerda Deutsch Schottlaender, Breslau, Germany

Dear Gerda and Heinz,

We have finally done it!! We got an approval for a visa for you both!! It took a long time and a few things still have to be taken care of, but we hope everything will be fine. I am sure you are as excited as we are that before long we will all be together.

Erwin

July 25, 1939
From: Heinz Schottlaender, Breslau, Germany
To: Erwin Deutsch, La Paz, Bolivia

Dear Erwin,

I received your telegram, "Immigration from Minister approved, will receive numbers after you deposit $350 to Banco Central." We are in pretty good health and are winding up our affairs. Unfortunately, there is little money left. It will be a long time until I get my exit permit but one cannot lose patience. We are so happy that your parents' trip went smoothly. Many thanks for your efforts and troubles on our behalf. Now I have to figure out how in the world I can come up with the needed $350!

Yours, Heinz

August 1, 1939
From: Gerda Deutsch Schottlaender, Breslau, Germany
To: Erwin Deutsch, La Paz, Bolivia

Dear Erwin,

We are so happy that you got approval for a visa for us and we thank you for your efforts. How we will come up with the $350 is the big question but I'm sure we will find a way. Do you think the Bolivian government will keep their word if it takes several months for us to get out? If not, will the money be lost or will we get the $350 back?

With all my love, Gerda

August 24, 1939
From: Gerda Deutsch Schottlaender, Breslau, Germany
To: Margot Deutsch Prinz, St. Louis, Missouri

Dear Margot:

Yesterday we heard about the non-aggression pact between Germany and the Soviet Union. This was completely unexpected. I hope this pact will bring some sense to the world and all will be good in the end! Today, we heard on the radio that the leader of Bolivia died. I hope this does not mean bad news for us. I am happy that our parents are gone from here. Lots of luck in your business. I think of you so very much.

Gerda

August 29, 1939
From: Gerda Deutsch Schottlaender, Breslau, Germany
To: Stefan and Frieda Deutsch, La Paz, Bolivia

My Dear Parents,

Everything is at a standstill, but things will be decided within the next few hours. No matter the outcome, there is nothing we can do. In case of war, we think Heinz will be drafted as a worker and I, too; something we would gladly want to do. It would be better than to be a bystander. For that, we are still too German. My dear parents, stay well.

Your Gerda

September 5, 1939
From: Gerda Deutsch Schottlaender, Breslau, Germany
To: Stefan and Frieda Deutsch, La Paz, Bolivia

My Dear Parents,

I hope you have been receiving my letters because we haven't heard from you in a while. Here the situation is much worse. I hope the war won't last too long because it's impossible now to think of leaving Germany. We believe that Heinz, and I, too, will be drafted in the Work Corps. Many of our friends have already been drafted.

Gerda

September 26, 1939
From: Gerda Deutsch Schottlaender, Breslau, Germany
To: Margot Deutsch Prinz, St. Louis, Missouri

Dear Margot,

So much has changed that I don't think we will be able to leave now. None of the ocean liners are leaving, and the few foreign ships only take foreign money and it is very dangerous to go by ship. I hope you receive this letter.

I am enclosing a letter to our parents; please mail it for me; it is faster and safer. They sent us a telegram asking if we could leave Germany if they deposit the money for us. This is very touching, but we cannot leave here in the foreseeable future. We have no friends here any longer. I think of you a lot. We are fine and I hope you won't worry too much about us.

Your Gerda

October 26, 1939
From: Stefan Deutsch, La Paz, Bolivia
To: Heinz and Gerda Deutsch Schottlaender, Breslau, Germany

My Dear Children!

Gerdele, you write that Mother should be content living with some of her children in Bolivia. But we cannot be happy while you are so far away and until you are out of Germany. We think of you day and night. Last year was the first time in my life that I could not congratulate you for your birthday. I hope this letter will reach you in time, and I pray to God that we will be able to see each other again. I can see from your letter to Mother how lonely you are. We are lonely too, but we have to be patient. Stay well, best greetings and kisses, Your Father

October 30, 1939
From: Heinz Schottlaender, Breslau, Germany
To: Kurt and Margot Deutsch Prinz and Martin Deutsch,
    St. Louis, Missouri

My Dear Margot,

I just received your letter of *September 16* which was opened by the censor!! That's why it took so long. There is no way for us to tell what will happen regarding our leaving. It looks almost hopeless.

Everyone receives rationing coupons; there is an 8 p.m. curfew; windows must be blackened out and nobody can go out. In spite of it, we are feeling good.

Warm regards, Your Heinz

December 4, 1939
From: Heinz Schottlaender, Breslau, Germany
To: Stefan and Frieda Deutsch, La Paz, Bolivia

Dear Parents-in-Law,

Emigration does not look good for us. The main obstacle is, as before, the exit permit.

In July, we asked for a revision of the value of our estate, but as of today, the officials in the Finance Office have not acted. A lot of tax cases are still unsolved and in dispute. But as long as this revision is not completed, the emigration tax is figured according to the *original* value of the estate, which is not what we Jews can get today. Therefore, the emigration tax is so large that the fortune left to me won't cover the asking amount. We intend to have another meeting with the authorities. I will suggest that I turn over my *entire* inheritance for security to the Finance Office, which would get everything I own except what I need for my own emigration. Since I cannot pay more than I own, I hope they will understand and give me the exit permit.

Always, Your Heinz

December 9, 1939
From: Heinz and Gerda Deutsch Schottlaender, Breslau, Germany
To: Erwin Deutsch, La Paz, Bolivia

Dear Erwin,

Finally, our tax problems have been resolved and our prospect is better to get the exit permit in the first few months of 1940. I *beg* of you to expedite our visas. I advised my brother to wire you the needed $350 so you can continue with everything else.

I'm adding this to Heinz's letter. Hopefully, we will receive the visas soon and I ask you again, *as soon as the money* is there, to take the necessary steps *as quickly as possible*. It is of the *utmost importance* that you act fast. Many, many thanks, my dear Erwin.

Lots of love, Heinz and Gerda

December 13, 1939
From: Heinz Schottlaender, Breslau, Germany
To: Erwin Deutsch, La Paz, Bolivia

Dear Erwin,

Today we went to the Italian ship line and were told that no ship is leaving in March. But one will leave from Genoa on April 6, 1940, and that date suits us fine. That gives us enough time to take care of things; everything takes longer than one thinks. The main thing is that we have our visas in our hand; I hope you will be able to get them for us. Chile closed its borders; our chances to go there are nil.

We embrace you with all our love, Heinz

December 26, 1939
From: Gerda Deutsch Schottlaender, Breslau, Germany
To: Stefan and Frieda Deutsch, La Paz, Bolivia

My Dear Parents,

We sent you the $350 quite a while ago and can't understand why we haven't heard from you or the Bolivian government. Erwin was supposed to cable us our numbers. What's happening? Is it not going through?

Gerda

January 10, 1940
From: Stefan Deutsch, La Paz, Bolivia
To: Heinz and Gerda Deutsch Schottlaender, Breslau, Germany

Dear Heinz and Gerda,

As soon as the $350 arrives, it should all go fast. You can be sure when we receive it, we will try our best to get your immigration numbers as soon as possible. You have no idea how happy we are that you straightened out your tax problems. God willing, we will take you in our arms in April and our fondest wish will be fulfilled!

Your loving Father

January 27, 1940
From: Heinz Schottlaender, Breslau, Germany
To: Stefan and Frieda Deutsch, La Paz, Bolivia

Dear Parents,

We have just received your long-awaited telegram: "Received the money, will send numbers in a week." We are so happy!

Heinz

February 15, 1940
From: Stefan and Frieda Deutsch, La Paz, Bolivia
To: Heinz and Gerda Deutsch Schottlaender, Breslau, Germany

My Dearest Children!

I am completely desperate! We have not been able to receive your immigration numbers. The government promised them no later than February 3rd. In the meantime, we have our Carnival and everything is closed. I was promised we would have them by the 12th, but we are getting nothing but phony promises. Erwin and I go every day to the Immigration Office at 10 a.m. and are promised that if we come back at noon, we will get your papers. At noon a sign says come back at 4 p.m., and at 4 they tell you to come again at 7 p.m. From 7 it goes to 10 p.m., and this is how it goes, day by day. Although I get these excuses, I am convinced I will get it. The question is when? God willing, I will be able to send the cable to you before it is too late. Believe me, dear children, we aren't neglecting anything. We are all very desperate. I will only be happy when I have you here.

Kisses from your unhappy Father

February 19, 1940
Telegram from Stefan Deutsch to Heinz and Gerda Deutsch Schottlaender

    Immigration number for Gerda and
    Heinz Schottlaender definitely this
    week.

March 22, 1940
From: Stefan Deutsch, La Paz, Bolivia
To: Heinz and Gerda Deutsch Schottlaender, Breslau, Germany

Dear Gerda and Heinz,

You write that you are surprised that you still haven't received your immigration numbers. I'm surprised, too!! On account of the Carnival and new elections, everything is at a standstill. The newly-elected President promised us that we will receive the numbers the first week of April. Please be patient and I will be the same.

Your loving Father who is longing for you

April 8, 1940
From: Stefan Deutsch, La Paz, Bolivia
To: Heinz and Gerda Deutsch Schottlaender, Breslau, Germany

My Dear Heinz, Dear Gerda!

We received your letter and thank you for the birthday wishes. I swear by God the All-mighty that we are not neglecting any possibilities. There are so many unbelievable circumstances that you will see once you have your visas. For me there is only one wish: to be able to hug you, the sooner the better. That will be the best day of my entire life.

Your father who longs for you with a loving heart

April 15, 1940
From: Heinz Schottlaender, Breslau, Germany
To: Erwin and Steffi Deutsch, La Paz, Bolivia

My Dear Erwin and Steffi!

Unfortunately, today is April 15th and the Bolivian Consulate in Hamburg stops issuing visas on April 20th. Since the immigration numbers aren't here yet, I assume we will not get them in time and will not be able to come to Bolivia. It is terribly sad that you went through such trouble for nothing. But we cannot be disappointed. I thank you both for all you did. It would be best if you keep the money that my brother sent you liquid, so we can get it whenever we might need it. We hope to get the exit permit by the beginning of May. In any case, we will be packing our belongings by next week.

Many greetings, Heinz

April 22, 1940
Telegram from Stefan Deutsch to Heinz Schottlaender in Breslau

> Engineer contract, chemical factory.
> Immigration numbers <u>definitely</u>
> Friday.

April 25, 1940
From: Stefan Deutsch, La Paz, Bolivia
To: Heinz and Gerda Deutsch Schottlaender, Breslau, Germany

My Dear Gerda and Heinz!

I really don't know what to do anymore. Today I was promised that I will receive your immigration numbers. Nothing happened. Now I am promised for tomorrow. It's enough to drive one to despair. We got upset when we heard from Margot that you think we aren't doing everything possible for you. I assure you we did and continue to do everything possible. I don't blame you for not trusting us anymore, but you don't know the conditions here. We are in a bad mood and only talk about one subject—your visas. We are desperate. Stay well, a thousand regards and kisses from your very unhappy Father

April 26, 1940
From: Stefan Deutsch, La Paz, Bolivia
To: Heinz and Gerda Deutsch Schottlaender, Breslau, Germany

My Dear Children,

Your immigration is being worked on by three different sources. Although the new Minister closed immigration, we found a man who is building a chemical plant here. He has the right, by law, to bring people here to work for him. He applied for you and declared that both of you are his employees. He says the application was approved by the

Government and the immigration numbers will be issued this Friday. This is why we sent you the telegram stating that you have a contract to work and will get your immigration numbers by Friday. We are convinced the deal is on the up and up. If not, then I will have lost my faith in humanity and there is no sense in living. God willing, I will send the telegram with the numbers to you today. Greetings and kisses from your loving, desperate Father

May 14, 1940
From: Gerda Deutsch Schottlaender, Breslau, Germany
To: Stefan Deutsch, La Paz, Bolivia

My Dear Pops!

You are wrong if you think I don't believe you are doing everything within your power for us. On the contrary, I am convinced you are doing too much, overdoing it, hurting yourself and at the end of your nerves. You cannot jump over your own shadow, Pops; what can't be, can't be. You have to be sensible … it is all fate anyway. One has to take it as it comes and not let it wear you down. I know your only thought is to have us with you and that you have been working toward that. Don't despair. We will see each other soon regardless of the problems, maybe in another country and then you will have traveling to look forward to!! With love and faith, wishing you everything good, I remain your loving Gerda.

May 18, 1940
From: Stefan Deutsch, La Paz, Bolivia
To: Heinz and Gerda Deutsch Schottlaender, Breslau, Germany

My Dear Children,

I don't know what to say. I made you so many promises, but nothing has worked out. I can't tell you how many tears I have shed and how many sleepless nights I endured. Mother's nerves are shattered. The deal with the owner of the chemical plant did not materialize. He seems to be a crook. The borders for Jewish immigration to Bolivia are closed but we don't know how long this will last. We are trying another deal with a Mr. Winkler, a rancher who got a permit to sell land to Jewish immigrants, allowing him to bring over 15 Jewish families. Should this not work out, I don't know what to do.

All my best and lots of kisses, Father

June 3, 1940
From: Gerda Deutsch Schottlaender, Breslau, Germany
To: Margot Deutsch Prinz, St. Louis, Missouri

My Dear Margot,

I wish you had not sent my last letter to you on to Father. He believes we think he is not doing enough. He is the wrong person to do all this since he can't be understood well by strangers and he is too nervous and excitable. I cannot understand why Steffi and Erwin do not take care of this. That constant optimism that things will be okay! ... Even if we had the immigration numbers, we could not get a visa anymore. Until further notice, everything is closed. Even if we had a visa, we could not get out, since Stalin does not let any one of us through his country. Therefore, it is all useless at this time. Brazil does not work either, and the Philippines denied our efforts. The Aid Agency did not even submit our papers, since they claim there are no positions for engineers. Impossible to understand! Please don't tell this to our parents. It's no use to excite them and would not do Mother's health any good. We are now trying for Ecuador and just have to wait. On the 15th it is your birthday, and I wish you above all that we will see each other soon. Best greetings to all of you with hugs from your Gerda.

June 12, 1940
From: Heinz Schottlaender, Breslau, Germany
To: Stefan and Frieda Deutsch, La Paz, Bolivia

Dear Parents-in-Law,

Gerda and I are very unhappy about your state of mind. You see that getting into Bolivia is impossible; therefore, I'm asking you to stop all efforts. You are chasing a phantom. I assume the money is lost, and you feel responsible and depressed. You are not doing us any favors if you fight a lost cause. I beg you not to continue any efforts for our emigration. We received a report from the tax official here who says my tax problems will drag. We won't get our exit permit for some time, contrary to earlier expectations.

Heinz

June 13, 1940
From: Stefan Deutsch, La Paz, Bolivia
To: Heinz and Gerda Deutsch Schottlaender, Breslau, Germany

My Dear Children!

It will be one year tomorrow since we were last together. Those were beautiful, and at the same time, sorrowful, days. It is a comfort that I did not know then that you would still be in Germany; otherwise, I would not have been able to say goodbye. I cannot get over the fact that I am unable to help you, of all people, who did so much for us and the rest of the family. I will not rest until we are successful. I decided to go the President. If that does not work, I see no way out. My dear Heinz, I do not have the will power to get over my failure so easily. If I don't succeed, I will not get over it as long as I live. Every possibility I pursued without hesitation, sometimes with a 100% guarantee, and always it was a disappointment. He who loves his children the way I love you, and who wants to thank them for all the love and sacrifice they have shown us, cannot come to peace with himself. Martin and Kurt are also very good to us and send us a few dollars every month. I am blessed by God to have such wonderful children and children-in-law, but only in matters of your immigration has God deserted me. Nevertheless, I have not lost faith, and I pray daily to God to help me, not to abandon me. With best regards and many kisses, I am your loving Father.

July 20, 1940
From: Stefan Deutsch, La Paz, Bolivia
To: Heinz and Gerda Deutsch Schottlaender, Breslau, Germany

Dear Gerda and Heinz,

You write that I should quit efforts to get visas since it seems hopeless. Are you saying this so I won't have so much work and tension? Or don't you want to come here anymore? Do you really think I would stop trying, that my worries would lessen? No, my children, then you don't know your father very well. I will only be relieved when I have your immigration secured. The worst would be if you, young people, aren't taken care of, that you don't get out. We are old, so everything else is unimportant. I will continue the efforts and hope you won't blame me. I am worried that you still don't have exit permits because then you can't get your passports either. This is very serious.

Your father

November 26, 1940
From: Gerda Deutsch Schottlaender, Breslau, Germany
To: Stefan and Frieda Deutsch, La Paz, Bolivia

My Dear Parents,

I have a great surprise for you. I am pregnant and think that the baby will be born the end of June! We are elated and wish that you could be here with us. I am doing fine except some morning sickness. I could use Margot's baby things, but I am sure she will need them again, or maybe Steffi will need them!

Your Gerda

January 15, 1941
From: Stefan Deutsch, La Paz, Bolivia
To: Kurt and Margot Deutsch Prinz and Martin Deutsch, St. Louis, Missouri

My Dear Martin, Margot, and Kurt,

We are still at an impasse with Gerda and Heinz's affairs. It is terrible. If we didn't have all these worries, we could be very content here in Bolivia. Thanks to all of you and your help, we are able to live comfortably. That swine, Hitler, marched into Italy; many people protest, but it looks like Mussolini is finished. We hear that 1000 Jews were murdered in Romania. It is despicable. People here receive letters from Jews in camps who ask for food packages because they are starving. My biggest fear is that Gerda and Heinz will be transported to a camp and then there would be no hope for them to leave. People write that no one can leave Germany now even if they have visas.

Your Father

February 2, 1941
From: Gerda Deutsch Schottlaender, Breslau, Germany
To: Margot Deutsch Prinz and Martin Deutsch, St. Louis, Missouri

My Dear Good Margot, My Dear Martin!

I wrote you on December 18th and just noticed you wrote me on the same day. ... Isn't it funny we both felt the need to talk to each other at the same time! In the meantime, you must know I am expecting a baby at the end of June. The first three months I was nauseated, but not anymore. I gained quite a bit of weight so my dresses don't fit anymore. Too bad you are not here, or rather, that I am not there; you could give me good advice. I got some baby clothes from acquaintances, but not enough, so we have to advertise in the paper, asking for used ones. Unfortunately, when we were first married, I didn't buy anything because I was superstitious, and now it is so difficult. But I am thrilled to be having a baby! For the fun of it, we named it, Emil or Emilie, but in reality, from the names we are allowed by the Nazis to choose, we would pick only Denny for a boy and Zilla or Tana for a girl. Too bad that we cannot be out of here by the time the baby is born. But it does not look good to get any visas, and the date for receiving our exit permit has been moved far into the future. An official here is giving us a tremendous amount of trouble even though there is enough collateral for any unresolved financial questions.

As always, Your Gerda

March 2, 1941
From: Gerda Deutsch Schottlaender, Breslau, Germany
To: Stefan Deutsch, La Paz, Bolivia

My Dear, Good Father,
I hope this letter gets to you in time for your birthday. I wish you all the best, health and a comfortable life. Our prospects to leave are zero! The possibilities for an entry into the Philippines are not good because one needs a minimum of $1200, and then only a temporary permit is granted. But where could one get that much money?
Love, Gerda

April, 1941
From: Frieda Deutsch, La Paz, Bolivia
To: Margot Deutsch Prinz, St. Louis, Missouri

Dear Margot,
Regarding Gerda and Heinz's immigration, things look very bad. And on top of the worry, what is that scoundrel going to do to the rest of Jews in Germany? I wish one could wake up in the morning and Hitler and his consorts would be annihilated and the world would be at peace. But, unfortunately, a lot of misery will befall many good people. One cannot even think about it.
Your loving Mother

May 15, 1941
From: Gerda Deutsch Schottlaender, Breslau, Germany
To: Margot Deutsch Prinz, St. Louis, Missouri

Dear Margot,

I want to congratulate you on your birthday! You know I wish you only the best. Last week we had a sunny day and I hung out all the baby clothes. Now we are ready! We are so excited, as you can imagine.

Now some good news! We finally got our exit permit, thanks to Heinz's enormous efforts. We are trying our best for Ecuador again, but it takes a long time to get an answer. We were advised by the Consulate to send all the necessary papers, and we wait.

With all our love, Gerda

June 26, 1941
From: Heinz Schottlaender, Breslau, Germany
To: Stefan and Frieda Deutsch, La Paz, Bolivia

Dear Parents,

I want to give you the good news that Gerda gave birth to a boy! Her first pain came at 11 p.m. on the 24th after she was busy all day in the garden. At midnight, we drove to the hospital, at 4 p.m. the midwife arrived, and then the doctor, at 5:30 p.m. Shortly after 6:30 he was born. All is fine. He has dark blond hair, weighs six and one-half pounds, and is 52 cm. long. He is in perfect health and cries very little. His name is Denny.

July 22, 1941
From: Stefan Deutsch, La Paz, Bolivia
To: Heinz and Gerda Deutsch Schottlaender, Breslau, Germany

My Dear Heinz and Gerda,

We were thrilled to get your letter. We are only sad that we cannot be with you to enjoy Denny and that Mother cannot help you. Heinz, I hope that Denny will grow up to be as good a Jew as your father and grandfather and also Grandfather Deutsch. A special kiss for Denny from his grandfather, and for you, greetings and a thousand kisses from your loving Grandfather and father who longs for you.

September 18, 1941
From: Gerda Deutsch Schottlaender, Breslau, Germany
To: Margot Deutsch Prinz, St. Louis, Missouri

My Dear Margot,

I will bring you up to date about the baby. You have no idea how happy I am to have him. I am a real crazy mother, so in love with this little boy. He had lots of hair from the beginning, now the new hair is flour white, silky. His eyes are dark blue but I think he will have brown eyes one day. He looks like Heinz did as a child and will be as tall, which I always hoped for! Soon he will be three months old, how time flies! Heinz is a proud father who changes his diapers and feeds him. We are satisfied with our life here since there is no way to leave. I missed all of you very much during my delivery and thought of you a lot.

Stay well, Gerda

September 25, 1941
From: Gerda Deutsch Schottlaender, Breslau, Germany
To: Stefan and Frieda Deutsch, La Paz, Bolivia

My Dear Parents,

Right now I am sitting on the porch and my little Denny is right next to me. I am afraid that Ecuador is not possible. We contacted the Consul of Ecuador in Berlin, because all of a sudden the Consul in Hamburg tells us that he is not allowed to issue visas for entry to Ecuador, even though he told us to fill out all the forms, etc. I guess he does not give a darn. We are still trying to get into Brazil and also Santo Domingo. Everything is pretty hopeless.

Erwin's home sounds very nice. I envy him that he has banana trees in his yard. Here we can't get any apple or banana baby food. They tell us to mash up potatoes which they say are just as good!! Today our Denny is three months old. He never cries, sleeps all night, and has a great appetite. All in all, he is a fantastic little boy. We are taking lots of movies of him that we hope to show you one day.

Lots of kisses from your Gerda

December 19, 1941
From: Stefan Deutsch, La Paz, Bolivia
To: Heinz and Gerda Deutsch Schottlaender, Breslau, Germany

My Dear Good Children,

All of us, Mother, Erwin, Steffi, and I have, since January 10th, 1940, only one wish, to get your visas. The lawyers gave us hope, but there was no way to tell if and when we were going to get the numbers. I went to the lawyer on Friday, and he said, "Come on, let's go right away to the Ministry, you have your immigration numbers!" I thought my heart stopped for joy. We went to the Ministry, and, after a few minutes, which seemed like hours, I received the cable for your immigration numbers. I was so excited that everyone thought I might pass out. But how could it have been otherwise after the struggle of 1 year, 11 months and 8 days, to finally get it in the last minute? Now, my dears, hurry up, and don't overlook anything. See how quickly you can leave. Cable us as soon as you have your visas and what the possibility for ship passage is. Please answer as soon as possible, because, as you can imagine, we have only one thought, that you will be able to make it out.

Your loving father

February 13, 1942
From: Stefan and Frieda Deutsch, La Paz, Bolivia
To: Heinz and Gerda Deutsch Schottlaender, Breslau, Germany

Dear Gerda and Heinz!

We are extremely worried that we haven't heard from you since December 7, 1941. We sent telegrams to the Consulates in Hamburg and Berlin, advising them that we have approval for you to enter Bolivia. I wrote to you on December 19th and 29th. We have not received any word from you acknowledging those letters. We sent a telegram to the Consulates on February 9th, asking them to let us know if the family Schottlaender received authorization to immigrate. We are beside ourselves and desperate and don't know what to do! We are sending this letter to the Red Cross and the Jewish Committee in Switzerland in the fervent hope that they will be able to forward this to you. I am, forever, your loving father.

April 9, 1942
From: Stefan Deutsch
To: Swiss Jewish Agency

    Inquire whether Schottlaender
    Breslau obtained visa from
    Bolivian Consul Berlin on account
    immigration permit December 19 Stop
    Inform SOPRO [Society for Helping
    Jewish Refugees] La Paz stop

June 10, 1942
From: Mr. Pahlke, Nazi Administrator, Adolf Hitler Platz, Berlin
To: Mr. Eckersdorff, Schottlaender Attorney, Breslau
The Central Administration of the Dr. Paul Schottlaender heirs, Heinz Schottlaender, sent me your letter of 4/21/42 with your query on liquidation of property for Mr. Schottlaender. The fortune of Mr. Schottlaender became the property of the German Reich.

July 1, 1942
From: Stefan Deutsch, La Paz, Bolivia
To: Victor Schottlaender, San Bernardo, Chile

Dear Mr. Schottlaender,

Mr. Capauner was kind enough to give me your address. I come to you for a great favor. My acquaintances here have heard from their relatives in Germany through friends or relatives in Chili. Since I have not heard from my children, your cousin Heinz and his wife, since December 7, 1941, I ask you to please dispatch the enclosed letter per airmail.... I got the visas on December 19, 1941, unfortunately, several months too late. I informed Heinz through every source available, letters, telegrams, direct and through the consuls but have not heard from him since December 7th. I don't know if Heinz received the cables, if he got the visas. I do not know if they are still in Breslau. I hope, dear Mr. Schottlaender, that you will not mind forwarding my letters; you can imagine the shape we are in. If you hear anything about Heinz, please let me know.... Many thanks and regards to your family.

    Yours, Stefan Deutsch

August 1, 1942
From: Stefan Deutsch, La Paz, Bolivia
To: Victor Schottlaender, San Bernardo, Chile

Dear Mr. Schottlaender,

I received your letter on the 28th of July. Many thanks! Let's hope Heinz will get the letter and that I will receive mail from him. Your brother in Basel was so kind to try to get my children into Switzerland but without success. It is regretful that the reason for the failure was the non-existence of a permit to enter another country. I hope your intuition that Heinz, Gerda, and the child are not in Breslau anymore is wrong. I cannot imagine that thought; that would be terrible. Again, many thanks for your efforts.

Stefan Deutsch

August 7, 1942
From: Stefan Deutsch, La Paz, Bolivia
To: Victor Schottlaender, San Bernardo, Chile

Dear Mr. Schottlaender,

You can imagine how your news affected me. You were, unfortunately, right; the children are not in Breslau. I did not want to believe it. Thanks for letting me know and for your words of consolation. Unfortunately, there is no consolation for me. I cannot think that the children might be in a ghetto. Even if it might be true that they are safer in a ghetto than in Germany, it is terrible not to know where and how they are. Here it is said that if one knows where they are, it is easier to get them out than from Germany. If you know of any way to find out where they are, please don't spare any expense, I will reimburse everything. When I think back to our incarceration in Buchenwald, and remember how impatient we were waiting for our release even though we knew it would come, I can imagine how desperate the children must be that they can not get out until the end of the war. And this can drive one to insanity. With God's help, this terrible war will have an end soon, and these criminals will be punished. I must fight until I get the children out. I want to live to be able to accomplish that. Please help me. My wife and I will not rest until we know where the children are. Many thanks, and let me hear from you soon.

Yours, Stefan Deutsch

Received in Bolivia on August 26, 1942:
February 16, 1942
From: Heinz Israel and Gerda Sara Deutsch Schottlaender
Breslau, Germany
To: Stefan Deutsch, La Paz, Bolivia
Telegram via International Committee of the Red Cross March 26, 1942

> Dear Parents,
> Received Bolivian visa No connection
> with any ships Won't give up trying
> Immigration to Brazil not possible
> Trying to get deposit back All
> three of us are well
> Gerda
> Heinz

August 29, 1943
From: Stefan Deutsch, La Paz, Bolivia
To: Margot and Kurt Prinz, Cape Girardeau, Missouri; Martin Deutsch

My Dear Children,

The news of the war is mixed. But when you get a letter from the Red Cross, as Mother wrote you, that the children were sent to the East on May 4, 1942, how can you avoid being desperate? Even this is unconfirmed. One doesn't know where they were sent. I hope they weren't sent to the hell of the Warsaw Ghetto and that Heinz, since he is an engineer, was sent to a labor camp, and Gerda and the baby were able to join him. Let's hope that they will outlive the war! Now it is four weeks to the High Holidays and a difficult time for me.

Stefan

July 14, 1945
From: Stefan Deutsch, La Paz, Bolivia
To: Gerhard Schlesinger, Rio de Janeiro, Brazil

Dear Mr. Schlesinger!

Two years have passed since we have heard from each other. Now, finally, the war has ended, but I have not been able to find out the fate of our beloved ones in Germany. I have not heard anything about Heinz, Gerda, and the child and assume that you have not gotten any news either. It is terrible to live in this uncertainty; one does not know what to do. We received from my children in St. Louis the entry permit to the U.S.A. and will probably leave here in September. Please answer me if you hear anything or can give me any advice if there is a source where one can inquire.

Regards, Stefan Deutsch

December 14, 1947
From: Gertrud Leuschner, Hanover, Germany
To: Stefan and Frieda Deutsch, St. Louis, Missouri

Dear Mr. and Mrs. Deutsch,

In the quiet evening hours on this Sunday, I am sending you my heartiest greetings. I received your address only a short time ago. This is why I am sending you this report only now.

Today, I want to go back a few years in order to give you a report about the terrible year of 1942. At that time, it was not possible to send an honest report.

As you know, I worked with Heinz in Breslau to determine what was left of his estate. In the winter of 1941-42, Heinz met a man who promised to help all three of them flee across the border into Switzerland. Everything was worked out in detail. Gerda and Heinz were convinced that their plan would work. Heinz bought, through an ad in the newspaper, a knapsack that I picked up for him, since Heinz had to wear the yellow star.

On Monday, April 15, I arrived in Breslau. I met Gerda, who was terribly upset, because on Sunday, Heinz had been picked up by the Gestapo while working in the garden. He was forced to leave without a coat and as dirty as he was from working. He asked to say good-bye to his son, who was asleep at the time, and Heinz started to cry quietly.

The people who picked him up informed him that the man who had arranged for their flight to Switzerland had already been picked up for his actions. Gerda was devastated and afraid that she might never see him again. She was riding to the Jewish Agency to see what could be done for Heinz and to talk to someone who helps people leave Germany. I went to the house to take care of my beautiful Denny.

The next day, the Gestapo informed us that Gerda and Denny would be picked up on April 29th. I quickly drove to the Immigrationburo [immigration bureau] to speak to someone in the hope that Heinz and Gerda could be spared.

I stayed with Gerda the last night. We slept only 2 or 3 hours. We tried to be brave and not shed any tears to make the good-bye easier. I took Denny downstairs and held him. I saw tears in his eyes, but he did not cry as he might have if he had felt something terrible was going to happen. I said good-bye and promised to bring clean diapers for Denny. Gerda and Denny were taken to the Jewish Community Center in Breslau.

When I came the next day, I could not find Gerda. Other people were lying on straw, but Gerda and Denny were not there. I finally found a nurse who told me that they were sent to Wallstrasse. I found them there, and, since Gerda was freezing, I gave her my warm ski jacket.

On my next trip, I was told that Gerda and Denny were sent to yet another location. I went the next day. The building was roped off and I could not see anyone. Someone said they were transported on Monday by train. Heinz's mother also tried to find them but was not allowed in. We talked about how to send food to Gerda and Heinz as soon as we would hear where they were.

But there was never a word from them. All hope, and the long wait, for a sign of life from your children seems to have been in vain, because by now there would have been some kind of communication from them.

Already in 1944 there was a rumor in Breslau that Gerda and her child were not alive. A man claims to have talked to Heinz at a labor camp in Poland. He said that Heinz had to transport heavy cement blocks and was very hungry. This man also claimed that he was able to smuggle some bread to Heinz, who was very thankful, but they were not able to talk.

The last years have brought such terrible heartache to so many people; almost everyone had to pay an unbelievable price due to the incredible actions of the Nazis. But the misery that we suffered when we were forced to leave our Homeland is no comparison to what you, my dear friends, had to endure.

You can be assured that all of us did everything we could to help. Gerda and I were close friends. She always came to me for help and advice. One can only hope that these two wonderful people and that sweet child did not suffer too much.

Yours, Gertrud Leuschner

Prelude

Albert Halper

I was coming home from school, carrying my books by a strap, when I passed Gavin's poolroom and saw the big guys hanging around. They were standing in front near the windows, looking across the street. Gavin's has a kind of thick window curtain up to eye level, so all I saw was their heads. The guys were looking at Mrs. Oliver, who lately has started to get talked about. Standing in her window across the street, Mrs. Oliver was doing her nails. Her nice red hair was hanging loose down her back. She certainly is a nice-looking woman. She comes to my father's newspaper stand on the corner and buys five or six movie magazines a week, also the afternoon papers.

When I passed the poolroom, one or two guys came out. "Hey, Ike, how's your good-looking sister?" they called, but I didn't turn around. The guys are eighteen or nineteen and haven't ever had a job in their life. "What they need is work," my father is always saying when they bother him too much. "They're not bad; they get that way because there's nothing to do," and he tries to explain the meanness of their ways. But I can't see it like my father. I hate those fellas and I hope every one of them dies under a truck. Every time I come home from school past Lake Street they jab me, and every time my sister Syl comes along they say things. So when one of them, Fred Gooley, calls, "Hey, Ike, how's your sister?" I don't answer. Besides, Ike isn't my name anyway. It's Harry.

I passed along the sidewalk, keeping close to the curb. Someone threw half an apple but it went over my head. When I went a little farther, someone threw a stone. It hit me in the back of the leg and stung me but it didn't hurt much. I kept a little toward the middle of the sidewalk because I saw a woman coming the other way and I knew they wouldn't throw.

I came up to the newsstand and put my school books inside. "Well, Pa," I said, "you can go to Florida now." So my Pa went to "Florida," that is, a chair near the radiator that Nick Pappas lets him use in his restaurant. He has to use Nick's place because our own flat is too far away, almost a quarter-mile off.

I stood around, putting the papers on the stand and making a few sales. The first ten minutes after coming home from school and taking care of the newsstand always excites me. Maybe it's the traffic. The trucks and cars pound along like anything and of course there's the Elevated right up above you which thunders to beat the band. We have our newsstand right up against a big El post and the stand is a kind of cabin which you enter from the side. But we hardly use it, only in the late morning and around two p.m., when business isn't very rushing. Customers like to see you stand outside over the papers ready for business and not hidden inside where they can't get a look at you at all. Besides, you have to poke your head out and stretch your arm to get the pennies and kids can swipe magazines from the sides, if you don't watch. So we most always stand outside the newsstand, my father, and me, and my sister. Anyhow, I like it. I like everything about selling papers for my father. The fresh air gets me and I like to talk to customers and see the rush when people are let out from work. And the way the news trucks bring all the new editions so we can see the latest headlines, like a bank got held up on the South Side on Sixty-third Street, or the Cubs are winning their tenth straight and have a good chance to cop the pennant, is exciting.

The only thing I don't like is those guys from Gavin's. But since my father went to the police station to complain, they don't come around so often. My father went to the station a month ago and said the gang was bothering him, and Mr. Fenway, he's the desk sergeant there, said, "Don't worry any more about it, Mr. Silverstein, we'll take care of it. You're a respectable citizen and

taxpayer and you're entitled to protection. We'll take care of it."
And the next day they sent over a patrolman who stood around
almost two hours. The gang from Gavin's saw him and started to
go away, but the cop hollered, "Now listen, don't bother this old
fella. If you bother him any, I'll have to run some of you in."

And then one of the guys recognized that the cop was Butch,
Fred Gooley's cousin. "Listen who's talkin'!" he yells back. "Hey,
Fred, they got your cousin Butch takin' care of the Yid." They
said a lot of other things until the cop got mad and started after
them. They ran faster than lightning, separating into alleys. The
cop came back empty-handed and said to my father, "It'll blow
over, Mr. Silverstein; they won't give you any more trouble." Then
he went up the street, turning into Steuben's bar.

I am standing there hearing the traffic and thinking it over
when my little fat old man comes out from Nick's looking like he
liked the warm air in Nick's place. My old man's cheeks looked
rosy, but his cheeks are that way from high blood pressure and
not from good health. "Well, colonel," he says smiling, "I am
back on the job." So we stand around, the two of us, taking care
of the trade. I hand out change snappy and say thank you after
each sale. My old man starts to stamp around in a little while
and, though he says nothing, I know he's got pains in his legs
again. I look at the weather forecast in all the papers and some
of them say flurries of snow and the rest of them say just snow.
"Well, Pa," I tell my old man, "maybe I can go skating tomorrow
if it gets cold again."

Then I see my sister coming from high school carrying her
briefcase and heading this way. Why the heck doesn't she cross
over so she won't have to pass the poolroom, I say to myself; why
don't she walk on the other side of the street? But that's not like
Sylvia; she's a girl with a hot temper, and when she thinks she
is right, you can't tell her a thing. I knew she wouldn't cross the
street and then cross back, because according to her, why, that's
giving in. That's telling those hoodlums that you're afraid of their
guts. So she doesn't cross over but walks straight on. When she

comes by the pool hall, two guys come out and say something to her. She just holds herself tight and goes right on past them both. When she finally comes up, she gives me a poke in the side. "Hello, you mickey mouse, what mark did you get in your algebra exam?" I told her I got an A, but the truth is I got a C.

"I'll check up on you later," she says to me. "Pa, if he's lying to us we'll fine him ten years!"

My father started to smile and said, "No, Harry is a good boy, two years is enough."

So we stand around kidding and pretty soon, because the wind is coming so sharp up the street, my old man has to "go to Florida" for a while once more. He went into Nick's for some "sunshine," he said, but me and Syl could tell he had the pains again. Anyway, when he was gone we didn't say anything for a while. Then Hartman's furniture factory, which lately has been checking out early, let out and we were busy making sales to the men. They came up the sidewalk, a couple of hundred, all anxious to get home, so we had to work snappy. But Syl is a fast worker, faster than me, and we took care of the rush all right. Then we stood waiting for the next rush from the Hillman's cocoa factory up the block to start.

We were standing around when something hit me in the head, a half of a rotten apple. It hurt a little. I turned quick but didn't see anybody, but Syl started yelling. She was pointing to a big El post across the street behind which a guy was hiding.

"Come on, show your face," my sister was saying. "Come on, you hero, show your yellow face!" But the guy sneaked away, keeping the post between. Syl turned to me and her face was boiling. "The rats! It's not enough with all the trouble over in Europe; they have to start it here."

Just then our old man came out of Nick's and when he saw Syl's face he asked what was the matter.

"Nothing," she says. "Nothing, I'm just thinking."

But my old man saw the half of a rotten apple on the sidewalk, and at first he didn't say anything but I could see he was worried. "We just have to stand it," he said, like he was speaking to himself, "we just have to stand it. If we give up the newsstand where else can we go?"

"Why do we have to stand it?" I exploded, almost yelling. "Why do we—"

But Mrs. Oliver just then came up to the stand, so I had to wait on her. Besides, she's a good customer and there's more profit on two or three magazines than from a dozen papers.

"I'll have a copy of *Film Fan*, a copy of *Breezy Stories*, and a copy of *Movie Stars on Parade*," she says. I go and reach for the copies.

"Harry is a nice boy," Mrs. Oliver told my father, patting my arm. "I'm very fond of him."

"Yes, he's not bad," my father answered, smiling. "Only he has a hot temper once in a while."

But who wouldn't have one, that's what I wanted to say! Who wouldn't? Here we stand around minding our own business and the guys won't let us alone. I tell you sometimes it almost drives me crazy. We don't hurt anybody and we're trying to make a living, but they're always picking on us and won't let us alone. It's been going on for a couple of years now, and though my old man says it'll pass with the hard times, I know he's worried because he doesn't believe what he says.

And another thing, what did he mean when he said something two days ago when the fellas from Gavin's passed by and threw a stone at the stand? What did he mean, that's what I wanted to know. Gooley had a paper rolled up with some headlines about Europe on it and he wiggled it at us and my father looked scared. When they were gone my father said something to me, which I been thinking and thinking about. My Pa said we got to watch our step extra careful now because there's no other place besides this country where we can go. We've always been picked on, he said, but we're up against the last wall now, he told me, and we got to be calm because if they start going after us here, there's no other place where we can go. I been thinking and thinking about that, especially the part about the wall. When he said that, his voice sounded funny and I felt like our newsstand was a kind of island and if that went, we'd be under the waves.

"Harry, what are you thinking of?" Mrs. Oliver asked me. "Don't I get any change?" She was laughing.

And then I came down from the clouds and found she had given me two quarters. I gave her a nickel change. She laughed again. "When he looks moody and kind of sore like that, Mr. Silverstein, I think he's cute."

My old man crinkled up his eyes and smiled. "Who can say, Mrs. Oliver? He should only grow up to be a nice young man and a good citizen and a credit to his country. That's all I want."

"I'm sure Harry will." Mrs. Oliver answered, then talked to Syl a while and admired Syl's new sweater and was about to go away. But another half of a rotten apple came over and splashed against the stand. Some of it splashed against my old man's coat sleeve. Mrs. Oliver turned around and got mad.

"Now you boys leave Mr. Silverstein alone! You've been pestering him long enough! He's a good American citizen who doesn't hurt anybody! You leave him alone!"

"Yah!" yelled Gooley, who ducked behind an El post with two other guys. "Yah! Sez you!"

"You leave him alone!" hollered Mrs. Oliver.

"Don't pay any attention to them," Syl told Mrs. Oliver. "They think they're heroes, but to most people they're just yellow rats."

I could tell by my old man's eyes that he was nervous and wanted to smooth things over, but Syl didn't give him a chance. When she gets started and knows she's in the right, not even the Governor of the State could make her keep quiet.

"Don't pay any attention to them," she said in a cutting voice while my old man looked anxious. "When men hide behind Elevated posts and throw rotten apples at women, you know they're not men but just things that wear pants."

Every word cut like a knife and the guys ducked away. If I or my father would have said it, we would have been nailed with some rotten fruit, but the way Syl has of getting back at those guys makes them feel like yellow dogs. I guess that's why they respect her even though they hate her.

Mrs. Oliver took Syl's side and was about to say something more when Hillman's cocoa factory up the block let out and the men started coming up the street. The 4:45 rush was on and we didn't have time for anything, so Mrs. Oliver left, saying she'd be back when the blue-streak edition of the *News* would arrive. Me and Syl were busy handing out the papers and making change.

Then the *Times* truck, which was a little late, roared up and dropped a load we were waiting for. I cut the strings and stacked the papers and when my father came over and read the first page, he suddenly looked scared. In his eyes there was that hunted look I had noticed a couple of days ago. I started to look at the first page of the paper while my old man didn't say a word. Nick came to the window and lit his new neon light and waved to us. Then the light started flashing on and off, flashing on the new headlines. It was all about Austria and how people were fleeing toward the borders and trying to get out of the country before it was too late. My old man grew sick and looked kind of funny and just stood there.

In a little while it was after five and Syl had to go home and make supper. "I'll be back in an hour," she told me. "Then Pa can go home and rest a bit and me and you can take care of the stand." I said all right.

After she was gone, it seemed kind of lonesome. I couldn't stop thinking about what my father had said about this being our last wall. It got me feeling funny and I didn't want to read the papers any more. I stood there feeling queer, like me and my old man were standing on a little island and the waves were coming up. There was still a lot of traffic and a few people came up for papers, but from my old man's face I could tell he felt the same as me.

But pretty soon some more editions began coming and we had to check and stack them up. More men came out from factories on Walnut Street and we were busy making sales. It got colder than ever and my old man began to stamp again. "Go into Nick's, Pa," I told him. "I can handle it out here." But he wouldn't do it because just then another factory let out and we were swamped for a while. "Hi, there, Silverstein," some of the men called to him, "what's the latest news, you king of the press?" They took the papers, kidding him, and hurried up the stairs to the Elevated, reading all about Austria and going home to eat. My father kept staring at the headlines and couldn't take his eyes off the print where it said that soldiers were pouring across the border and mobs were robbing people they hated and spitting on them and making them go down on their hands and knees to scrub the streets. My old man's eyes grew small, like he had the toothache and he shook his head like he was sick. "Pa, go into Nick's," I told him. He just stood there, sick over what he read.

Then the guys from Gavin's poolroom began passing the stand on their way home to supper after a day of just killing time. At first they looked as if they wouldn't bother us. One or two of them said something mean to us, but my old man and me didn't answer. If you don't answer hoodlums, my father once told me, sometimes they let you alone.

But then it started. The guys who passed by came back and one of them said: "Let's have a little fun with the Yids." That's how it began. A couple of them took some magazines from the rack and said they wanted to buy a copy and started reading.

In a flash I realized it was all planned out. My father looked kind of worried but stood quiet. There were about eight or nine of them, all big boys around eighteen and nineteen, and for the first time I got scared. It was just after six o'clock and they had picked a time when the newspaper trucks had delivered the five-star and when all the factories had let out their help and there weren't many people about. Finally one of them smiled at Gooley and said, "Well, this physical culture magazine is mighty instructive, but don't you think we ought to have some of the exercises demonstrated?" Gooley answered, "Sure, why not?"

So the first fella pointed to some pictures in the magazine and wanted me to squat on the sidewalk and do the first exercise. I wouldn't do it. My father put his hand on the fella's arm and said, "Please, please." But the guy pushed my father's hand away.

"We're interested in your son, not you. Go on, squat."

"I won't," I told him.

"Go on," he said. "Do the first exercise so that the boys can learn how to keep fit."

"I won't," I said.

"Go on," he said, "do it."

"I won't."

Then he came over to me smiling, but his face looked nasty. "Do it. Do it if you know what's good for you."

"Please, boys," said my Pa. "Please go home and eat and don't make trouble. I don't want to have to call the policeman—"

But before I knew it someone got behind me and tripped me so that I fell on one knee. Then another of them pushed me, trying to make me squat. I shoved someone, and then someone hit me, and then I heard someone trying to make them stop. While they held me down on the sidewalk I wiggled and looked up. Mrs. Oliver, who had come for the blue-flash edition, was bawling them out.

"You let him alone! You tramps, you hoodlums, you let him alone!" She came over and tried to help me, but they pushed her away. Then Mrs. Oliver began to yell as two guys twisted my arm and told me to squat.

By this time a few people were passing and Mrs. Oliver called at them to interfere. But the gang were big fellows and there were eight or nine of them, and the people were afraid.

Then while they had me down on the sidewalk Syl came running up the street.

When she saw what was happening, she began kicking them and yelling, trying to make them let me up. But they didn't pay any attention to her, merely pushing her away.

"Please," my Pa kept saying. "Please let him up; he didn't hurt you. I don't want to call the police—"

Then Syl turned to the people who were watching and yelled at them. "Why don't you help us? What are standing there for?" But none of them moved. Then Syl began to scream:

"Listen, why don't you help us? Why don't you make them stop picking on us? We're human beings the same as you!"

But the people just stood there afraid to do a thing. Then while a few guys held me, Gooley and about four others went for the stand, turning it over and mussing and stamping on all the newspapers they could find. Syl started to scratch them, so they hit her, then I broke away to help her, and then they started socking me too. My father tried to reach me, but three guys kept him away. Four guys got me down and started kicking me and all the time my father was begging them to let me up and Syl was screaming at the people to help. And while I was down, my face was squeezed against some papers on the sidewalk telling about Austria and I guess I went nuts while they kept hitting me, and I kept seeing the headlines against my nose.

Then someone yelled, "Jiggers, the cops!" and they got off of me right away. Nick had looked out the window and had called the station, and the guys let me up and beat it away fast.

But when the cops came it was too late; the stand was a wreck. The newspapers and magazines were all over the sidewalk.

Then the cops came through the crowd and began asking questions right and left. In the end they wanted to take us to the station to enter a complaint, but Syl wouldn't go. She looked at the crowd watching and she said, "What's the use? All those people standing around and none of them would help!" They were standing all the way to the second El post, and when the cops asked for witnesses none of them except Mrs. Oliver offered to give their names. Then Syl looked at Pa and me and saw our faces and turned to the crowd and began to scream.

"In another few years, you wait! Some of you are working people and they'll be marching through the streets and going after you too! They pick on us Jews because we're weak and haven't any country; but after they get us down they'll go after you! And it'll be your fault; you're all cowards, you're afraid to fight back!"

"Listen," one of the cops told my sister, "are you coming to the station or not? We can't hang around here all evening."

Then Syl broke down. "Oh, leave us alone," she told them and began wailing her heart out. "Leave us alone. What good would it do?"

By this time the crowd was bigger, so the cops started telling people to break it up and move on. Nick came out and took my father by the arm into the lunchroom for a drink of hot tea. The people went away slowly and then, as the crowd began to dwindle, it started to snow. When she saw that, Syl started bawling harder than ever and turned her face to me. But I was down on my hands and knees with Mrs. Oliver, trying to save some of the magazines. There was no use going after the newspapers, which were smeared up, torn, and dirty from the gang's feet. But I thought I could save a few, so I picked a couple of them up.

"Oh, leave them be," Syl wept at me. "Leave them be, leave them be!"

The Gathering Storm

The End

Ida Fink

Translated from the Polish by Philip Boehm and Francine Prose
They were still standing on the balcony, although it was the middle of the night and only a few hours kept them from dawn. Down below lay the dark, empty street; the trees in the square looked like black tousled heads. Once again it was quiet, too quiet after what had happened. From time to time a streetcar rumbled through the city center; a car rolled quietly past. The night was heavy, humid: one of those midsummer nights when not a single leaf trembles, and the asphalt, overheated during the day, exhales its steamy breath.

He slid his hand along the iron railing of the balcony and touched the girl's hand. Her hand was cold; she kept her fingers clenched.

"You see," he said. "It was nothing."

She wasn't looking at him, she was looking out over the roofs of the city, peering into the thick darkness; she sensed that he, too, was straining to listen. He said it was nothing, and yet he was listening.

"Don't be afraid, let's get some sleep." And again he said, "It was nothing."

"I'm not afraid," she answered loudly, angrily; her words spattered down onto the street like tiny, hurried footsteps. "And I'm not a child. Don't treat me like one. And don't lie to me. I can see that you're listening, too."

"But you are a child." He laughed. "My beloved little child ..."

"Don't make me mad. And anyway—" She stopped in midsentence.

They heard a noise, at first far away, then clearer, close by—it was just a truck.

"Do you remember when we first realized that something was happening?" she asked, after the silence returned. Her voice was high-pitched and clear. The boy shut his eyes and thought, I love her, I don't want her to be afraid.

"Tell me," she insisted, "do you remember?"

"Of course. I could sing the exact moment for you, except you know how I sing."

"Don't joke now. This is an important night."

He put his arm around her; he could feel her body shaking. "It's an important night, love—because it's our night . . ."

In the darkness, he caught a glimpse of her angry expression. She was in no mood for either jokes or tenderness.

"I remember," he added hastily, and in an instant the music of that first moment surged inside him.

He recalled it exactly. The strings were growing quieter, preparing the way for the soloist. During the first measures of the larghetto, which he liked so much, he began to notice a faint buzz coming from the direction of the city. As if swarms of locusts were flying in from far away. Maybe not locusts, but simply the dense tremolo of the strings, rising to a forte, closer and closer, fleeing before the storm. The orchestra, which had once again picked up the piano theme, seemed muted, and the whole audience turned as if swept by a great wind toward the rumbling, now a loud and brutal thunder. He saw the pianist hesitate and watched his fingers attack the silent keyboard: by now, neither the piano nor the orchestra could be heard above the din. Then the tanks came rolling up the street alongside the park, their treads clanging and clattering. The storm crested and subsided. Once again it was quiet, and the full whisper of the strings reached the very last rows, where they were sitting.

"I remember," he said once more. "What an idea, to have a concert in the park!"

"Piotr," the girl whispered. She had never called him by his real name before, preferring instead the nickname Piotrus. "Piotr, think about it . . . three months of happiness . . . so little . . ."

For a moment he didn't realize she was talking about them; when he finally understood and tried to answer, the words stuck in his throat.

"And you go on insisting that nothing has happened. Why do you want to hide your head in the sand? People have been asking each other all week: When is it going to happen? Everyone knows that it is, that it's just about to . . ."

He managed to remain calm. "You're not making sense, you're upset. Look, the whole city is sleeping, all the lights are out. That proves that nothing has happened."

As if to spite him the darkness resounded with dull thuds. They raised their heads and listened. It was the same ominous music that had overpowered Chopin in the park. Tanks were once again riding down the city streets. Lights flickered on; voices could be heard through the open windows. She looked into his eyes.

"Let's go inside," she said.

She went back into the room and carefully locked the door to the balcony, as if she could lock out all the evil events of the night.

"Do you remember the first time I came here?" she asked, stopping in the middle of the room to look around. Piotr felt a chill run through him: Then, too, she had run into the room with rapid little steps, stopped still, and looked all around. Was she now unconsciously replaying that night?

"Do you remember? It was March, a very wet March, the snow was melting. Everything you were painting was green, and being in your room was like lying in the grass."

She was already looking back! Already recalling the past! He wanted to tell her, Don't say "was." Don't say: "You *were* painting." Say "is." Say: "You *are* painting."

"And you were playing Bach," he said.

"And I was playing Bach," she repeated. And added, "I'm so sad that it's already over."

"Stop it!" he shouted. "How can you say that! Nothing is over, we're still together, we're going to stay together. Always. Calm down. I'll make some coffee."

His hands were shaking. In the mirror he saw a pale face that looked nothing like his own. The girl was saying, "Why lie? It's the end. The end of youth, the end of love, of your paintings, of my music. We were very happy, but there's no need to lie. Isn't it better to accept that we had three months of great happiness? And now they're over."

She met his gaze, read his answer. His face was chalk-white, taut with pain.

A low thrumming of windowpanes jarred her from her sleep. She bolted up in bed, wide awake, fully aware of what was happening. The room itself was now half dark; the windows had become glowing rectangles of gray. She waited. After a few minutes she heard a heavy, dull rumbling, as if the earth were sighing. The windows once again began to hum, but their music was immediately overwhelmed by a new explosion.

She glanced at her watch. It was almost four. Carefully, so as not to wake the boy, she moved over and leaned back against the wall. She watched him lying there, defenseless as a child and, like a child, unconscious of the evil that had been unleashed. She studied the rough darkness of his body, the hawklike profile of his young face. Gently she stroked his hair.

"Keep sleeping," she whispered.

She bent over him and stayed that way, keeping watch, guarding his last peaceful moments of sleep. The dawn advanced, followed by the sun. The war was fifteen minutes old.

The Threshold

Ida Fink

Translated by Philip Boehm and Francine Prose

The wooden porch was glassed in on all sides with huge panes. Until recently, curtains had hung in the windows, as yellow as the noonday sun. Not a restful color, but bright and warm; it complemented the nasturtiums that bloomed in the beds Mother tended all by herself. This year there were no nasturtiums either. Stripped of curtains and flowers, the front of the house looked strange and pathetic. Even these tiny changes showed how different things were now. The gate, usually latched with such care, hung by one hinge, lopsided, like someone about to faint. The windows were sealed tight, though it was the height of summer. The path in front of the house meandered toward the meadows and the river, past lush gardens and one-storied cottages. It was early morning, the beginning of July 1941, the first quiet, calm morning after days of intense worry. One week before, the Russians had fled the town. One week before, the Germans had marched in. The first pogrom had already taken place.

Elzbieta sneaked out onto the porch. It was cold; rivulets streamed down the windowpanes. She sat in a wicker armchair—pale, but calm. She was thinking about her parents, whom the war had caught by surprise in L.; she wished that they would return as soon as possible. Once they came back, she thought, peace and order would return, too; everything would be the same as before . . . or almost the same. Elzbieta was still very young.

Every day she took Czing on his leash and went for a walk outside the town.

"It's safest by the river," she explained to Kuba. "The Germans never go down there—after all, these days there aren't too many Jews interested in swimming."

It was quiet by the river. The poplars glistened in the sun, gray-green, slender as columns; the water flowed lazily, covered with spreading blooms of gray spawn. The sand was hot.

They often stayed out the entire afternoon and went back just before dark, when the empty streets sighed with relief and fatigue after another long day. As they made their way through town, they could hear drunken voices coming from the bars, loud songs sung in a harsh foreign language.

"I never liked German even in school," she confessed to Kuba. "Now tell me if I wasn't right."

Kuba smiled and said nothing. He was much older; he knew more than Elzbieta, and had a better sense of the world. He put his arm around her and hugged her gently. She did not resist. It gave her a feeling of security.

"Let's go to the farmer's tomorrow to buy potatoes," she told him one day as they said good-bye in front of the porch. "I have to get them before my parents come back." At the thought of her parents she could hardly hold back her tears. Not now, maybe later, at night, when no one could see . . .

The next day they brought the potatoes in a wheelbarrow.

"Two sacks! That'll last a long time," she told Kuba happily. "We'll make pierogi and potato pancakes. Do you like pierogi?"

The furrow in Kuba's forehead disappeared when he heard her voice and looked at her young face, tanned by the summer sun.

Her aunts and uncle disapproved of her behavior. Elzbieta kept her distance from them, just as she distanced herself from their incessant concern with all the frightening and incomprehensible events. She locked herself in her own world and kept the others out. Even though they all lived under one roof, they hardly ever saw one another. Elzbieta refused to cross the threshold of their room, which seemed haunted by the spirit of that terrible time.

In vain they tried to reason with her, to explain things, to open her eyes, as they said. "Everything just slides off her like water off a duck! At a time like this, she wants to go walking. At a time like this."

The pastures smelled of chamomile and wild thyme. She lay next to Kuba on the trampled, fragrant grass, passing the hours.

"I just can't," said Elzbieta, "I just can't accept . . ." Kuba took a box of tobacco out of his pocket, rolled a cigarette, and lit it.

"What can't you accept?" he asked.

She sat up and looked all around her, as far as she could see. The forest off to the east was slowly turning black. She saw herself in the meadow with flowers in her hair. She heard herself laughing. "Why are you laughing?" her teacher had asked at the school's spring outing. She hadn't wanted to say.

"What can't you accept?"

Instead of answering, she asked: "Tell me, Kuba, . . . you really love life, too, don't you?"

They walked along the riverbank, just as in the old days, down by the little beach, and then across to the pastures. They bought apples from the farmer and ate nothing else all day. In the evening Agafia made pierogi and put a steaming bowl of them on the table next to the window. Outside the window were lilacs, beyond the lilacs was the garden, and beyond the garden was the river.

Sometimes, when she lay awake in the darkness, she could make out bits of conversation coming from her aunts' room. Mostly cries and sighs. Then she would cover her ears with her pillow and burst into tears. Puzzled, Czing would lick her feet.

Two young SS men had been ransacking the house for over an hour. They stuffed their suitcases with the table silver, the kilims, the paintings, the porcelain. Elzbieta's uncle was at work; only the women were at home. When all their pleas were answered with harsh threats and warnings, the aunts took refuge in their room, but not even that room was spared. Since Elzbieta was the legal owner of the house, the Germans ordered her to assist with the looting, to show them around and explain where everything was. Nor did they overlook the attic, where they found the painting of a naked woman, which Elzbieta's parents had received on some occasion and stashed out of sight. They couldn't bear to look at it and only brought it out when the hapless person who gave it to them was about to visit. The SS men were very taken by the painting. They laughed as they used their riding crops to touch the breasts of the woman posed so nonchalantly.

Finally, when the whole house looked as if a battle had been fought there, they demanded a bottle of wine and two glasses. "I'll take it to them," Agafia whispered to Elzbieta.

Elzbieta sneaked out onto the porch. It was cold; rivulets streamed down the windowpanes. She sat there pale and very weary. "Come back," she pleaded with her absent parents. She could hear, from inside, the Germans' vulgar laughter and Agafia's angry mutter. A moment later she heard the sound of shattering glass; the Germans must have smashed the wineglasses. Then she heard steps. They were leaving. They shouted at her. She stood up, her back to the house, facing the shadowy street. "*Wo ist dein Vater?*"— "Where's your father?"—one of them remembered to ask. She didn't look at him. She focused on the spreading chestnut in their neighbor's garden.

"*Dein Vater!*"

"My father is at work," she lied, still looking at the tree. And at that moment she glimpsed something moving: A cat?

The first thing she noticed was the boyish face, the frightened eyes. How did he get here? A whole week after the fighting? And so young!

Then he emerged completely, his uniform in tatters, without a cap, his hair disheveled as if he had just woken up. He looked around. The little street was empty. She stifled a cry.

"*Bitte,*" she said with effort, inviting the SS men back into the house. "There's still one more room. . . ."

"What?" shouted the older one. "Go have a look, Hans."

The Russian boy was approaching slowly; he seemed hardly able to walk. He was so close that she could make out the insignia on the uniform, the cuts on his hands.

"We've gone through the whole house," reported the younger one.

"*Na, dann los*"—"let's go!"

They pointed to the bulging suitcases and instructed her not to touch them. They would be right back with the car. Then they headed for the porch door. She thought quickly, I have to stop them until he passes. I have to stop them.

"*Bitte*," she said shyly.

"Quiet!" the older one shouted, convinced that she was going to beg them not to take something.

Just in front of the porch, the Russian finally saw them. He ducked and ran.

The younger SS man cried out and chased after him. "Come on." The older one pushed Elzbieta in front of him. "You will translate."

"They want to know where you were hiding," Elzbieta explained, her voice soft and kind.

"*Schneller, schneller!*"

The soldier didn't speak. Elzbieta couldn't bear to look into his eyes.

"Don't be afraid," she said, "I won't tell them anything, don't be afraid . . ."

The boy moved his lips and mumbled a few words: The only word Elzbieta understood was *zhizn*—"life."

"What did he say? Translate!"

"Let him go," she cried despairingly, "*ich bitte, ich bitte . . .*"

The older SS man peered at her. His eyes were sky blue. "How old are you?

"Fifteen."

"I'm twenty. And I've already shot seventeen people. This one'll be my eighteenth. Have you ever seen how it's done?"

She tore herself away with all her strength but then felt the strong arm of the SS man around her neck and something cold jabbing into her cheek.

"*Schau mal*—look, it's so simple. . . ."

The last thing she saw before she shut her eyes was the boy's final, bewildered gaze.

That evening she and Agafia buried him beneath the chestnut tree in their next-door neighbor's garden. Inside her aunts' room the light was already burning. A pot of kasha was cooking on their makeshift stove, filling the whole room with its aroma. Several people were sitting around the table.

". . . and then they killed Goldman and his little son . . . ," her uncle was saying quietly.

Elzbieta crossed silently into the room and took her place at the table.

An Evening Guest

Elie Wiesel

Translated from the French by Steven Donadio

Like all the persecuted Jewish children, I passionately loved
the prophet Elijah, the only saint who went up to heaven alive,
in a chariot of fire, to go on through the centuries as the herald
of deliverance.

For no apparent reason, I pictured him as a Yemenite Jew: tall,
somber, unfathomable. A prince ageless, rootless, fierce, turning
up wherever he is awaited. Forever on the move, defying space
and nature's laws. It is the end which attracts him in all things,
for he alone comprehends its mystery. In the course of his fleeting
visits, he consoles the old, the orphan, the abandoned widow. He
moves across the world, drawing it in his wake. In his eyes he
holds a promise he would like to set free, but he has neither the
right nor the power to do so. Not yet.

In my fantasy I endowed him with the majestic beauty of Saul
and the strength of Samson. Let him lift his arm, and our enemies would fling themselves to the ground. Let him shout an
order, and the universe would tremble: time would run faster so
that we might arrive more quickly at the celestial palace where,
since the first day of creation, and, according to certain mystics,
long before that, the Messiah has awaited us.

A Yemenite Jew, I no longer know why. Perhaps because I had
never seen one. For the child I then was, Yemen was not to be
found on any map but somewhere else, in the kingdom of dreams
where all sad children, from every city and every century, join
hands to defy coercion, the passing years, death.

Later on, I saw the prophet and had to admit my error. He was a Jew, to be sure, but he came from no farther away than Poland. Moreover, he had nothing about him of the giant, the legendary hero. Pitiful, stoop-shouldered, he tightened his lips when he looked at you. His movements betrayed his weariness, but his eyes were aflame. One sensed that, for him, the past was his only haven.

It was the first night of Passover. Our household, brightly lit, was preparing to celebrate the festival of freedom. My mother and my two older sisters were bustling about the kitchen, the youngest was setting the table. Father had not yet returned from synagogue.

I was upset: we were going to partake of the ritual meal with only just the family, and I would have preferred having a guest as in preceding years. I recovered my good mood when the door opened and father appeared, accompanied by a poorly dressed, shivering, timid stranger. Father had approached him in the street with the customary phrase: *Kol dichfin yetei veyochal* (Let him who is hungry come eat with us).

"I'm not hungry," the stranger had answered.

"That makes no difference; come along anyway. No one should remain outside on a holiday evening."

Happy, my little sister set another place. I poured the wine.

"May we begin?" my father asked.

"Everything is ready," my mother answered.

Father blessed the wine, washed his hands, and prepared to tell us, according to custom, of the exploits of our ancestors, their flight from Egypt, their confrontation with God and their destiny.

"I'm not hungry," our guest said suddenly. "But I've something to say to you."

"Later," my father answered, a bit surprised.

"I haven't time. It's already too late."

I did not know that this was to be the last *Seder*, the last Passover meal we would celebrate in my father's house.

It was 1944. The German army had just occupied the region. In Budapest the Fascists had seized power. The Eastern front was at Körösmezö, barely thirty kilometers from our home. We could hear the cannon fire and, at night, the sky on the other side of the mountains turned red. We thought that the war was coming to an end, that liberation was near, that, like our ancestors, we were living our last hours in bondage.

Jews were being abused in the streets; they were being humiliated, covered with insults. One rabbi was compelled to sweep the sidewalk. Our dear Hungarian neighbors were shouting: "Death to the Jews!" But our optimism remained unshakable. It was simply a question of holding out for a few days, a few weeks. Then the front would shift and once again the God of Abraham would save his people, as always, at the last moment, when all seems lost.

The *Haggadah*, with its story of the Exodus, confirmed our hope. Is it not written that each Jew must regard himself, everywhere and at all times, as having himself come out of Egypt? And that, for each generation, the miracle will be renewed?

But our guest did not see things that way. Disturbed, his forehead wrinkled, he troubled us. Moody and irritated, he seemed intent upon irritating us as well.

"Close your books!" he shouted. "All that is ancient history. Listen to me instead."

We politely concealed our impatience. In a trembling voice, he began to describe the sufferings of Israel in the hour of punishment: the massacre of the Jewish community of Kolomai, then that of Kamenetz-Podolsk. Father let him speak, then resumed the ancient tale as though nothing had happened. My little sister asked the traditional four questions which would allow my father, in his answers, to explain the meaning and import of the holiday. "Why and in what way is this night different from all other nights?" "Because we were slaves under Pharaoh, but on this night God made us free men." Discontent with both the question and the answer, our guest repeated them in his own way: "Why is this night not different from other nights? Why this continuity of suffering? And why us, always us? And God, why doesn't he intervene? Where is the miracle? What is he waiting for? When is he going to put himself between us and the executioners?"

His unexpected interruptions created a feeling of uneasiness around the table. As soon as one of us opened his mouth, our guest would cut us short:

"You concern yourselves with a past that's three thousand years old and you turn away from the present: Pharaoh is not dead, open your eyes and see, he is destroying our people. Moses is dead, yes, Moses is dead, but not Pharaoh: he is alive, he's on his way, soon he'll be at the gates of this city, at the doors of this house: are you sure you'll be spared?"

Then, shrugging his shoulders, he read a few passages from the *Haggadah*: in his mouth, the words of praise became blasphemies.

Father tried to quiet him, to reassure him: "You're downhearted, my friend, but you must not be. Tonight we begin our holiday with rejoicing and gratitude."

The guest shot him a burning glance and said: "Gratitude, did you say? For what? Have you seen children butchered before their mother's eyes? I have, I've seen them."

"Later," said my father. "You'll tell us all about that later."

I listened to the guest and kept wondering: who is he? what does he want? I thought him sick and unhappy, perhaps mad. It was not until later that I understood: he was the prophet Elijah. And if he bore little resemblance to the Elijah of the Bible or to the prophet of my dreams, it is because each generation begets a prophet in its own image. In days of old, at the time of the kings, he revealed himself as a wrathful preacher setting mountains and hearts on fire. Then, repentant, he took to begging in the narrow streets of besieged Jerusalem, to emerge, later as student in Babylonia, messenger in Rome, beadle in Mayence, Toledo, or Kiev. Today, he had the appearance and fate of a poor Jewish refugee from Poland who had seen, too close and too many times, the triumph of death over man and his prayer.

I am still convinced that it was he who was our visitor. Quite often, of course, I find it hard to believe. Few and far between are those who have succeeded in seeing him. The road that leads to him is dark and dangerous, and the slightest misstep might bring about the loss of one's soul. My Rebbe would cheerfully have given his life to catch one glimpse of him, if only for the span of a lightning flash, a single heartbeat. How then had I deserved what is refused so many others? I do not know. But I maintain that the guest was Elijah. Moreover, I had proof of this soon afterward.

Tradition requires that after the meal, before prayers are resumed, a goblet of wine be offered the prophet Elijah, who, that evening, visits all Jewish homes, at the same moment, as though to emphasize the indestructibility of their ties with God. Accordingly, Father took the beautiful silver chalice no one ever used and filled it to the brim. Then he signaled my little sister to go to the door and ask the illustrious visitor to come taste our wine. And we wanted to tell him: you see, we trust you; in spite of our enemies, in spite of the blood that has been shed, joy is not deserting us, we offer you this because we believe in your promise.

In silence, aware of the importance of the moment, we rose to our feet to pay solemn tribute to the prophet, with all the honor and respect due him. My little sister left the table and started toward the door when our guest suddenly cried out:

"No! Little girl, come back! I'll open the door myself!"

Something in his voice made us shudder. We watched him plunge toward the door and open it with a crash.

"Look," he cried out, "there's no one there! No one! Do you hear me?"

Whereupon he leaped out and left the door wide open.

Standing, our glasses in our hands, we waited, petrified, for him to come back. My little sister, on the brink of tears, covered her mouth with both hands. Father was the first to get hold of himself. In a gentle voice he called out after our guest: "Where are you, friend? Come back!"

Silence.

Father repeated his call in a more urgent tone. No reply. My cheeks on fire, I ran outside, sure I would find him on the porch: he was not there. I flew down the steps: he could not be far. But the only footsteps that resounded in the courtyard were my own. The garden? There were many shadows under the trees, but not his.

Father, Mother, my sisters, and even our old servant, not knowing what to think, came out to join me. Father said: "I don't understand."

Mother murmured: "Where can he be hiding? Why?"

My sisters and I went out into the street as far as the corner: no one. I started shouting: "H-e-e-y, friend, where are you?" Several windows opened: "What's going on?"

"Has anyone seen a foreign Jew with a stooped back?"

"No."

Out of breath, we all came together again in the courtyard. Mother murmured: "You'd think the earth swallowed him up."

And Father repeated: "I don't understand."

It was then that a sudden thought flashed through my mind and became certainty: Mother is mistaken, it is the sky and not the earth that has split open in order to take him in. Useless to chase after him, he is not here anymore. In his fiery chariot he has gone back to his dwelling-place, up above, to inform God what his blessed people are going to live through in the days to come.

"Friend, come back," my father shouted one last time. "Come back, we'll listen to you."

"He can't hear you anymore," I said. "He's a long way off by now."

Our hearts heavy, we returned to the table and raised our glasses one more time. We recited the customary blessings, the Psalms, and, to finish, we sang *Chad Gadya*, that terrifying song in which, in the name of justice, evil catches evil, death calls death, until the Angel of Destruction, in his turn, has his throat cut by the Eternal himself, blessed-be-he. I always loved this naïve song in which everything seemed so simple, so primitive: the cat and the dog, the water and the fire, first executioners then victims, all undergoing the same punishment within the same scheme. But that evening the song upset me. I rebelled against the resignation it implied. Why does God always act too late? Why didn't he get rid of the Angel of Death before he even committed the first murder?

Had our guest stayed with us, he is the one who would have asked these questions. In his absence, I took them up on my own.

The ceremony was coming to an end, and we did not dare look at one another. Father raised his glass one last time and we repeated after him: "Next year in Jerusalem." None of us could know that this was our last Passover meal as a family.

I saw our guest again a few weeks later. The first convoy was leaving the ghetto; he was in it. He seemed more at ease than his companions, as if he had already taken this route a thousand times. Men, women, and children, all of them carrying bundles on their backs, blankets, valises. He alone was empty-handed.

Today I know what I did not know then: at the end of a long trip that was to last four days and three nights he got out in a small railway station, near a peaceful little town, somewhere in Silesia, where his fiery chariot was waiting to carry him up to the heavens: is that not proof enough that he was the prophet Elijah?

Under Occupation

Fear of Fear

Ilse Aichinger

Translated from the German by Cornelia Schaeffer

The mirror was like a big, dark escutcheon. In the middle was the star. Ellen laughed happily. She stood on her toes and crossed her arms behind her head. That wonderful star, that star in the middle.

The star was darker than the sun and paler than the moon. The star had big, sharp points. In the twilight its radius was undefined, like the palm of a stranger's hand. Ellen had taken it secretly out of the sewing box and pinned it to her dress.

"Never in the world!" her grandmother had said. "Be happy you're spared that. You don't have to wear it, like the others." But Ellen knew better. Allowed, that was the word: allowed. She sighed deeply and felt relieved. When she moved, the star in the mirror moved too. When she jumped, the star jumped and gave her a wish. When she stepped backward, the star went with her. She put her hands to her cheeks for the happiness of it all, and closed her eyes. The star remained. For a long time it had been the most secret idea of the secret police. Ellen reached for the hem of her skirt and whirled in a circle, dancing.

Damp darkness rose out of the cracks between the boards. Her grandmother had gone away. She had turned the corner, like a rolling ship. As long as she could still be seen, her umbrella drove like a black sail against the wet wind. Indecisive rumors blew frostily down the alleys of the island. Her grandmother had gone away to discover more information.

Information?

Ellen smiled thoughtfully at the star in the mirror. Her grand-mother wanted certainty. Between two mirrors. How uncertain all certainty. Only uncertainty was certain, and had become more and more certain since the creation of the world.

On the floor above, Aunt Sonya was giving piano lessons,. Secretly. In the room to the left, two boys were fighting. Their clear, angry voices were very audible. In the room to the right, the deaf old man shouted to his bulldog: "Do you have any idea what's happening, Peggy? They don't tell me anything, No one tells me anything!"

Ellen got two saucepan lids out of the cupboard and clanged them angrily. The janitress was shouting in the courtyard. It sounded like: *pack—pack—*.

Ellen stared for a moment at the empty gray walls that rose out of the mirror behind her and the star. She was at home alone. Strangers lived in the rooms to the right and the left. She was alone in this room. And this room was home. She took her coat from the hook on the door. Her grandmother might be back soon; she had to hurry. The mirror was like a big, dark escutcheon.

She tore the star from her dress with trembling hands. One had to light the way when it was as dark as this, and how better to light it than with a star? She would not have this forbidden her, not by her grandmother nor the secret police. Quickly, with big, uneven stitches she sewed the star to the left side of her coat. Then she put it on, slammed the door behind her, and ran down the stairs.

She stood beneath the house portal for a moment, breathing deeply. Fog hung in the air. Then she flung herself into the late autumn. She loved it, without knowing it, because it enfolded everything in something deep and dark; and out of this all things rose like something marvelous; it returned to them a notion of the intangible, lending mystery to bareness. It wasn't open and dazzlingly showy like spring—see, I'm coming—it was withdrawn, like someone who knows more—come to me.

Ellen ran. She ran through the foggy old streets, past things unconcerned and smooth, and threw herself into autumn's concealed arms. The star on her coat gave her wings. Her shoe soles slapped noisily on the hard pavement. She ran down the streets of the island.

The cake in the half-lit bakery-shop window brought her to a stop. The cake was white and shiny, and written on it in pink sugar was "Happy Birthday." The cake was for George; it was like peace itself. Folded red curtains surrounded it on all sides, like translucent hands. How often they had stood here and stared. Once it had been a yellow cake and once a green one. But today's was the best of all.

Ellen pushed open the glass door. She entered the bakery like a foreign conqueror, walking up to the counter in long strides.

"Good evening," said the saleswoman absently. Then she lifted her eyes from her fingernails and was silent.

"Happy birthday," said Ellen. "That's the cake I'd like."

Her hair was long and wet on the collar of her old coat. The coat was much too short, and her plaid skirt showed two hands' breadths beneath it. But that wasn't it. It was the star that was responsible for the turn of events. Bright and calm, it was resplendent on the thin dark-blue cloth, as though convinced it was in the heavens.

Ellen laid the money on the counter; she had saved for weeks. She knew the price.

All the clients stopped doing what they were doing. The saleswoman leaned her thick red arms on the silver cash register. Her glance soaked up the star. She saw nothing but the star. Behind Ellen somebody got up. A chair was pushed against the wall.

"Please, the cake," said Ellen again, pushing the money nearer the cash register with two fingers. She didn't understand this hesitation. "If it costs more," she mumbled unsurely, "if maybe it costs more now, I'll fetch the rest. I still have some at home. And I can hurry. . . ."

She lifted her head and saw the saleswoman's face.

What she saw was hatred.

"If you're still open that long—" stammered Ellen.

"Get out of here!"

"Please," Ellen said anxiously, "you're making a mistake. I know you're making a mistake. I don't want you to give me the cake; I want to buy it! And if it costs more, I'll pay, I mean I'm ready to—"

"Nobody's asking you," explained the saleswoman icily. "Get out! Go! Now! Or I'll have you arrested!"

She removed her arms from the cash register and started walking slowly around the counter.

Ellen stood very still, looking at the woman's face. She wasn't sure she was really awake. She ran her hand over her eyes.

The saleswoman stood close before her. "Go! Can't you hear me? Be happy I'm going to let you go!" She was screaming.

None of the customers budged. Ellen turned toward them, looking for help. It was then they all saw the star on her coat. Some began to laugh jeeringly. Others produced pitying smiles. No one helped her.

"It costs more," said one of the customers.

Ellen looked down. Suddenly she knew the price of the cake. She had forgotten it. She had forgotten that people wearing the star weren't allowed in the stores and still less in a bakery that served coffee and cakes at tables. The price of the cake was the star. "No," said Ellen, "no, thank you."

The saleswoman reached for her collar. Somebody pushed open the glass door. In the dimly lit display case was the cake. Like peace.

The star was searing. It burned through the blue sailor coat and drove Ellen's blood to her cheeks. So one had to choose. One had to choose between one's star and all other things.

Ellen had envied the children with the star—Herbert, Kurt and Leon, all her friends, but she hadn't understood their fear. Now the saleswoman's grip brushed the back of her neck like a shudder. Since the edict she had fought to have the star, but now it burned like flaming metal through her coat and dress to her skin.

And what was she going to tell George?

Today was George's birthday. Panels had been laid into the tabletop so it would be as large as possible, and it was covered with a big bright cloth the color of apple blossoms. The lady who lived in the room beside the kitchen had lent it to George for his birthday.

George thought it strange to be lent something for his birthday. Lent. The thought wouldn't leave him. He sat, stiff and alone, at the place of honor and waited for his guests; he froze. His bed and his father's had been pushed to the wall in order to make room. Still, they would not be able to dance, as Bibi wanted. George wrinkled his brow and laid his hands on the table before him. He was sad that he wouldn't be able to offer his guests everything they wanted. The big black cake stood helplessly among cups, as though it had been enthroned against its better judgment. It was all a mistake; it wasn't chocolate, it was just black.

George sat very still. He had waited so long, unreasonably happy, for this day. He was as happy as his parents had been fifteen years earlier when they carried him out of the lighted hospital, down the street into the falling dusk. George was glad to have been born. But his gladness had never been as enormous as this last year.

For weeks they had talked about his birthday party; for weeks they had planned and talked it all over with one another. To make it more of a celebration, his father had lent him a dark-gray suit. A narrow leather strap held his trousers up. The jacket was broad and double-breasted, and from George's shoulders it hung down, quite calm and unconcerned. If only the star hadn't been there, the big yellow star on the handsome jacket!

It spoiled all George's joy.

The star was the color of the sun. It had unmasked the sun, that beloved, beaming constellation of childhood. If you scrunched up your eyes, it grew a black rim that expanded and contracted. In the middle it said "Jew."

Despairingly George laid his hand over it, then let it fall. Veils floated out of the still courtyard, through the dull window panes, and tried to muffle the star. The secret police had forbidden hiding the star. So the dusk became punishable, like the moon, as often as its mocking light was thrown over the blacked-out city.

George sighed. His guests rang the bell. He jumped up and ran around the table.

"Are you all here?"

"Ellen's missing."

"Maybe she isn't coming any more."

"Maybe she doesn't want to come."

"Maybe it's not a good thing to be with us."

"I don't believe that," said George thoughtfully. The veils still drifted through the panes. And the cake still stood, black and unhappy, in the middle of the table.

"Ellen's bringing another cake," said George urgently. "A real one. Ellen doesn't have to wear the star. She just pushes open the door, puts the money down on the counter, and says, 'The cake, please,' and she gets it. That's possible. You can have anything if you don't wear a star."

Bibi laughed, but it didn't sound as though she was really laughing. The others sat in a circle and tried vainly to make conversation with quiet and noncommittal voices like grownups; as though they couldn't hear the crying in the room next door, and as though they weren't afraid.

George stood up, pulled in his belt, and laid his hands flatly and unsurely on the tablecloth. He coughed and drank a swallow of water. He wanted to make a speech and he wanted to do it ceremoniously. He wanted to say: I thank you most sincerely for coming; it makes me very happy. I want to thank Bibi and Hannah and Ruth for the three silk handkerchiefs which I really need. I want to thank Kurt and Leon for the leather tobacco pouch; I'd been wishing for one for a long time. When the war's over, I'll pull it out of my pocket suddenly and we'll all smoke a peace pipe. I want to thank Herbert for the red water ball; it belongs to us all now. Next summer we'll play dodge ball again.

George wanted to say all that. That's why he stood up and laid both hands on the tablecloth. That's why he kept tapping his fingers on the edge of the table. He was rapping for silence.

The children had been silent for quite some time, but not the young man next door. His crying drowned George's words in his mouth, as a wind will blow out one match after another.

George wanted to make a great speech. He wanted to say everything, but now he only said, "Somebody's crying," and sat back down again.

"Somebody's crying," repeated Kurt sullenly.

A spoon fell on the floor. Bibi slipped under the table and picked it up.

"Isn't it silly," said Herbert, "to cry like that? Because of nothing and nothing."

"Nothing and nothing," said Leon despairingly, "that's it. That's it, I tell you."

"Have some cake!" called George. It was supposed to cheer them up but it sounded rather frightening. They all took some cake. George watched them anxiously. They ate quickly, forcing themselves; the cake was too dry. They gagged. "Ellen will be here soon with the other cake," said George. "It's always good to have the best last—"

"Ellen isn't coming," interrupted Kurt. "She doesn't want to be seen with us any more."

"Because of the star."

"She's forgotten us."

Ruth got up and went around pouring tea, quietly and quickly without spilling any. The children's lost eyes met over the white cups. Herbert pretended something had gone down the wrong way and began to cough.

George went slowly from one to the other, slapping them on the shoulder as he went by and saying "Old man" or something like it, and laughing. The others laughed with him. As soon as they stopped even for a second they could hear the crying next door very clearly. Kurt wanted to tell a funny story, and turned over a cup by mistake.

"It doesn't matter," said George. "It doesn't matter at all."

Bibi jumped up and laid her napkin under the wet spot.

The veils coming in through the windows changed from gray to black.

Bibi whispered something to Kurt.

"No secrets on my birthday!" muttered George irritably.

"Just be glad you don't know," Bibi called across the table in her clear, somewhat loud voice. "Be glad, George, it's nothing for your birthday." Bibi was happy when she could have a secret. She thought no further than that—about what it contained. If it was a secret, she was pleased.

The crying next door went on and on. Suddenly Hannah jumped up. "I'm going to ask him," she called excitedly. "I'm going to ask him. Right now."

George blocked the door. He spread his arms and pressed his head against the wood, a living barricade against the crying which is always next door if you can hear it. Hannah grabbed his shoulders and tried to push him away.

"I've got to know, you hear me?"

"It's none of our business. It's bad enough that we have to live door to door with strangers. Why they laugh or cry is none of our business."

"It is our business," Hannah shouted, beside herself. "It always has been our business, only we thought we were being tactful. But now it's become urgent." She turned to the others. "Help me. You've got to help me! We've got to make certain!"

"You can't ask for certainty," George said softly. "That's what grownups do, almost all of them, and that's why one dies. Because one demands certainty. However much you ask, it will always remain uncertain. Always, you understand? For as long as you live." His fingers were cramped on the door jamb. After a while his arms grew limp and threatened to drop.

"You're sick," said Hannah. "You're sick, George."

The others stood around in a silent circle.

Herbert pushed to the front.

"Do you want to know what Bibi said just now? I know! I heard it. Shall I tell you? Shall I?"

"Tell!"

"Don't tell!"

"Herbert, if you do—"

"Bibi said—she said—"

"I don't want to know!" screamed George. "Today's my birthday and I don't want to know!" His arms finally dropped. "Today's my birthday," he repeated exhaustedly, "and you've all wished me happiness. All of you."

"He's right," said Leon. "Today's his birthday and that's all. Let's play something."

"Yes," said George, "please." His eyes began to shine again. "I've gotten out the cards for Old Maid."

"What'll we play for?"

"For honor."

"For honor?" Kurt jeered. "Whose honor? In that case you might as well play for the star."

"You're beginning all over again," said George stiffly.

"So now I'll tell you," Herbert stammered. "Now I'll tell you what Bibi told me. She said"—and before she managed to put her hand over his mouth he went on—"Bibi said: the star means death."

"That's not true!" said Ruth.

"I'm scared," said Hannah. "I still want to have seven children and a house on the Swedish coast. But sometimes, lately, my father runs his hand over my hair, and then, before I can turn around, he starts whistling—"

"The grownups," Herbert said excitedly, "the grownups in our houses speak to each other in foreign languages."

"They always do that," said Leon. "They always have." Then his voice changed. "It's all becoming clearer."

"Unclearer," said Ruth.

"It's clouding over," explained Leon. It seemed to him as though he was telling a secret he would have done better to keep. Give yourself over to uncertainty so that you may find something sure.

The others turned away. "May we, George? It's getting stuffy in here." They threw open the window and leaned out. It was as dark and deep as the sea. The courtyard was unrecognizable.

"If we were to jump now?" Kurt said hoarsely. "One right after the other. It would take just a moment, and then we wouldn't be afraid any more. Not afraid. Just think of it!"

The children closed their eyes and saw themselves clearly, jumping one after the other. Black, quick and straight, as though there were water below.

"Isn't that good?" said Kurt. "They'll find us all soft and motionless. Some people say the dead laugh. Then we'll be laughing at them."

"No!" screamed Herbert. "No, you can't do that!"

"Mama won't let you!" jeered Kurt.

"It's something everyone has to know for himself," Ruth said quietly, out of the dark room. "You don't throw away what you get as a birthday present."

"And today's my birthday," announced George. "You're all very impolite." He tried with all his strength to lure the others away from the window. "Who knows whether we'll be together next year? Maybe this is our last party."

"Next year!" Kurt said bitterly.

Despair again fell over the children.

"Please have some cake!" screamed George, frantically. If only Ellen were here. Ellen might have helped him. Ellen would have persuaded them to come away from the window. But she wasn't here.

"Suppose we did it," Kurt pressed on. "Suppose we did it now! We've nothing to lose."

"Nothing but the star."

Ellen was terrified.

The veil of fog tore open, and the sky became a high, arched mirror. It no longer reflected a figure—no outline and no definition; no question and no fear. Now it reflected only the star. Glimmering, calm and relentless.

The star led Ellen through damp, dark streets, away from George, away from her friends, away from all her desires, in a direction that was the opposite of all other directions, where all became one.

Giddily she reeled along, her arms spread, stumbling after the star. She leaped and reached, but nothing was within her reach. The star hung on no wires.

Had her grandmother's warnings been right?

"Don't you dare take out that star—be glad it doesn't apply to you! No one knows what the star means. And no one knows where it leads."

No, and you weren't supposed to know. You weren't allowed to know. You had only to follow it, and this decree applied to them all.

Therefore why should one be afraid? What was the use of a prophet as long as there was the star? Wasn't it within the star's power to dissolve time and break through fear? Ellen suddenly stopped. She seemed to have arrived. Slowly her glance left the star and wandered down the sky until it met the rooftops. And from the roofs it wasn't a long way to numbers and names. It was all the same; they hid themselves from the star.

Ellen stood in front of Julia's house. Julia, whom no one mentioned, whom they had shut out after she had shut herself out. She didn't want to belong to them; fear was written in their faces. They were bound to misfortune. Even long ago, on the quay, Julia hadn't wanted to play with them. She should have worn the star, but she didn't. Since the law about the star had been enforced Julia no longer went out into the street.

She no longer counted herself among the children with the star. "I'm going to leave my house only to go to America!"

"You won't get a visa. I didn't get one."

"Not you, Ellen, but I'll get one. I'm going to leave with the last train, with the very last train."

Since then Ellen hadn't seen Julia any more. Julia was the name of everlasting success, while Ellen was the name of incomprehensible, everlasting failure. Besides, the children considered a visit to her as betrayal. But her grandmother had said, not so long ago: "I think Julia's going to America. You should say good-bye to her."

"Say good-bye? To her? Maybe you want me to be cheerful and wish her a happy trip?"

Ellen groaned and pulled up her coat collar.

A few seconds later she was folded into a pair of arms and told, among many quick, tender kisses, that Julia had been granted a visa for America only a few hours ago.

Julia was sixteen years old and wore long silk underpants; she occupied herself sorting handkerchiefs according to color.

Ellen sat on a light-green stool, all pale and stiff, trying to keep down her tears. She pulled her legs in under her so she wouldn't dirty the scattered clothes.

A big truck stood in front of the window.

"I used to play at packing," said Ellen heavily.

"Play!" exclaimed Julia.

"I haven't done it for a long time," said Ellen.

"Why are you crying?" asked the older girl, in amazement.

Ellen didn't answer. "Green with white rims!" she said instead, picking up a pair of sunglasses with admiration. "Are you going to take along a prayer book?"

"A prayer book? That's a strange idea, Ellen! That's a product, I believe, of your development."

"Most ideas come from your development," muttered Ellen.

"What would I need a prayer book for?"

"Maybe . . ." said Ellen, "I thought, in case the ship sinks. In that case it would be a good idea to have. . ."

Julia dropped her handkerchiefs and stared at Ellen in fright. "Why should the ship sink?"

"Aren't you scared?"

"No!" screamed the older child angrily. "No, I'm not scared. Why should I be scared?"

"It's possible," Ellen persisted calmly. "It's possible, you know. Ships do sink."

"Maybe that's what you want to have happen to me?"

Both of them were breathing heavily. And before either of them came to their senses they had pulled each other down to the floor. "Take it back!" They rolled under the piano. "You're envious of me. I'm going off on a huge adventure!"

Pain lent Ellen strength. While Julia pinned her arms to her sides, she butted her head against Julia's chin. But since the older girl was bigger and much more agile, it was quite easy for her to defend herself. So she held on and whispered cruelly: "The ocean is blue-green. They're waiting for me on the pier. And in the west there are palm trees."

"Stop it!" gasped Ellen, and she tried to gag Julia with her hand. But Julia burbled on about college and golf, straight through Ellen's fingers, and when she let go for a moment Julia said clearly:

"Three people have vouched for me."

"Yes," screamed Ellen bitterly. "And nobody will vouch for me."

"Nobody could vouch for you."

"Thank heaven not," said Ellen.

Exhausted, they both fell silent.

"You envy me," said Julia. "You've always envied me."

"Yes," replied Ellen. "That's true. I've always envied you. Even way back when you could walk and I couldn't, when you had a bicycle and I didn't. And now? Now you're going to sail across the sea and I'm not. Now you're going to see the Statue of Liberty, and I'm not—"

"Now I'm going off on a huge adventure. A bigger adventure than you'll ever have," said Julia triumphantly.

"No," said Ellen quietly, and she let go. "I think the bigger adventure is not to have all those things."

Julia reached again for Ellen, pressed her shoulders to the wall and looked at her with fear. "Do you want my ship to sink? Yes or no?"

"No!" Ellen shouted impatiently. "No, no, no! Then you'd have the bigger adventure, and besides—"

"Besides?"

"Then you couldn't give my mother my love." She stopped, terrified, and the end of the battle took place in silence.

Anna opened the door and stood outlined against the dark. She was wearing a pale scarf, and laughing. "Like drunken sailors!" she said calmly. She lived in the same house and sometimes came upstairs. She was older than Julia.

Ellen jumped up, bumped her head against the edge of the piano, and called: "I can see your star gleaming!"

"I washed it yesterday," replied Anna, "If I've got to wear it, it might as well gleam." She leaned her head against the doorjamb. "Really, everybody should wear stars!"

"Not me," said Ellen bitterly. "I'm not allowed to wear one! I've got two wrong grandparents too few. And so they say I don't belong."

"Oh, you know," said Anna and she laughed again. "Maybe it's all the same whether you wear it on your coat or in your face."

Julia picked herself up slowly and painfully. "In any case, you wear it twice—on your coat and in your face. Do you always have a reason for being so cheerful?"

"Yes," replied Anna. "Don't you?"

"No," said Julia hesitatingly. "Even though I'm going to America next week. But Ellen envies me."

"Why?" asked Anna.

"It's clear as anything," murmured Ellen.

"Perfectly clear," said Anna. "America. I just wanted to know specifically."

"The ocean," stammered Ellen in confusion. "And freedom."

"That's less specific," replied Anna quietly.

"How do you do it?" Ellen said. "I mean, do you have a special reason?"

"What do you mean?"

"What I said a minute ago—you gleam."

"I've no special reason," said Anna slowly.

"Yes, you do!" insisted Julia. "Why did you come?"

"I came to say good-bye to you."

"But I only got the visa today, and you couldn't have known—"

"No," Anna said heavily. "I didn't know. Still, I came to say good-bye."

"I don't understand you."

"I'm going away too."

"Where?"

Anna didn't answer.

Ellen jumped up. "Where are you going?"

Julia was pink with pleasure, "We'll go together!"

"Where are you going?" repeated Ellen.

Anna gazed quietly at her very pale, tormented face.

"Do you envy me, Ellen?"

Ellen turned away her head, yet she felt obliged to look.

"Yes or no?"

"Yes," said Ellen softly, and it seemed to her as though in her despair her words remained hanging in the room. "Yes, I envy you."

"Be careful!" called Julia jokingly. "Now she'll start a fight with you."

"Leave her alone," said Anna.

"She's right," murmured Ellen tiredly. "But my mother's over there. And freedom."

"Freedom, Ellen, is where your star is."

She pulled Ellen to her. "Is it really true? Do you envy me?" Ellen tried to pull herself away, biting her lips, but she couldn't.

Again she turned away and again she felt obliged to look at this face. There she saw for a moment a break in the shine. In Anna's face she saw fear, deathly fear, and a tortured mouth.

"No," stammered Ellen in terror. "No, I don't envy you. Where are you going?"

"What's the matter with you both?" said Julia impatiently. Anna stood up and pushed Ellen away. "I came to say good-bye."

"Can we travel together?"

"No," said Anna. "Our directions are different." She leaned against the wall and tried to find words.

"I've been—I've been ordered to Poland."

This was what they didn't dare mention: her grandmother, Aunt Sonya, all of them, all of them. This was what they trembled before. For the first time, Ellen heard it aloud. All the fear in the world was locked in it.

"What are you going to do?" asked Julia, rooted.

"Go," said Anna.

"No, I don't mean that, I mean—what are you going to hope for?"

"Everything," said Anna. And the shine of an enormous hope flooded over the fear in her face.

"Everything?" Ellen asked softly. "Did you say everything?"

"Everything," repeated Anna quietly. "I've always hoped for everything. Why should I stop now?"

"That's . . ." stammered Ellen, "that's what I meant. That's what the star means—everything!"

Julia looked from one to the other in confusion.

"Wait!" said Ellen, "I won't be long. I'm just going to get the others."

And before someone could stop her she had slammed the door behind her.

Startled, they moved away from the window.

"Come with me!"

"Where to?"

"If you want to know what the star means. . . ."

They were weakened by fear and asked no more questions, so glad they were to be pulled away from the sucking void.

They ran behind Ellen silently. They no longer saw the small heavily laden vans at the edge of the railroad in the dark, nor the tearful faces nor the smiles of the uncaring guards. Like Ellen, they saw only the star. They stopped short in front of Julia's house.

"Not to Julia!"

"No," said Ellen, and she opened the door.

Julia had put away the scattered handkerchiefs. When she greeted the children, she never mentioned her visa and she didn't look them in the face.

"We'd never have come to see you," said Bibi in her high voice. "It's Ellen's doing."

"Never!" repeated the others.

"We'd have found this easy to do without," said Kurt.

Their heavy shoes left tracks on the clean floor.

"Anna's here," said Ellen.

Anna: it was like a breath; like taking and giving at the same time.

Anna was sitting on the trunk and she smiled a greeting. They lost their constraint. "Don't you want to sit down?"

They sat down in a circle on the floor. Steerage passengers. It suddenly seemed as if they'd been traveling a long time.

"What do you want to know?"

"We want to know what the star means."

Anna looked quietly from one to another. "Why do you want to know that?"

"Because we're scared." Their faces flickered.

"And what are you afraid of?" asked Anna.

"Of the secret police!" They all said it together.

Anna lifted her head and looked at them all. "Why, of all things, are you afraid of the secret police?"

The children were silent in confusion.

"They forbid us to breathe," said Kurt, and he grew red with anger. "They spit at us and chase us."

"Very strange," said Anna. "Why do they do that?"

"They hate us."

"Have you done something to them?"

"Nothing," said Herbert.

"You're in the minority. You're relatively smaller and weaker than they are. You're unarmed. And still they can't seem to stop."

"We all want to know what the star means!" shouted Kurt. "What's going to happen to us?"

"When it gets dark," said Anna, "when it gets very dark, what happens then?"

"You're afraid."

"And what do you do?"

"You defend yourself."

"You lash out at things, do you?" said Anna. She paused. "And then you notice that it's no use. It gets darker still. Then what do you do?"

"You look for a light," shouted Ellen.

"A star," said Anna. "It's very dark around the secret police."

"You think—you really think that's true?"

Restlessness spread among the children. Wildly, whitely, their faces gleamed.

"I know!" George jumped up. "I know now. I know!"

"What do you know?"

"The secret police is afraid!"

"Of course," said Anna. "The secret police is fear. Living fear, nothing else." The shine on her face deepened.

"The secret police is afraid!"

"And we're afraid of them!"

"Fear of fear—they cancel out."

"Fear of fear, fear of fear!" said Bibi and laughed.

They started jumping around the big trunk.

"The secret police has lost its star."

"The secret police follows a strange star."

"The one they've lost and the one we wear is the same!"

"Suppose we're wrong to be glad," said Bibi, stopping suddenly. "Suppose it's still true, what I've heard?"

"What have you heard?"

"That the star means death."

"How do you know that, Bibi?"

"Because my parents thought I was asleep."

"Maybe you understood wrong," murmured Ellen. "Maybe they meant that death means a star?"

"Don't let yourselves be led astray," said Anna softly. "That's all I can tell you. Follow the star. Don't ask grownups; they won't tell you the truth, not the deep truth. Ask yourselves. Ask your angel."

"The star!" said Ellen, with glowing cheeks. "The Wise Men's star—I knew it all the time!"

"Be sorry for the secret police," said Anna. "They're afraid of the King of the Jews again."

Julia stood up and said as she drew the curtains, "How dark it's gotten!"

"So much the better," said Anna.

A Chicken for the Holidays

Bernard Gotfryd

At the time the Nazis occupied our city in September of 1939 my father owned a used-furniture business that he had taken over from my grandfather shortly before the war. One afternoon around October of 1940, some months before the ghetto was established, a Polish farmer came in with his wife to purchase an antique bed. They settled on a huge, very old bed with an exceedingly heavy, tall bedstead. When the time came to pay for it, the couple realized they were short of money. Perhaps, my father suggested affably, they could compensate him with some provisions from their farm instead. It was agreed that one of us would visit before long—the farm was about one hour's walk from the city—to collect our debt. I happened to be present during the transaction and was introduced by my father to the farmer, Mr. Dombroski; I helped him load the bed onto his wagon. He thanked me for my help and left, obviously pleased with the acquisition.

Some months went by, but none of us ventured out to the farm. Eventually my father gave up on the idea entirely because of the danger of crossing the city limits without a proper pass, and because passes were impossible to get.

Shortly before the Jewish High Holidays I heard my mother mention how nice it would be to have a chicken for the holidays. Immediately I thought of Mr. Dombroski's agreement with Father and started plotting a trip to the farm. I would have to walk; there was no public transportation in rural areas, and Jews were no longer allowed to ride or own bicycles, under penalty of death. It was the time of martial law: no hearings, no trials, and no excuses.

I asked my Polish friend George about the safest way of walking to the Dombroskis' and if he would like to accompany me. He refused. "It's an insane idea," he told me. I even thought of asking a German soldier I knew, a client at the photo studio where I worked, if he would escort me, but thought it to be presumptuous on my part. Although I knew how risky it was to cross the city line without a pass, alone or with a companion, I became obsessed with the idea. I wasn't going to let George or anyone else discourage me. The anticipation of adventure and the risk involved must have appealed to me, but above all I could visualize my family at the holiday dinner eyeing a cooked chicken at the center of the table. My mouth started watering at the mere thought of being able to savor a chicken giblet, as in the old days. Chickens were hard to come by and were very expensive. Open markets were banned, and farmers didn't bring their produce into town for fear of having it confiscated.

Only two days remained before the holidays. I started out on a rainy afternoon without revealing my plans to anyone—not even to my mother. The chicken was going to be a surprise. As soon as I crossed the city line, so as not to attract attention, I took off the arm band with the Star of David and briskly followed the road toward the Jewish cemetery. To be caught without the arm band was punishable by death. Soon, for safety reasons, I got off the road and walked along narrow, muddy paths or crossed pastures full of puddles. The rain intensified; the sky began to darken. Flocks of crows pecked away at the wet fields, taking off noisily at the slightest motion only to land again seconds later.

As I neared the cemetery I saw a military truck surrounded by people in uniform. Instinctively I took a detour through the woods; I had to avoid anyone in uniform at all cost. When I stopped for a moment to orient myself I realized how insane I was to be there, but I wasn't about to turn back at that point. I continued along the edge of the woods for some time until I came to a clearing covered by fog. Suddenly a salvo of rifle shots rang out from the direction of the cemetery. I stopped behind a hollow tree and virtually pressed myself into it. I was mortified.

The sky turned a dark gray; it was still raining. There was not a living soul in sight, not the slightest sound save for the wet leaves and rustling twigs underfoot; I felt as if I was alone in the world. The fog was all around me; like a procession of floating ghosts it kept spreading, enveloping every tree at the edge of the forest.

Still there was no farm in sight. Momentarily I lost my way. I wasn't sure if I really knew the country as well as I thought I did. Just then I started hearing children's voices. I stopped and turned to look, but nobody was there. I didn't think I was hallucinating, for I could still hear the voices, a whole chorus. I looked up and saw the wind-whipped treetops move in a wild dance, twirling and rotating; they were creating all sorts of weird squeaking sounds. It was eerie.

I looked at my watch; it was after six o'clock. There wasn't much time left to find the farm and get back to the city before curfew, which would begin at eight. A wild rabbit frightened me as it sped by, leaping over the brush. As I walked on I could hear the pounding of my own heart.

Some minutes later, through a thick haze, I saw the farmhouse in a clearing between the woods and a small lake surrounded by weeping willows. As I came closer to the fence a dog started barking; moments later a woman opened the door of the house. It was Mrs. Dombroski. She didn't recognize me at first, but when I told her who I was she pulled me inside.

"Oh, yes, I remember you now," she said in her high-pitched voice. "Sure, sure, I know, I know. Please come inside.

"We were wondering why no one ever showed up, so here you are. Well, my husband should be right back, and he will give you something. Maybe some fresh milk? Sit down at the table, please." I was starved and exhausted. "Thank you, ma'am," I said, and I sat down on a wooden bench. At the other end of the room I saw the huge bed they had purchased from my father, piled high with richly embroidered pillows. The bedstead reached almost to the ceiling. I was wondering what had happened to the milk Mrs. Dombroski had offered me.

Mrs. Dombroski seemed to need to talk. She moved about in her long, colorful skirt, chattering ceaselessly; everything she said, she said twice. When she finally stopped talking I asked her if I might have a live chicken.

"A live chicken?" she repeated twice after me. "And how will you carry it back to the city so that a patrol won't stop you?" she asked. "It's dangerous to carry anything live, you know. You may get arrested, or even shot. Who knows? I will be happy to give you one, but it would be easier to kill it here and take it back dead." I needed a live chicken, however, so that it could be slaughtered according to the kosher law.

"I would rather have it live," I told her stubbornly. "I can hide it under my brother's raincoat. It's a big raincoat, and there shouldn't be a problem." I didn't think I could explain that for a chicken to be kosher it would have to be slaughtered according to the laws of kashruth, for which Mrs. Dombroski couldn't be responsible.

Mr. Dombroski soon returned; after hearing me out he decided to let me have a live chicken. In the event I was stopped, he said, it would be my responsibility.

"You are not to tell anyone where you got the chicken. Chances are that you could be accused of having stolen it, which would only make matter worse," he said.

Finally Mrs. Dombroski gave me a tin cup of fresh milk and a thick slice of home-baked bread. I hadn't had fresh milk in months, and the bread tasted like cake. When I thanked her for her hospitality she just waved her hand at me, saying, "I would like to give you more, but I'm afraid too much fresh milk would make you sick." Then she went out, to return with a gray-yellow bird, not very big, with scared eyes. It kept turning its head nervously without making a sound. She had tied its feet and wings with strap of cloth to prevent its escape. The chicken fit under my raincoat with feet tied behind my belt; I would have to support it with my left hand through the raincoat pocket. The Dombroskis silently stuffed my empty pockets with bread and potatoes, and Mr. Dombroski walked me to the road. I must have looked ridiculous loaded down with so many provisions.

"If they catch you," Mr. Dombroski said, "you don't know me, and I don't know you." "I won't tell a thing," I assured him. "And don't forget to tell your father that we're even. The chicken is worth much more than I owe him." He wished me luck and went back to his house. I took a shortcut, bypassing the woods, and trudged along a narrow, muddy road. I feared that I might not be able to make it back on time if I was to return through the woods; in any event, my shoes were covered with thick mud, and my feet were wet and cold.

It was past dusk; the visibility was bad. The whole landscape seemed to be drowning in the rain, which had long since penetrated every inch of my raincoat. A farmer drove by, his horse and wagon splashing me with mud. The chicken kept quiet, and it kept me warm, and as I got closer to the city line the fog started to lift, exposing the contours of a row of low-lying houses. I leaned against a tree to rest and slipped on my arm band. I realized I was just as scared wearing the arm band as I was without it.

By the time I crossed the city line it was almost dark. At a street intersection a German soldier in an SS uniform emerged from a house and blocked my way. I stopped and recognized him immediately: It was Schultz, a Pole-Volksdeutsch of German descent who had volunteered for the Waffen SS. Some weeks before he had come to the studio to be photographed, and I had taken care of him.

"Where are you off to at this hour?" he asked me.

"I'm on my way home after visiting a sick friend, sir," I lied. "I just realized how close it is to curfew. By the way, I do remember you from the photo studio," I added very casually. Suddenly I felt the chicken move. I wanted only for it to keep quiet; it would have been disastrous had Schultz discovered a chicken under my raincoat.

"Yes, yes, I remember you, too," Schultz answered impatiently, waving me off. "Now hurry home," he yelled. I didn't have to be told twice; I had never walked so fast before.

As soon as I left Schultz the chicken grew restless and noisy; I thought it must have been scared by the SS man's yelling. I tried to caress it with my free hand; I held its beak, but nothing helped. I was desperate; the walk back was the most risky of all, and I knew there was no turning back. I remembered a story my grandmother had told me years before about a young peasant girl who in the middle of the night got lost in the woods while looking for a doctor to attend her sick mother, and who in desperation asked God to guide her.

"Please, God, help me, too, and keep this chicken quiet," I started praying under my breath. "I must get this chicken home alive so we can celebrate the holidays. Please make it keep quiet."

For the next few moments I thought God had heard me. The chicken was silent, though not for very long. Suddenly she let out a loud, attention-getting cluck; fortunately there were no pedestrians in earshot. The streets were nearly deserted.

"Dear God," I continued, "how can you let this chicken jeopardize my life? Please get us home safely. My family is waiting for me."

The chicken's clucking was getting louder. I panicked, tightened my grip around the chicken's neck, and held on until the bird quieted. I felt its legs moving up from behind my belt, its whole body stiffening as if it was trying to free itself. I felt awful.

Just then I saw a German police patrol on the opposite side of the street, walking in my direction. I hid inside the gate of a building until they passed, but they stopped directly across from me to talk to a woman. It was eight minutes before curfew. I broke out in a new sweat. Should I leave the dead chicken in the yard and climb some fences so as to get home faster? Or should I wait a bit longer? After a minute I looked out again, but the patrol was still there with the woman, pointing now at the building in which I was hiding. I was trapped.

Without giving it another thought, with the little strength still left in me, I pulled myself over the fence behind me, the dead chicken dangling from my belt, and sped off through yards and orchards, climbing more fences, some lined with barbed wire, until I reached our street. A friendly stray dog came close, sniffing at the chicken. He followed me to the gate of our building, where I was greeted by a long line of German soldiers waiting their turn at Stasia's whorehouse. Stasia was an enterprising Polish woman who—with the help of the German authorities—had taken over three adjoining sheds, evicting the tenants and converting the sheds to a pleasure house catering exclusively to the German army.

"*Wie gehts dier?*" one of them asked in a sort of friendly tone of voice. "*Danke, sehr gut, mein Herr,*" I answered, and I ran home.

It was past curfew by the time I got to our apartment. My worried mother stood at the door waiting for me. "Where were you?" she demanded with tears in her eyes. "Why all this mud all over you? Did you know how many arrests and executions for curfew violations there are every night?"

As soon as I entered the apartment I pulled out the dead chicken and deposited it on the doormat, as if in explanation.

"I'm sorry, Mother, but the chicken had to be strangled," I said. "It was making too much noise."

"Where did you get a chicken?" Mother asked.

When I told her the whole story tears started running down her face. She came closer to embrace me and held me in her arms. I could feel her tears on my neck, behind my shirt collar, and the strength of her caring arms. It gave me a jolt of renewed self-confidence, moving me to tears.

"I think what you did was extraordinary," Mother said, "and all thanks to the Almighty for bringing you back alive. You committed no crime, and you must promise me never to risk your life again. We would survive even if it meant having a meatless holiday."

"It wasn't very risky," I lied to her. "No one stopped me, and it was nice to be out in the country, even though it rained a lot."

"But now," Mother was saying, "I'm sorry to tell you that in spite of the risk you have taken to make this a better holiday for all of us, we can't eat an unkosher chicken. We'll probably give it to the janitor's family. It would be a shame to throw it away."

"But Mother," I interrupted, "it's wartime, and there's a food shortage. Does it really matter that the chicken isn't kosher? Who'll know? Won't God forgive us?" I pleaded with her, but Mother was unrelenting. "In wartime or peacetime," Mother answered, "we're a people who must abide by the laws, or else we'll cease to be a people. That's the best explanation I can give. But let me assure you that you're a dear son, and I'll always love you."

The chicken went to the janitor's family; weeks later his wife was still talking about it, reminding my mother what a tasty and fat bird it had been.

Grandson

Clara Asscher-Pinkhof

Translated from the Dutch by Terese Edelstein and Inez Smidt

Grandma is made of porcelain. You hardly dare to shake her hand with your strong boyish grip because you are used to grasping so tightly and grandma's hand would certainly fall into pieces if you did that.

She has not been able to move her legs for years. He has never seen her walk, at least, and he is eleven years old. When he was little, he had asked his mother anxiously several times if grandma's legs were whole, because things that were broken were so dreary to him. Grandma's legs are whole, it is just that she cannot move them. If they had been broken it would not have been as easy to love her so very much as he does now. He *would* have loved her, except he would have had to have tried his utmost; but he does not have to do that now.

She lives in a very big house. All the people there are sick or are incapacitated in some way, which is why they live in that house. When he goes to grandma's room, he meets all of those people. He looks the other way, then, but nevertheless he says hello to them because they are nice people and because they cannot help that they are so eerie to look at. He is glad when he comes to grandma and sees her lying so whole and white and clean in her bed. She reaches her thin, white hand out to him and smiles at him with her small, white face. Everything about her is white and smooth and fine. He would like to stroke her if his hands were not so strong and so black. When he is with grandma, he always has the feeling that he should have washed his hands just one more time.

Her voice is just as thin as her hands. She asks him things that
no other adult may ask, for then he would rudely say "yes" or
"no" and think to himself, "You're asking only because you don't
know what else to say to me, but you don't care in the least what
I say." But he knows that grandma cares very much—that is the
difference. Therefore he explains everything to her in a voice that
is much softer than the one he uses outside this room. Then she
looks at him with her sweet eyes—the only thing about her that
is not white—and she nods when she understands him. He knows
for certain that she never nods before she has comprehended it.
Therefore he loves to tell her the things that are actually intended
for boys and not for white, porcelain grandmas.

Then one Monday morning when he is on his way to school,
he comes past the square where grandma's big house is and is
held back. He may not go past. He does not find this unusual
because there is so much that is no longer allowed. It does not
matter if you are late for school when something like this happens; you make a detour because there is nothing else you can
do, and you do not run because the schoolmaster does not mind
if you come late.

But then he sees the big vans parked in front of grandma's
building and suddenly he knows that something very terrible is
happening. He walks a few steps to the front but is shoved back.
No one may come closer, including himself, even if this horrible
thing is going to happen to his own grandma.

People are being carried out of the house and shoved into the
vans. Crippled people—people who cannot move their arms or
legs—people who must let themselves be carried quietly and
shoved and driven away because they cannot do anything else. He
cannot see who they are, he can only hear some of them crying
very loudly and fearfully. He would like to run away if his legs
were not so weak, like grandma's. He knows that grandma will
not cry, at least not loudly. He will not hear her voice, and he

will not see her face, but one of those being carried out there and shoved into the van is grandma—and he cannot stop it.

When his legs can move again and his head is no longer buzzing and whirling, he penetrates through the crowd of people standing behind him, watching, and with dragging feet walks past the detour to school. He does not care anymore, oh, he does not care about anything anymore. If a bomb falls, he does not care; if he comes home and father and mother have been taken away, he does not care; if the schoolmaster no longer wants him in the class, he does not care; if no one wants him anymore, he does not care—for grandma, who is made of porcelain, has been bound up and shoved into a big van.

He rings the bell of the school and is let inside. He takes his coat off because he does that every day. He knows where to find his classroom because he goes inside there every day.

Each pupil has his language lesson in front of him and is writing quietly.

How strange. How can you just sit there and write your language lesson when your grandma has been shoved into a van? But oh, he does not care.

The schoolmaster says something to him. Perhaps he is asking him something. He has not understood exactly.

Now the schoolmaster asks again, and he understands this time.

"Why are you so late?"

Strange. A strange question.

The teacher asks him again.

Then he speaks, and his voice is loud and hoarse as it goes above the large, quiet class.

"I couldn't get by."

White Lie

Clara Asscher-Pinkhof

Translated from the Dutch by Terese Edelstein and Inez Smidt

It is difficult enough for everyone in the city to get food, but it is even more difficult for the Jews. The Jewish fish stores are not permitted to sell fish, and the Jewish greengroceries may not sell fruit but only those vegetables that are left over in the city. The fish stores have merely a few jars of mustard and a little beet salad displayed in the windows. The greengroceries have a lot of turnips at the moment because the people in the city cannot eat all the turnips up. A while ago there were absolutely no vegetables left over. At that time he and father found a little spot one afternoon, a spot where a "Jews forbidden" sign did not stand but that was green nevertheless, and there they picked nettles together. They tasted all right when mother had cooked them—you would almost say that the nettles had been bought in a store.

Of course, you are not permitted to go into a non-Jewish fish store or grocery store, not even between three and five, thus it is difficult enough. And just once they would so like to eat some fruit. Some people get fruit in a package sent from outside the city, but oh, that is dangerous, for if the men in green come after eight o'clock to take you away and if they find apple peelings in your garbage can, even though you say that you have gotten apples from outside the city, nevertheless you and everyone else in the house will be punished. One time they themselves received a fish from a friend of father's who is not Jewish and who thus is allowed to fish. When the fish was eaten, they threw the bones into the toilet because it would have been dangerous to have thrown them into the garbage can. And someone rang their doorbell that evening! Luckily it was not the police but a person who wanted to go to some neighbors of theirs but who came to their house by mistake. They were frightened nevertheless, and happy, too, that there were no fishbones lying in the garbage can!

Now mother wants so very much to have apples for father's birthday, and there is a way to get them, but it is a bit dangerous. He wants to get them just because it is dangerous. He is eight years old but is so small that he could pass for six. And six years old is not much different from five, and if you are five, you do not have to wear a star. Of course he always wears a star, but he has a sweater without a star. Understand? And he is blond, too. He can walk into a non-Jewish grocery and buy two kilograms of apples! Easy enough!

Mother does not find it as easy as he does. He might meet people there who know that he is a little Jewish boy. There might be people there who ask him what his last name is, and their last name sounds Jewish.

"If they ask you why you aren't wearing a star, say that you're five."

"All right," he nods, reassured. He is suddenly happy with his small size, which he has always found so terribly humiliating.

"And if they ask you your name, say that . . . say that it's Dejong. That can be both."

"Dejong," he repeats softly. There are Jewish children at school whose names are DeJong, but mother says that it can be both, so that is all right. Dejong.

All is going well. No one asks him why he is not wearing a star. Being without a star is really a pleasant feeling. When he sees a man in green, he thinks, "He can't do anything to me because he doesn't know that I'm Jewish." It really is a pleasant feeling.

He must wait a long time in the store. There are many women who come before him. When it is his turn, he comes to the counter, his head just reaching above it.

"Two kilograms of apples," he says immediately. He has such a craving for apples.

While she is weighing the fruit, the woman begins to talk to him. She is friendly because he is so small. "What is your name, little one?"

He must reflect a bit.

"DeJong," he says.

"No," smiles the woman. "I mean your first name."

He has not counted on this. His first name? He does not know whether Jopie is a Jewish name or whether it can be both. Still it would be better not to say Jopie. But what, then?

"Come on, tell me," nods the woman.

"Jesus," he says hoarsely.

Daily Life in the Ghetto

A Cupboard in the Ghetto

Rachmil Bryks

Translated from the Yiddish by S. Morris Engel
Hershel Zeif was an emaciated man with a pale, peaked face and lusterless eyes. A native of Kalisz, he had been married in Lodz just before the war. He and his wife, luckily, were able to bring with them into the ghetto their entire wedding outfit, all their clothes, as well as twin beds, a table, several chairs and a clothes cupboard.

For a long time Hershel Zeif ran to the Civil Administration every day looking for work. After a while he became exasperated with the false promises of the officials and decided that if you had no "shoulders" (protection) you couldn't get anything. Now he and his wife spent most of the day in bed—he in one of the twin beds, she in the other—writhing from hunger and cold, like all their neighbors.

Mrs. Zeif was small and thin, with hollow cheeks and big black eyes. She was a quiet woman who never raised her voice. Silently, within herself, she endured the grief and agony of hunger and cold. Both she and her husband were positive that the war would end any day.

When the sun rose higher and lavished its rays, also brightening their window, Hershel and his wife hung their wedding clothes out to air. There was Zeif's black winter coat with a velvet collar; a blue capote with a vent in back; trousers with a crease and cuffs; a pair of boots and a pair of shoes; a half-dozen white shirts; undershirts; a pair of soft leather bedroom slippers and a hard black hat, round as a coin, with a crescent brim like a new moon.

Mrs. Zeif had a black winter coat; a light summer coat; a suit; several dresses; a plush hat and a hand-knitted hat; underclothes; linens and four pairs of shoes.

All these things were brand new, they had never been worn. They were coated with green mildew. After several days in the sun the mildew whitened and then vanished. But after a few days in the house the green mildew appeared again. They decided to air their wedding clothes every day, sunny or not, just as long as it didn't rain. They made a pact: one day he hung his clothes outside the sunny window for several hours—the next day she hung hers. The sun never reached the other window, because it was in a corner opposite a high wall.

When Zeif saw that the mildew was gone a smile of pleasure lit up his haggard face: "Yes, the war might end any minute. God can do anything, and we'll go home in our new clothes. Yes, yes, my dear Henye." His wife nodded in agreement: "That's right."

Hershel Zeif invited his neighbor Bluestein into his house. "Guess how my wife cooked supper today," he said in his weak voice, looking into Bluestein's eyes with a mischievous smile, like a schoolboy trying to confuse a friend with a difficult riddle.

Bluestein looked around, in all the corners, and saw that all was as before: the mouldings of the door and windows and floor had long ago been swallowed up by the tiny kitchen stove. The floor itself could not be ripped up, because it was the second story and they would fall through. Besides, one of "Emperor" Rumkowski's men came by every few days to inspect the floor. Bluestein also saw that the beds, the clothes cupboard, the table and chairs were all there. The beds, by the way, were new and modern. The Zeifs had gotten them in exchange for their old oak beds, and were even paid for the difference in weight.

Bluestein wracked his brain. He wanted to guess the answer, he didn't want to be fooled.

"Come on, guess! You can't guess, can you?" Zeif teased him. "I know!" Bluestein cried confidently. "With the board you got from the tinsmith."

"Ha-ha! A likely story! Why don't you say with last year's snow? That board was used up long ago—even the ashes are gone," Zeif shouted triumphantly.

This was what had happened. It had rained in, and Zeif had to put pans on the beds. After much pleading, the administrator of the buildings in the neighborhood sent him a tinsmith to fix the roof. The tinsmith climbed into the attic, and immediately Zeif heard boards being pried loose over his head. Soon the tinsmith climbed down calmly, with a pile of boards under his arm. Zeif started to shout: "You're a robber! You've ruined me! I almost died until you finally got here! Instead of fixing the roof so it shouldn't rain in on me, you destroyed it and are taking home the wood!? You've made it worse! Don't you have any feelings?"

"Oh, come on now," the tinsmith replied calmly, "why should you eat your heart out over such a little thing? The house isn't even yours. Until it rains again the war might end. Look how hot it is. You know it rains very seldom in the summer, and when it does, it's hardly more than a drizzle. The roof doesn't even get wet. Anyway, we are having a dry summer, and by the fall we'll all have forgotten that there was ever a war, with a ghetto, with an 'Emperor' Rumkowski."

"God forbid the war should last until the fall," Zeif interrupted him. "It's lasted almost two years already."

"Of course. Now take a board for yourself for fuel and it'll bring you luck—you'll see the end of the war," and he thrust a board under Zeif's arms.

Zeif thought: "As I live and breathe, the man is right." Aloud, he said: "What can I do with you? Shall I report you to the 'Emperor's' police? How can I?" He seized the board with both hands and pointed to Bluestein: "But *he's* the one you have to watch out for. He sees that nobody steals any wood."

The tinsmith grew a little frightened, but Bluestein looked at him pityingly and he felt better. Zeif added: "Don't be afraid. I should live so long what a nice man he is, huh, Mr. Bluestein? I swear he would never hurt anyone."

The tinsmith left quickly with his bundle and Zeif went into the house with the board and broke it into small pieces for several days' fuel.

"Mr. Bluestein, can you guess what my wife used for fuel when she cooked supper tonight? You can't guess, can you?"

"No," said Bluestein firmly.

Zeif opened the clothes cupboard with the expression of an inventor demonstrating his work. Bluestein saw that everything was ship-shape. The glassware, the china; even the paper shelving lay flat and smooth, and the linens were arranged in neat piles. Bluestein wondered: "What is he trying to show me?"

Zeif could no longer refrain from boasting. Quickly he lifted up the paper shelving and pointed: "See? Why do I need whole boards on the shelves? The wooden strips are enough." He cut an arc through the air with his thumb, chanting in talmudic fashion: "So I removed the boards. I chopped up three boards, split two of them into strips, put four strips on each level, laid out the shelving paper with the clothes and all the rest of the things and there are my shelves. Can you tell the difference? Now my wife will be able to cook and cook for a long time." He pointed to the bunches of wood which he had divided into four tiny strips each. "More than that isn't necessary. I'm like 'Emperor' Rumkowski with his rations. I dole out rations to my wife. And, thank God, we have what to cook." He showed Bluestein a big heap of cabbage roots.

Not far from Zeif's house there was a large field which the Agriculture Division had rented to one of Rumkowski's officials—formerly a rich man. After the cabbage was picked, Zeif dug out the roots, which were hard and bitter, and also took home the wild cabbage leaves that grew near the roots.

Two weeks later Zeif called Bluestein again and said: "Well, be smart and guess with what my wife cooked her cabbage stew today."

The same game was reenacted. Bluestein pondered, searched, examined every corner of the house and couldn't find any clues to the riddle. Finally Zeif solved it for him. He flung open the door of the cupboard. "Why does a cupboard need a back wall when it stands against a wall? I removed the rest of the wall and now I'll have fuel for a long time."

From the roots and wild leaves Mrs. Zeif prepared appetizers, fish, meat, soups, tsimmes. She let the cabbage cook a while and then put in a lot of bicarbonate of soda, because soda boils up in hot water. She thought: "It is cooking and at the same time the soda draws out the poisons." (The cabbage roots don't get soft even over the biggest fire.)

From the poison Zeif made "marinated herring" (his own invention). He removed the bulbs from the roots, salted them heavily and let them stand. Then he mixed a little vinegar and water, added some paprika ersatz and saccharin. Into this mixture Zeif dipped his scrap of ersatz bread and sighed with pleasure: "Ah—ah—delicious," smacking his lips as in the good old days over a savory roast. He hummed a hasidic tune, drumming his fingers on the table in rhythm. "Oh, a delicious marinated herring! Henye, our enemies should never enjoy it!" And his wife nodded in agreement as they ate with relish.

Two weeks later Zeif called in Bluestein again and asked: "Well, guess how my wife cooked today? This time you must guess!" and he pointed to the cupboard that was covered with a blanket. "See? Today I got still smarter! Why does a cupboard need a door? What's bad about this? Anything wrong? With the door my wife will be able to cook for a long time, and the cupboard is still a cupboard!"

Bluestein touched the cupboard with one finger and it began to sway back and forth.

Zeif defended the dignity of the cupboard: "That's nothing! Who's going to fight with it? A cupboard doesn't have to be strong, man!"

Bluestein's heart ached because of Zeif's decency—and he agreed that Zeif was a smart, practical man, a real inventer. Zeif tried to smile, but a grimace distorted his face.

The next day Mrs. Zeif, sobbing with terror, called in Bluestein: "Mr. Bluestein, look what's happened to my husband!"

Zeif lay in bed, unable to move. Overnight he had grown so swollen and his head and face so huge, that it covered the entire pillow. The bed was too narrow for his body.

Zeif said in a weak voice: "Look what happened to me! And all because I have no 'shoulders!' "

Bluestein tried to console him. "Don't worry, Mr. Zeif, the war will end any day now, and we'll go home together."

"Yes, Mr. Bluestein, my wife and I haven't even used up our wedding outfit."

"Listen to me, Mr. Zeif, sell some of your wedding clothes and buy yourself some bread and a bit of meat. When you go back to the city you'll get new clothes, maybe even better ones."

"We'll never sell anything from our wedding outfit. I just told you, we didn't even replace any of it. To spite the Germans we'll go home in those clothes!"

Bluestein didn't urge him, because he didn't want Zeif to doubt that the war would end any day. He said lightly:

"Don't worry about the swelling, it's nothing," but he was sure that Zeif would soon lose the battle with his hunger. At the door he said: "Mr. Zeif, in the middle of the night I'll come running in to tell you that the war is over!" and he left the house. He recalled that he had read in the forbidden *Deutsche Zeitung* the speech which Hans Greizer, may his name be blotted out, delivered to the Hitler youth on May 1, 1940, the day when the ghetto was sealed off with barbed wire:

"The Jews are finished," Greizer said. "Hunger will turn them into mad dogs. They will bite chunks of flesh from each other. They will devour themselves!"

"It's true, we are dying out because of hunger," Bluestein thought, "but we have not become wild beasts. Not only are we not biting chunks of flesh from each other, but we don't even want to exchange a single garment from our wedding outfits for a piece of bread and meat. We don't steal and we don't kill. No, he will not turn us into mad dogs! On the outside we look like corpses, but inside we have preserved the image of God."

Early next morning Bluestein went to see how Hershel Zeif was feeling. He was afraid that Zeif had not lasted the night, or that he had taken his own life because of his suffering and despair.

But Bluestein was surprised! Overnight Zeif had grown as thin as a rail, and his skin was like that of a corpse. He couldn't get off the bed. Again Bluestein consoled him: "See, the swelling is gone! That's a good sign. You're getting better, you'll soon be well. Be patient, Mr. Zeif, we'll go home together."

"Oh, I haven't lost faith yet! What's this nonsense about my getting well soon? I'm not sick! I was never sick in my life! I'm just a little weak from hunger. I have pain—but that's nothing. The hell with 'them!' Do you remember what Greizer, may his name be blotted out, said in those days? You should remember. He said: 'The Jews are finished.' Believe me, Mr. Bluestein, 'They are finished!' Last night I had a wonderful dream. I saw my father, of blessed memory, and—the war was over and I was beating up the Germans and 'Emperor' Rumkowski and his henchmen. How I took revenge! How I cooled my heart! I should be as sure of meeting my family again as I am sure that 'they' will die an unnatural death!" Zeif ranted in his weak voice.

"It's good, Mr. Zeif, good that you haven't lost faith! I admire you. You'll see, we'll go home together!"

Bluestein walked down the stairs with an aching heart, thinking: "Who knows what will happen to him? Hunger has already turned him into an obituary. The Angel of Death has placed his mark on him."

A little later Bluestein received the new ration which contained two kilos of potatoes. He brought one kilo to the Zeifs: "Mrs. Zeif, I'm lending you a kilo of potatoes. When you get your ration you'll give it back. Cook the potatoes right away. They'll be a good medicine for Zeif."

Husband and wife didn't know how to thank Bluestein. They showered blessings on him. With several slivers of wood Mr. Zeif boiled the potatoes half-raw in their skins. When they were eating, Henye tried to give the larger portion to Zeif and he tried to give the larger portion to her. After eating a few potatoes Zeif felt better: "See, Henye, all we need is faith. With God's help we'll survive the war. Do you have any wood left for cooking?"

"Yes, for a few more times," she replied with satisfaction.

"See, Henye, the cupboard is still a cupboard," he smiled.

And they dipped the unpeeled potatoes in salt and ate. Because the ghetto Jews said: "The peel is healthy. In the peel there is iron and under it there is sugar, and that's why cattle are so healthy and strong—because they eat the peel."

Bread

Isaiah Spiegel

Translated from the Polish by David H. Hirsch and Rosyln Hirsch

The little room where Mama Glikke has installed herself and her housekeeping, along with Shimmele and their two children, sits in the porch of the little house, its one narrow little window looking wistfully down at the small street that is already beyond the confines of the ghetto. The little street runs like a narrow tunnel outside the ghetto, next to the recently installed wire fences. The hovel itself—a wooden structure crumbling with age, sagging with the rains and snows of many generations—bows its roof ever closer to the top of the fence, like a person who laments: "Oh—oh, what I have lived to see. . . . Oh my, such a fate. . . ." None of the roofs of the neighboring stone houses has taken up the rain-song of the autumn night, the joyful caresses of the glittering snow—and the clear strolls of silvery moons—as has the old, crumbling roof on the old, sinking hovel.

From the narrow little window, "they" can always be seen below. For days, now, and months, the black, shiny military boots have been pacing the bridge, back and forth, day and night, without ceasing. The Kraut pacing here with his gun keeps on looking at the warped little house and at the tilted roof. None of those inside the house approach the little window. The window is open just a crack, because when the Kraut below sees an open window, or the shadow of a head—he shoots at it. As a matter of fact, at this moment the little window in Glikke's house is just the slightest bit ajar. It is a hot July day. Through the narrow opening in the window wafts a dry, hot wind.

The room itself is white, calcined, with a wooden pole that descends straight down to the stove. The paint is peeling from the walls, littering the ragged floor, which here and there is missing a few boards. The Gentile who had lived in the apartment before them, and who left before the Jews had been herded into the ghetto, took some of the floor with him when he left and took the stove apart too. When they moved in Mama Glikke had quickly set up a second stove, which now stands propped up on some red bricks emitting billows of smoke from the crevices every time Mama decides to cook a hot meal. Not a stick of furniture, no closet, no beds. When the family had fled here, Mama Glikke had even brought a decent cabinet with her from the old place in the city. Back there, at home, a pair of silver Sabbath candelabras used to stand in the cabinet, behind glass doors. But, as it happened, the cabinet fell apart on the journey, as they were rushing into the ghetto, and now the two Sabbath candelabras are lying on the floor in a corner near the window, in a pile of junk, among empty pots and torn clothes.

Set in the right wall of the room is a little wooden door, and beyond the door a tiny chamber, dark and narrow, where Mama has stored a bit of firewood, and also the sides of the collapsed cabinet. A cold gloom pervades that tiny chamber with its perpetual evening twilight; behind the slanted studs old green spiders are spinning their webs. The Gentile who used to live here kept pigeons in the tiny chamber. A triangular opening had been cut out of the front wall facing the street, and through this hole in the wall the Gentile's doves would fly in and out. You could still find little grains of oats in the soil of the black earthen floor of the little chamber. The door in the little chamber is always closed. Mama does not let the children, who are constantly digging holes in the earthen floor, into the room. It sometimes happens that in that chamber, in the cut-out opening, a pigeon will alight on the edge of a board. She has blundered here because of a familiar wind or cloud. She still can't divorce herself from the old home, from the old chamber under the crumbling roof.

She bends her head into the empty, dark chamber. She stands trembling, frightened, with her red little feet on the board's edge, and with surprised, innocent eyes she soon flies away, beating her wings outside the window as if to bid a farewell: "Stay healthy! Who knows if we will see each other again?"

The mother and the father divide their day as follows:

At the crack of dawn, as soon as the sun appears on the eastern rim of the ghetto, Mama Glikke takes two huge pots and positions herself somewhere in a courtyard behind a fence. Mama stands there for hours, sometimes till late at night. There is a kitchen there where they cook dinners for many people. The boys who carry water from the pump to the kitchen know, by this time, that the desperate eyes of Mama Glikke are staring through a crack in the fence. After the soup has been portioned out, the boys take two pots from her and ladle out a bit of turbid, diluted liquid. Though hunger gnaws at Mama's bowels, as if someone were tearing her flesh with a pair of pliers, and although she has been standing at the fence staring through the crack all day, still Mama does not taste a drop of the soup until she has entered the little room. With two pots tucked under her scarf she runs across the ghetto like an athlete. She is terrified that, God forbid, she may spill a drop of soup, a spoonful of holy victuals. She runs, and the two corners of her scarf flutter behind her like the wings of a large, frightened bird.

The labors of the father, Shimmele, are quite another matter. Sickly, with a chronic, juicy cough and melting, running eyes, as if overflowing with tears, he, the father, sits all day in the room with the children, wrapped in his *tallis* and *tfillin*. He starts his prayers as soon as Glikke leaves, and does not take off the *tfillin* till just before evening. The children are afraid of the father. The last few days he just stands for hours on end next to the wall, wrapped in *tallis* and *tfillin*, without moving an inch. They imagine that father has been dead for a while, that out of the blue he has decided to give up his soul, that he is standing there with his face to the wall, stony, frosty, a dead man. And when he suddenly turns from the wall and gazes into the room after many hours of stony silence—the children see that their father's face is white as snow, his eyes soaked in tears. He sits down in the remotest corner of the room, covered with *tallis* and *tfillin*, and waits for the mother to walk through the door. And at his feet lie Avremele and Perele, terrified and lost.

Since they started rationing bread in the ghetto hunger has haunted the room. At the beginning everybody shared: mother, father, and children. When they picked up their ration of bread and laid it on the table, it would lie there for a long time till the fastidious and fluttering mother took the knife, said a blessing, and tremblingly sliced the bread. Father and the children would gather around her, and after everyone had received a portion sufficient to assuage the initial pangs of hunger, mother would wrap the bread in a white cloth and stash it away so that no one would be able to find it. The bread would have to last for a long, long time. As if out of spite, when bread entered the room hunger grew apace, tearing at the guts like a peverse imp. In dreams, fresh round loaves would swim into view and bring satisfaction. They knew that somewhere in the room a radiant treasure lay hidden. Oh, God, if only it were possible to cut slice after slice from the loaf and not be terrified at knowing that with every slice the loaf gets smaller and smaller, if only they could sit down and eat to their hearts' content. But that one could only dream. In the meantime they cursed every bite of bread that touched the palate. The bread did not satisfy. With each bite, hunger's curse sharpened. They examined each crumb of bread lying in their hands as if it were a diamond. And before putting it to the tongue they feasted their eyes on it, drawing a sad, sated joy from the sight of the Lord's bounty.

Once there was a stroke of misfortune.

That time, mother had denounced and cursed this wretched life all day. Something happened that almost caused father to hang himself out of shame in the little chamber. After that misfortune he spent whole days just lying on the floor, moaning. Who could have predicted such a thing? Mother just kept repeating: "Now there is nothing lower for him to stoop to, oh Master of the Universe, except to cut a chunk of meat out of the children and cook it."

They did not know how it came to pass, and even the father himself did not know how things had come to such misfortune and disgrace.

There was no way that Shimmele could figure out what the power was that urged him to it. He just did not know.

At that moment a tornado had raged in his heart. It could not have been his very own hands that in the darkness of the chamber stuffed the children's bread into his own mouth. No. . . no. That wasn't the father any more. It wasn't Shimmele, but some kind of enchanted shadow that had separated itself from him, that had issued from his hands and feet, some kind of accursed *dybbuk* who used the father's hands and fingers to tear at the dark, chestnut-flour loaf and salivate over it dozens of times. Wet, half-chewed chunks fell from his stuffed mouth and lay in his palms. From there they were popped right back into the mouth that had spit them out in unnecessary haste. And when that was done, he remained standing, benighted and petrified, his head buried in his hands.

The same day the father ate the children's bread, Mama Glikke came home late. She found both children lying in a corner, famished. When she noticed that a quarter of a loaf was missing, she raised a racket, and it was only then that Shimmele crawled out of the little chamber. When she read the truth in his downcast eyes, she squawked like a slaughtered chicken:

"A father, eh? A fa—ther, is it? *Murderer!*"

And from that moment on the mother walked around worried and anxious, till she found a solution: she sewed little sacks out of shirts and stuffed the sliced portions of bread into the sacks; in that manner she traversed the streets, with both sacks hanging over her heart.

The mother calls Avremele: Umele. He is slight in stature, with a thin, narrow little head and protruding ears. He is the spitting image of his father. His eyes also have a moistness about them, and if you were to look closely, knowing his elderly father, you would see from Umele's pinched expression and pointed chin that he will turn out exactly like the old man. Though Umele has not yet reached his twelfth birthday there is already set within his countenance a trace of his father's agedness and brokenness. Like the old man, he always keeps his hand on his bowed forehead, thinking of something. A restless shadow hovers over his pale, transparent cheeks. The few ghetto months have completely transformed the children. They are no longer children, but ancients, on whose faces sit the ravages of heavy years.

Umele is sitting on the floor, and next to him, at his side, his little sister, Perele. Perele has a slight limp; her thin, sandy-colored hair cascades down her narrow shoulders. They are both sitting in the corner near the Sabbath candelabras, gazing across at the opposite corner, where the father is busy with something or other. The mother left the room very early in the morning, taking with her the little sacks of bread, and now they are hoping that the father will leave the room soon, so that they can go back into the little chamber.

But it is a long, long time before the father leaves. He just keeps on looking at an open book. Since that day when the great disgrace occurred he has not been able to look the children straight in the eye. Buried in the pages of his book, he seeks something there with his tiny pinpoint eyes, and every now and then he gives vent to the accumulated air in his lungs with a great, deep sigh, and remains lying with his face buried in the book as if his throat had been cut. He doesn't move for a long time, dozes off, then wakes up abruptly when he hears the crash of the book that has fallen out of his hands onto the floor.

Now the children watch as the father picks up the book, rummages around in his pocket looking for his key, and lets himself out the door.

Bread

When the two of them, Umele and Perele, see that they have been left alone, their eyes light with glee. Umele runs quickly to the door of the little chamber and pulls out the nail that is keeping the door fastened. The two of them run into the chamber, but as she is running Perele trips on the threshold. She gets up and, with her dragging foot, chases after Umele. By this time, Umele is already standing in the darkness of the chamber, near the wall that faces out onto the street. Umele had found a crevice in the wall.

In the wooden wall there are two crevices, one slightly removed from the other. At one of these crevices, Umele now stands and watches.

Down below, on the other side of the street, across from the wires stand a little store and the display window of a bakery. Umele's eye aims directly into the window. Brown shiny loaves and white roundish rolls are set out for display. Avremele had discovered that treasure yesterday, when the mother happened to leave the chamber door ajar. And what a treasure! If you really squeezed your eye right up close to the crevice you could see clearly: roundish fresh loaves and light wholesome rolls. There might be four loaves lying in the window and perhaps ten or more rolls. The sun, as it happens, is just opposite the window, shedding its light directly on the treasures. Umele is taking it all in with his left eye, while his tongue is swimming in streams of sweet saliva. When the left eye tires he switches to the right, then back to the left, and still later back to the right. Suddenly he sees a hand from inside the store removing one of the loaves. He lets out a sigh. Behind him stands Perele, tugging at his hand, and she keeps asking:

"Let me look, let me look too. I'm hungry too."

Umele doesn't budge.

Suddenly he cries out in a strange voice:

"Don't take it, don't take it, don't take it!"

Across the way the hand has once again swept two loaves and a whole pile of rolls. A single loaf of bread and two rolls remain in the window. Umele still can't tear himself away from the crevice.

When Perele stubbornly grabs hold of his arm and will not relent, he flares up in anger and shouts:

"I don't want to and that's it. Leave me alone."

Through the crevice that Perele has been looking out of one can see a little shop. Laid out majestically in the display window is a pure white cheese, and nothing else. It is possible, by raising oneself a little higher on one's toes, to see part of a field, where a cow is grazing. From Umele's vantage-point there is only bread and rolls. Umele stands praying to God not to let the hand reappear. He murmurs a verse his father had taught him long before the ghetto. And that fragment has to accomplish everything. If you are ill, it can help; if you are very hungry and you say it with real feeling—your hunger disappears in the wink of an eye. Umele earnestly recites that holy verse now, and waits. The loaves and rolls are so close now, almost within reach. He can even see, at this point, two little holes in the bread. And he notices that a fly has alighted on one of the rolls, a large fly with large shimmering wings.

"Umele, would you like some cheese?" Perele does not stop her nagging. "Let me in, let me in. If you don't Mama will. . . ."

God forbid that Mama should find out about this. No, Mama must not know about this, because if she does, then the whole treasure is lost. It will no longer be possible to come into the little chamber and gorge oneself on rolls and loaves of white bread. Okay, he'll let her in just for a short while, only a minute.

"Not for a long stay, Perele, all right? I don't like cheese." He moves away slowly and peeps through the other crevice.

Through the crevices the eye can escape into a free, uncaged world. Just a single leap over the fence and you are free. You can go wherever you want: to the courtyard, from the courtyard to the open fields, from the fields to the forest, further and further. The childish eyes float out of the little chamber. First of all, across the road into the shops. Now Umele can see the flat white cheese,

Perele the last shiny rolls. How those rolls laugh their way right up to the children; they come so close to the crevice, so close to the eye, that Perele actually licks her little lips. You can smell the sweetness of the rich, black poppyseeds. Perele's lips are already tasting the sweetness, and just look, she runs her tongue across her lips and really—she feels as if she had taken a lick of those sweetish poppyseeds.

Suddenly Perele lets out a scream. Across the street, the hand has just pulled the last of the bread and rolls out of the window . . . now the window is empty. Umele runs over to the crack—and really he sees that the window opposite has become a complete void.

Perele watches Umele sink to the ground, tears running down his cheeks. She is now standing at her own crevice, and in the field she sees a cow with black spots.

Perele turns her head back into the chamber. She feels something soft sliding around in her throat interfering with her breathing.

"Umele," she asks, "would you like to look at some cows?"

And when Umele fails to answer she sits down next to him and her eyes also start to overflow. The two of them sit there for a long while, mute, while with their fingers they dig into the dark earth of the chamber floor, till the ominous dusk settles on the little roof and the mother finds them nestled against each other, fast asleep.

That day the mother sealed the door with a nail, and from that moment on all was lost. And anyway, a couple of days later something happened that made the children forget all about the treasure they used to see through the window.

It happened in the morning, on a day of incessant, soaking rain. Swollen black clouds had settled over the ghetto. The mother was occupied with something in the corner of the room, when a neighbor came running and cried out to her in a panic: "Glikke, they've picked up Shimmele!"

At first the mother just stood there, not understanding a single word. But when the neighbor poured out the whole tale in a single breath, saying, "It has begun already," and explaining that today they started the first transports of Jews, picking up people in the streets and loading them into wagons—at that point the mother went limp, right where she was standing, giving a toss of her head and fainting dead away on the spot.

Now the panic really started. More than half the men who lived in the court, who had just happened to be out on the street, were missing. But that was just a prologue to the awesome black days that were about to descend on the ghetto.

That very same evening, Mama Glikke is to be seen going around with a wet headdress wrapped around her head. The window, draped in black, looks like a mirror covered to protect the soul of a corpse lying in the room. The father's *tallis* and *tfillin* hang in shame in a corner. Who needs them now? Who will now bind the thongs around the arm? The mother walks around all day, eyes swollen with weeping. The children drag around behind her, desperately hungry. Suddenly, the mother reminds herself of something. A ray of joy creeps into her swollen eyes. From a remote corner she takes out a whole loaf of bread and lays it on the table. That bread lights up the entire room, as if the sun has just peeped above the horizon. With deliberation she plunges the knife into the hard loaf of bread and, swallowing the new salty tears streaming down her cheeks, she keeps up an uninterrupted monologue:

"Eat, children, eat. It is your father's bread, your father's whole loaf of bread. . . ."

And for the first time in many, many months, the children joyfully eat to their hearts' content, as does Mama Glikke.

That night they all sleep peacefully and soundly, and father, Shimmele, appears only to Umele in a dream. Umele sees him praying over a large, thick book.

The Last Morning

Bernard Gotfryd

I very clearly remember the day I saw my mother for the last time. It was Sunday the sixteenth of August, 1942, a beautiful day with a clear blue sky and hardly a breeze. That morning she got up very early, earlier than usual, and quietly, so as not to wake us, she went out to the garden. I was already up. I watched her through the kitchen window. She sat down on the broken bench behind the lilac tree and cried. I always felt bad when I saw my mother cry, and this time it was even more painful.

My mother was going to be forty-four years old at the end of August. She never made a fuss over her birthday, as if it were her own secret, and so I never knew the exact date. She was of medium height, rather plump, with a most beautiful face. She had large brown eyes and long, dark brown hair sprinkled with gray, which she pulled back into a chignon. She smiled at people when she spoke and looked them straight in the eye.

When she came in from the garden she walked over to me and caressed my face as she used to do some years before the war, when I was a little boy. Now I was in my teens. Then she went over to the kitchen stove and started a fire. The wood was damp, and the kitchen filled with smoke. There was no more firewood left; this was the last of the broken-down fence from around our garden. She stood next to the stove fanning the smoke and asked me to open the door and the windows to let the smoke escape. Her eyes were red and teary, but when she turned to face me she smiled.

Soon the rest of the family was up, and Mother served a chicory brew with leftovers of sweet bread she had managed to bake some days earlier. There was even some margarine and jam, a great treat. We sat wherever we could, since the table was too small for the five of us. Because of limited table space my grandmother and my aunt ate their meals in their own room. None of us had much to say that morning. We just stared at one another as if to reaffirm our presence.

Suddenly my mother lifted her eyes and, looking at my father, asked him, "What are you thinking about?" My father, as if he had just wakened from a deep sleep, answered, "I stopped thinking, it's better not to think." We looked at him oddly. How could anyone stop thinking?

My mother got up from the table and started to tidy up the room. Then she asked me to go up to the attic and find her small brown suitcase for her. I found the suitcase, and, alone in the attic, I hugged it many times before I brought it to her.

The tension in the house nearly paralyzed me. It was stifling. I left in a hurry and, running all the way, went to investigate the ghetto square. It was still early in the morning, and clusters of people were congregating at street corners, pointing up at the utility poles. During the night the light bulbs had been replaced by huge reflectors. The ghetto police were out in force, preventing people from gathering. I noticed a poster reminding all inhabitants of the ghetto to deliver every sick or infirm member of their families to the only ghetto hospital. Noncompliance called for the death penalty.

My paternal grandmother was recovering from a stroke. She was able to walk with the help of a cane. I trembled at the thought of having to turn her in. The Nazis were preparing something devious. I knew the hospital wasn't big enough to absorb all the sick people in the ghetto.

My mother studied my face when I came back from the square. There was a frightened look in her eyes. She asked me what was happening out there, what people were saying, and I lied to her. I didn't mention the reflector bulbs, but I could tell that she knew what was coming.

She had her suitcase packed, and her neatly folded raincoat was laid out on the couch, as if she were going on an overnight trip the way she used to before the war. No one said much. We were communicating through our silence; our hearts were tense. My father took out the old family album and stood at the window, slowly turning the heavy pages. I looked over his shoulder and saw him examining his own wedding picture. He pulled it out of the album and put it inside his breast pocket. I pretended not to see.

My mother started preparing our lunch, and I helped her with the firewood. There was no more fence left, and somebody had just stolen our broken bench. I found an old tabletop that Father kept behind the house, covered with sheets of tar paper. It was dry and burned well. I didn't tell my mother where the wood had come from; I was afraid she might not like the idea of putting a good table to the fire.

It was past noon, and my mother was busy in the kitchen. She found some flour and potatoes she had managed to save and came up with a delicious soup, as well as potato pancakes sprinkled with fried onions. Was this to be our last meal together? I wondered.

Some friends and neighbors with scared expressions on their faces dropped in to confirm the rumors about the coming deportation and to say good-bye. The Zilber family came, and everybody cried. I couldn't bring myself to say good-bye to anybody; I feared that I would never see them again.

It was getting close to four o'clock in the afternoon when my grandmother, dressed in her best, came out of her room. She was ready, she said, if someone would escort her to the hospital. My brother and I volunteered. She insisted on walking alone, so we held her lightly by the arms in case she tripped. She walked erect, head high; from time to time she would look at one of us without saying a word. People passed us in bewilderment. They seemed like caged birds looking for an escape. An elderly man carrying a huge bundle on his shoulders stopped us and asked for the time. "Why do you need to know the time?" I inquired. He looked at me as if upset by my question and answered, "Soon it will be time for evening prayers, don't you know?" And he went on his way, talking to himself and balancing the awkward bundle on his shoulders.

When we reached the hospital gate my grandmother insisted we leave her there. She would continue alone. With a heavy heart I kissed her goodbye. She smiled and turned toward us, saying, "What does one say? Be well?" Then she disappeared behind the crumbling whitewashed gate of the hospital. I needed to cry but was ashamed to do so in front of my older brother. Determined to prove how tough I was, I held back my tears. We walked back in silence, each of us probably thinking the same thing.

I'll never forget coming back to the house after escorting Grandmother to the hospital. My mother was in the kitchen saying good-bye to one of her friends. I had never seen her cry as she was crying. When she saw us she fell upon us, and through her tears she begged us to go into hiding. She begged us to stay alive so that we could tell the world what had happened. Her friend was crying with her, and I felt my heart escaping.

A neighbor came in to tell us that the ghetto was surrounded by armed SS men, and it was official that the deportation was about to begin. The ghetto police were on full alert, and it was impossible to get any information out of them.

My brother and I turned and ran out of the house. Without stopping we ran the entire length of the ghetto until, dripping with sweat, we arrived at the fence. On the other side of the fence was a Nazi officers' club; farther off in the middle of a field stood a stable. By now the Ukrainian guards with their rifles were inside the ghetto. We scaled the fence behind their backs and made it across to the other side. We entered the stable through a side door. As far as I could tell, no one was there. The horses turned their heads and sized us up. My brother decided we should hide separately, so that if one of us was discovered, the other one would still have a chance. I climbed up on the rafters and onto a wooden platform wedged in between two massive beams. There was enough hay to cover myself with, and I stretched out on my stomach. Through the wide cracks between the boards of the platform I could scan the entire stable underneath me. I also found a crack in the wall that allowed me a wide view of the street across from the stable.

A mouse came out from under a pile of straw, stopped for a second, and ran back in. I lay there trying to make sense of every sound. As I turned on my side I felt something bulky inside my pocket. I reached for it and discovered a sandwich wrapped in brown paper. My mother must have put it there when my jacket was still hanging behind the kitchen door.

As I replaced the sandwich I heard the door open and saw a man enter. He walked to the other end of the stable and deposited a small parcel inside a crate. Then he started to tend to the horses while whistling an old Polish tune. He must be the caretaker, I thought. He appeared to be still young, even though I couldn't clearly see his face; he walked briskly and carried heavy bales of hay with ease. I feared the commotion he was causing might attract attention; he kept going in and out, filling the water bucket for the horses to drink. I was getting hungry. I was about to bite into the sandwich when on one of his trips he looked up at the spot where I was hiding. I froze. Could it be that he had heard me move? I couldn't imagine what had made him look up, and I broke out in a sweat. I held on to the sandwich but was too upset to eat it. Every time he opened the door it squeaked, and the spring attached to it caused it to shut with a loud bang. He spoke to the horses in Polish with a provincial accent and called each horse by its name. He lingered with some of them, slapped their backs or gently patted their necks. How I envied him. Why was he free while I had to hide?

I started to recall the events of the entire day. I realized I had run out of the house without saying good-bye to my parents. Seized with guilt, I started sobbing.

I must have fallen asleep. When I woke up I heard loud noises coming from behind the fence. I looked through the crack in the wall; it was dark outside. Suddenly a loud chorus of cries and screams rang out, intermingled with voices shouting commands in German. Rifle shots followed, and more voices calling out names pierced the darkness. The cries of little children made me shudder.

I imagined hearing the screaming of my four-year-old cousin, who was there with his mother; my aunt, her sister, with her two beautiful little daughters. They were all there, trapped, desperate, and helpless. I thought of our friend Mr. Gutman, who some years before had claimed that God was in exile. I wondered where he was and what he was saying now. I worried about my grandmother and what they were doing to her at the hospital. Frightened and burdened with my misgivings, I resolved to go on, not to give in.

I heard the squeak of the door and looked down to see the caretaker slipping out. He blocked the door with a rock to keep it open. The sounds coming in from the outside were getting louder; the horses became restless and started to neigh. Rifle shots were becoming more frequent and sounded much closer than before. All these noises went on for most of the night—it felt like an eternity.

I could picture my mother in that screaming, weeping crowd begging me to stay alive, and I could hear her crying for help. Was my father with her, I kept wondering, and where was my sister?

It was almost daybreak when the noises began to die down. The sun was rising; it looked like the beginning of a hot August day. Only occasional rifle shots could be heard, and a loud hum that sounded as if swarms of bees were flying overhead; it was the sound of thousands of feet shuffling against the pavement.

Looking through the crack in the wall, I could see long columns of people being escorted by armed SS men with dogs on leashes. Most of the people carried knapsacks strapped to their backs; others carried in their arms what was left of their possessions. I focused on as many people as I could, hoping to recognize a face. I wanted to know if my mother was among them and kept straining my eyes until I couldn't see anymore. I wondered if my brother, at the other end of the stable, was able to see outside. As it was, we had no way to communicate.

I kept imagining the moving columns of people getting longer and wider until there was no more room for them to walk. As I pictured them they kept multiplying; soon they walked over one another like ants in huge anthills, and the SS men weren't able to control them any longer.

Suddenly I heard voices underneath me. Before I realized who was there I saw the caretaker climbing up toward my hiding place. I couldn't believe it. I stopped breathing. Two SS men wearing steel helmets and carrying rifles stood at the door watching the caretaker climb. He came close to the platform where I was lying and in a loud voice told me to get down. "They came to get you," he said. "I knew you were here hiding. You can't outsmart me." I was betrayed.

Next he walked right over to where my brother was hiding and called him out. The two of us took a terrible beating from the SS men before they escorted us back to the ghetto. The first thing I saw in the ghetto was a large horse-drawn cart on rubber wheels, loaded with dead, naked bodies. On one side, pressed against the boards, was my grandmother. She seemed to be looking straight at me.

No dictionary in the world could supply the words for what I saw next. My mother begged me to be a witness, however; all these years I've been talking and telling, and I'm not sure if anybody listens or understands me. I myself am not sure if I understand.

The following night my brother and I miraculously escaped the final deportation, only to be shipped off to the camps separately soon afterward. I never saw my mother again, nor was I ever able to find a picture of her. Whenever I want to remember her I close my eyes and think of that Sunday in August of 1942 when I saw her sitting in our ghetto garden, crying behind the lilac tree.

On Guilt

Bernard Gotfryd

A dim utility light from across the street shone through the curtainless window, outlining my father's dark, unshaven face. From my cot next to the window I could see his silhouetted figure against the wall. He spread his coat over an old, worn-out blanket he had found in an abandoned apartment. He kept turning and twisting most of the night, his body shaking as if in a spasm. I didn't think he ever slept. This went on every night, deep into the winter, the coldest I can remember. Curled up on a narrow iron bed, his head buried inside a soiled pillow, he would groan and whimper and sometimes break into a sob. Nights became unbearable; his groaning and crying out in his sleep got worse and worse.

I had never heard my father cry before. He was a tough and self-disciplined man, I thought, but since my mother had been taken away during the deportation, he wasn't the same; he seemed to be lost without her.

All the same, he never mentioned Mother. Was it too painful for him to talk about? I wondered. And why had he let her go alone? The questions had nagged at me daily.

At times he would take out his own wedding picture and look at it for the longest time. It was the only picture he had saved from the family album and the only thing he seemed to care about. He kept it in his breast pocket, neatly wrapped inside an old brown envelope, and never showed it to anybody. It was his personal property.

Then—as now—I had only a vague idea of what had taken place during the first night of the deportation; at my mother's insistence I had gone into hiding with my older brother, Michael. My sister stayed behind with my parents. Only reluctantly and with much apprehension, some months after the deportation, did she tell me what she had seen.

"It was still early in the evening," she told me, "when the SS and the ghetto police stormed into the house, ordered us out, and chased us on the double to the square. In the beginning I was with our parents, but in all the confusion, with thousands of people running and pressing against one another, we got separated. When I finally arrived at the square I somehow managed to find them again.

"The loud chorus of the Nazis shouting commands was interrupted only by the frequent crackling of rifle shots; huge dogs were everywhere. It was impossible to distinguish one voice from another; mothers were calling for their children, children were crying and screaming for their parents.

"People were being shot at close range," she continued, "and tiny babies were being crushed with rifle butts or being thrown against brick walls by intoxicated SS men and Ukrainians. It was one big death orgy. They were killing for sheer pleasure. No one was there to stop them. The sound of glass breaking, people climbing over one another or tripping over their belongings, desperately trying to find their loved ones, and the frightening screams went on for most of the night.

"It must have been around midnight when Mother was taken away by a tall SS officer and put with the group to be deported," she continued, "but some minutes later she was brought back by another SS officer, a shorter one. After a sharp exchange between the two Nazis Mother was taken away again by the tall officer, who, this time, also tore up her papers. I tried to intervene, pointing out to him that Mother had all her necessary working papers, that she was a talented seamstress, that she was young, only in her early forties, and healthy.

"He refused to listen, slapped my face, and threatened to deport me, too, unless I shut up. There was nothing more I could have done," she recalled. "I couldn't have gone with Mother even if I had wanted to. This was the moment when I realized that Father was nowhere to be seen. I feared that he had already been deported. I was in a different group by now, separated from Mother, whose group was across the square, closely guarded by Ukrainians, armed SS men, and dogs.

"In desperation," my sister continued, "I raised my arm with a handkerchief as high as I could, hoping that Mother would notice me. I even called her name, but I don't imagine she could have heard me. I tried to shout good-bye to her, just to let her know that I was there. I wasn't sure any longer where she was, but I assumed that she was still in that group to be deported. People were screaming and shouting louder and louder, and there were bloodcurdling screams. It is difficult to describe what went on that night. If there is a Hell, I thought, this is probably what it looks like.

"When dawn came a strange calm prevailed. Littered with torn books, abandoned knapsacks, shoes, and clothing, the square looked like a battlefield. Here and there loaves of bread or half-eaten sandwiches could be seen in the gutters. Dead bodies were scattered all over the place, and a nauseating odor—like a mixture of rotten vegetables, human sweat, and urine—hung over the whole square. Window shutters swung in the morning breeze, squeaking and banging loudly against the walls of the deserted houses."

My sister fell silent, closed her eyes, and covered her face with her hands, then looked at me again. "I can still smell the whole rotten scene," she said quietly.

Sometimes during that winter I could see my father talking to a stranger at a street corner or walking aimlessly by himself, looking at nothing in particular. He held his head low and kept his hands in his pockets, as if trying to hide something.

Occasionally, at the photo studio where I was working, I was able to buy some chocolate-filled wafers from my Polish black market contact and to smuggle them into the ghetto for my father. One cold, snowy evening I saw him standing in a doorway, displaying the chocolate wafers inside a cardboard box, trying to sell them. His hat was pulled over his eyes, his face wrapped inside a woolen scarf. That gray, miserable figure hawking chocolate wafers was my father. I realized how humiliating it would have been for him if he had seen me; I walked on quickly, hoping that he hadn't noticed me.

Some weeks went by, and spring was around the corner. One Sunday early in the morning my father asked me to go out with him.

"Let's go outside for a walk," he said quietly. "I would like to talk to you."

The ghetto was beginning to come alive as we went out into the narrow streets. It was a cold, crisp morning; the smell of freshly baked bread emanated from a bakery not far away. People were beginning to peek their frightened faces out of dark doorways and narrow passageways. First they stopped and looked to make sure it was safe. Somebody greeted my father, but he didn't hear. Lost in his thoughts, he kept walking, staring at the ground.

"I must tell you what happened during the night of the deportation," he suddenly began, "and how we lost Mother.

"You probably wonder why I didn't talk about it before," he said, almost in a whisper. "It's very painful for me to talk about it, but now the time has come for me to tell you. I hope you'll understand. Please listen.

"When the SS with the police chased us out of the house that evening, they made us run all the way to the square. It was very difficult for Mother to run over the cobblestone streets, but she held on to me, and somehow we made it. On the way we lost all our belongings, and it bothered us that we had nothing left, not even a toothbrush. The only thing I was able to save were two sandwiches inside my coat pockets.

"Once in the square we were told to form lines; then they broke the lines, only to start forming them again. It was confusing and tiring. We couldn't stand on our feet any longer; it must have been past midnight when our line got moving and the Nazis finally started checking our working papers.

"When I turned for a second to get out my papers I realized suddenly that your mother and your sister weren't with me. The two of them were gone, as if they had evaporated. This was when the Nazis decided to separate men from women, but I wasn't aware of it. I remained in the same spot. I looked around, called their names over and over, but as hard as I tried, I couldn't find them. It took some time before I realized what had happened. I got very panicky, and I kept asking people around me for help, but nobody paid any attention. Everybody out there was looking for some relative of his own.

"I still didn't understand how all this could have happened. I was left alone," he said, looking down at me with bloodshot eyes.

"I never even had a chance to give your mother the sandwich I kept for her in my coat pocket. I forgot all about it. She had nothing left, not even her pocketbook."

He started crying; in a desperate gesture full of false hope I muttered, "Oh, I'm sure she's alive and we'll find her soon."

My father just looked at me with an expression full of disbelief and answered, "I hope you're right, I just hope so."

It was extremely difficult for me to watch him suffer. At that moment I wished he had gone with Mother. At least then they would be together.

I tried to keep up his spirits whenever I could and told him all kinds of lies and stories about Allied air raids and attempted landings on the French coast. I kept reassuring him that the war would be over soon, that the Nazis would be punished for their crimes, that Germany was in the process of being devastated by the Allied air forces.

As it turned out later, I had very nearly spoken the truth, though I didn't know it then. I based my accounts entirely on rumors and underground fliers; I could tell that Father didn't believe me, but I kept up the stories nevertheless, hoping that I could turn them into fact.

One evening my father bluntly started a conversation with my sister about the deportation night.

"Do you remember the SS man who took away Mother?" Father asked her abruptly.

"Of course," she answered. "I still remember his horrible, scarred face and the way he slapped me on the cheek. It was all red afterward.

"But Father," she continued, "how could you have seen him when you claim you didn't see us? If you saw the SS man who took away Mother, then you must have been with us. I was right next to Mother, pleading with him to let her go, which was when he slapped me."

Father became somewhat disoriented. "You see," he explained, "from where I was standing I could only see his profile. I never saw him head-on, nor was I able to distinguish the people he was selecting. They all looked alike. I may have seen Mother and not recognized her. But I was calling for both of you. Or maybe I imagine I was, maybe because of my fear I thought I was, but now I'm not sure any longer. One thing I'm sure of is that I wanted to shout, and that I meant to shout. But I don't even know if I made a sound. And this uncertainty is my constant nightmare.

"I saw multitudes of people, but I couldn't recognize any of them. My papers were never checked, and I wound up with the group to remain. I still don't know how it all happened. I think I was swept along with that mob that was already checked out, and nobody noticed. It was a miracle that I wasn't deported," he said. "Or maybe I shouldn't say that," he added.

My father sighed heavily and started wiping his eyes. My sister took her coat and, without saying a word, went outside. It was past curfew. When I went after her she was standing in the dark hallway, crying.

"You are too hard on Father," I told her. "What are you trying to say with all this questioning?" I asked her.

"Don't you know? Do I have to spell it out for you? Unless you're too naïve to understand. I'm sure he abandoned us and saved himself," she answered through her tears as she walked to the other end of the hallway, sobbing.

I was dismayed. It felt as if someone had kicked me in the head; our father was not capable of such cowardice. I thought my sister was being dogmatic and unreasonable.

"Don't bother me anymore," she called over her shoulder.

"What's the point in torturing Father with all these questions?" I argued with her. "You know there wasn't a thing he could do to save Mother. Suppose he had gone, too. What good would that do us? Maybe I don't know what I'm talking about, but you ought to know, you were there. How could anybody save himself or anybody else? Wasn't it up to the Nazis whom to deport and whom to leave behind? You tried to intervene on Mother's behalf, and look what happened."

I could feel her tension and her pain. She stopped crying.

"Wasn't there something that kept telling you to save yourself?" I persisted. "Why did some people go into hiding and leave their families behind? Why the recriminations, why torture one another? What it comes down to is that we all want to stay alive. No one is guilty for it. Nor do we have the right to point fingers at anyone else."

"I just feel so sorry for Mother that she had to leave alone," my sister said, wiping her face. "If Father had gone with her, at least she wouldn't be alone, and that's what he should have done. She was his wife, and he owed it to her."

There was nothing else I could say. All I could do was to pity my father's predicament; it moved me to tears. I also realized how terribly we all missed Mother.

When I went back to the apartment Father was sitting on his iron cot reading a Nazi-controlled newspaper. "What is that you're reading?" I asked him. "Some more lies," he answered. "What's with your sister Hanka? Is she all right?"

"Yes," I said. "She needed some fresh air. It's so stuffy in here."

He gave me a funny look, the look he gave me when he didn't believe me, an expression I knew by heart.

The following day my father stayed home with a cold; normally he worked for the Nazis, moving and repairing furniture. That morning two armed Nazi gendarmes, assisted by several ghetto policemen, appeared in our yard escorting two young men. Father heard the commotion and looked out the window in time to witness some begging and pleading before the two men were placed against the brick wall of the adjoining building and shot point-blank from behind. When the shots rang out and the two men dropped to the ground Father nearly fainted, he told us that evening when we came home from work.

"This was the first time I ever witnessed an execution. It was a brutal, blood-chilling murder," Father said, shaking like a leaf. "I would never want to die in such a manner. God forbid," he said in an agitated voice.

"Do the Allies know what the Nazis are doing to us?" he asked me. In all my ignorance I assured him that they certainly knew and were only waiting for the right moment to strike back. Again he looked at me in disbelief, shaking his head. If he doubted my word, I wondered, why did he ask me such questions?

I remembered how two years earlier, when it was still possible, I had urged Father to leave Poland, but he had refused to listen. Instead he told me what World War I was like, and how much he had learned from it. "There is no sense running," he told me. "I have the experience. The best way is to stay put where your roots are." But two years later Father began to realize that this was a different war, a war against us, the Jews. By then it was too late; the borders were sealed.

When rumors started circulating about extermination camps and gas chambers Father refused to believe them. He accused the doomsayers of spreading panic and demoralizing our poor, broken people.

"Not the Nazis, not even Genghis Khan himself would do such a thing," he would insist. "This is the twentieth century, and the civilized world would not allow it."

The Nazis kept up their brutal tactics; executions and roundups were a daily occurrence. People continued to disappear. To survive another day was a miracle.

On Sundays, when nobody went outside the ghetto to work, my father stood near the gate and watched the street outside. He stood there for hours at a time, sometimes past curfew, the cop on duty warned me. When I tried to tell Father how dangerous it was to stand near the gate he gave me a scornful look and said, "You told me that Mother would come back one day, so let me stand there and wait for her."

"Yes, I did say she would," I answered, "but nothing is certain, and no one knows for sure when or by what means people will return."

"Well, then," he said, "if you don't mind, I'll be standing right there by the gate whenever I can, and regardless of what people think."

Shortly after, Father was taken to the Szkolna labor camp, next to the munitions plant at the other end of town. There was a shortage of labor, so the Nazis decided to replenish the Szkolna camp with people from the ghetto. Since I was still employed at the German-owned studio protected by the *Polizeiführer*, I remained in the apartment until the liquidation of the ghetto.

During the winter of 1943, after an unsuccessful escape attempt, I was apprehended and shipped to the Maidanek extermination camp. I lost touch entirely with Father and my brother, who were together at the Szkolna camp. Only two years later, when the war was over, did I hear news of them.

On a hot August day in 1944, during the evacuation of the Szkolna camp to Germany, my father was ordered by the SS to get on a horse-drawn wagon marked with the Red Cross insignia, as were all other prisoners too weak to march any longer. Some minutes later the wagon turned off the road and drove into a clearing in the woods. Everyone on the wagon, including my father, was machine-gunned and buried in a mass grave nearby. My brother was a witness. My father was forty-eight years old.

Choiceless Choices

A Conversation

Ida Fink

Translated from the Polish by Madeline Levine and Francine Prose

When he entered her room and slowly, carefully closed the door, and then began pacing the two steps between the window and the table, she realized that something had happened, and she guessed that it had to do with Emilia.

She was sitting beside the stove because it was already winter, which meant that almost six months had gone by since Emilia had taken them in. She rested her feet on a bundle of firewood that Michal had split, and softly clicked her knitting needles. She was making a stocking out of black sheep's wool. Emilia had taught her how to do that; she hadn't known how to knit before. She was grateful to her because she could do something useful—fill this unproductive time to which she had been condemned, isolated from the world and from people, imprisoned in this tiny room. At first, she had been grateful to Emilia for everything, and she was grateful to her now, too, but in a different way, in an abstract, cool, cerebral way.

Everything made her nervous: her husband's footsteps; his high, mud-caked boots; his jacket, which belonged to Emilia's husband, who had been missing since the start of the war; his sunburned face, which was also not his own, because in the past he had always been so pale—that pale, Slavic face, so unusual in his swarthy, black-haired family.

Because he was making her nervous, and not to make it easier for him, she asked him first, without raising her head, which was bent over the needles:

"Is it about Emilia?"

"What makes you think that?"

The rough way he asked and the fact that he was standing perfectly still convinced her that she was right. "Because I know. I have a lot of time, I think about things. I knew from the beginning that this would happen. Once I was standing near the window—don't be afraid, no one saw me—and I watched her. I saw how she looked at you, how she moved, her smile, it was completely obvious."

"Not to me. I had no idea until . . ."

"Why are you so upset? Calm down. You say you didn't know about it until . . ."

"Put down the needles," he said, furious. "I can't stand that clicking. And look at me, I can't talk like this."

"The clicking is what keeps me calm. It's a wonderful thing, this soft, monotonous clicking. I can talk while I'm doing it. You'd be surprised what I can do. So you had no idea . . ."

"Anna, why are you acting like this?"

"So you had no idea until . . ."

"Until she told me herself."

"How touching! And what did she tell you?"

"She just told me."

"That she can't take it anymore, that you are always together, and that since 1939, when her husband didn't return from the war, she has lived alone—poor thing. Is that right?"

"How did you know?"

"I told you, I just know. When did it happen?"

"A month ago."

"A month ago. And for a whole month you went on being together from dawn till night, together in the fields, together gathering wood in the forest, together going to town on errands . . . You know what? You really do look terrific, and she's very sharp, she spotted it right away that first evening. 'You can pretend to be my cousin, you're a born estate manager.' I never saw you as an estate manager, but that's probably because I never saw an estate manager in my whole life, I only read about them. She also sized me up right away. 'With your face, not one step outside this door . . .'"

"You're being unfair, Anna, ungrateful . . ."

"I know. And have you and she . . . ? You can tell me."

"No."

He stood there in his mud-caked boots and Emilia's husband's jacket, leaning against the wall, sunburned and so tall that his head almost reached the ceiling. He smells of fresh air, she thought. And also, he has changed, he's not the same man.

"Stop it!" he shouted. "Put that stocking down! We're leaving, we have to leave. Now, today, at once!"

She didn't want the sound of the needles to stop, but they fell out of her hands. A soft, almost imperceptible shiver ran through her. She recognized it.

"Leave? Why?" she asked in a frightened voice, and immediately began to shake. Earlier, before Emilia took them in, she used to shake like that constantly.

"Why, Michal?"

He didn't answer.

"Michal, why? Is she driving us out?"

"We have to leave, Anna."

"But Michal, for God's sake, where to? We have nowhere to go, we have no one. With my face, without money . . . I won't survive, you know it. Talk to her, ask her . . ."

Suddenly she raised her head and looked into his eyes. For a moment she seemed about to scream. She looked panic-stricken, horrified; then just as suddenly she lowered her eyes and straightened up. She was no longer trembling. She sat stiffly, and in her black dress, with her smoothly combed black hair, she looked like a nun. She picked up the stocking from the floor and set the needles in motion: her white hands began to dance rapidly and rhythmically to the beat of the metal sticks. She pressed her lips into a horizontal, dark-blue line.

"All right," she said after a moment.

Because her head was bowed, she didn't, couldn't see the flush that passed across the man's face and left it a shade paler. But she heard his loud breathing.

"All right. You can tell her that everything's all right."

"Anna . . ."

"Please go now."

At the sound of the door closing she trembled slightly, but she did not put down her work or raise her eyes. She sat stiff and straight, the needles clicked softly. After a moment, her lips moved silently. She was counting her stitches.

Aryan Papers

Ida Fink

Translated from the Polish by Madeline Levine and Francine Prose

The girl arrived first and sat down in the back of the room near the bar. Loud conversation, the clinking of glasses, and shouts from the kitchen hurt her ears; but when she shut her eyes, it sounded almost like the ocean. Smoke hung in the air like a dense fog and curled towards the roaring exhaust fan. Most of the customers were men and most of them were drinking vodka. The girl ordered tea, but the waiter, who had no experience with drinks of that sort, brought beer. It was sweet and smelled like a musty barrel. She drank, and the white foam clung to her lips. She wiped them brusquely with the back of her hand; in her anxiety she had forgotten her handkerchief.

Perhaps he won't come, she thought, relieved, then instantly terrified, because if he didn't come that would be the end of everything. Then she began to worry that someone would recognize her and she wished she could hide behind the curtain hanging over the door to the toilet.

When he entered, her legs began to tremble and she had to press her heels against the floor to steady herself.

"Good, you're here already," said the man and took off his coat.

"A double vodka!" he shouted towards the bar, "and hurry!"

He was tall, well built, with a suntanned face; his cheeks were a bit jowly, but he was good-looking. He was in his forties. He was nicely dressed, with a tasteful, conservative tie. When he picked up the glass she noticed that his fingernails were dirty.

"Well?" he asked, and glanced at the girl, who looked like a child in her plain, dark-blue raincoat. Her black eyes, framed by thick brows and lashes, were beautiful.

She swallowed hard and said, "Fine."

"Good," he said, smiling. "You see? The wolf is sated and the sheep is whole. As if there was a reason for all that fuss! Everything could have been taken care of by now."

He sat half turned away from her and looked at her out of the corner of his eye.

"Would you like something to eat? This place is disgusting but you must understand that I couldn't take you anywhere else. In a crummy bar like this even the informers are soused."

"I'm not hungry."

"You're nervous." He laughed again.

Her legs were still trembling as if she had just walked miles; she couldn't make them stay still.

"Come on, let's eat. This calls for a celebration."

"No."

She was afraid that she would pass out; she felt weak, first hot, then cold. She wanted to get everything over with as quickly as possible.

"Do you have it ready, sir? I brought the money . . ."

"What's this 'sir' business? We've already clinked glasses and you still call me sir! You're really something! Yes, I have everything ready. Signed and sealed. No cheating—the seals, the birth certificate—*alles in Ordnung*! Waiter, the check!"

He took her arm and she thought that it would be nice to have someone who would take her by the arm. Anyone but him.

The street was empty and dark; only after they reached the square did the streetlamps light the darkness and the passersby become visible. She expected that they would take a tram to save time, but they passed the stop and went on by foot.

"How old are you, sixteen?"

"Yes."

"For a sixteen-year-old you're definitely too thin and too short. But I like thin girls. I don't like fat on women. I knew you were my type the day you came to work. And I knew right away what you were. Who made those papers for you? What a lousy job. With mine you could walk through fire. Even with eyes like yours. How much did your mother give him?"

"Who?"

"The guy who's blackmailing you."

"She gave him her ring."

"A large one?"

"I don't know."

"One karat? Two?"

"I don't know. It was pretty. Grandma's."

"Aha, Grandma's. Probably a big stone. Too bad. So you see, I noticed at once that you had a problem, but I didn't know that you would admit it right away. At any rate, it's good that you happened to find me. I like to help people. Everybody wants to live. But why the hell did you spill it so fast?"

"I didn't care anymore."

"That's just talk! You knew I liked you, didn't you?"

"Maybe. I don't know."

"And why did your mother let the papers out of her hands?"

"They said that they wanted to check something and they took them away."

"And they said that they'd give them back once she came up with some cash. Right?" He laughed. "Was it always the same guys who came?"

"Yes."

"Naturally. Once you pay the first time, they'll keep coming back. They must have been making a pile. How much time did they give you?"

"Till the day after tomorrow. But we don't have any more money—really. The money I've brought for you is all we have."

He steered her through a gate and up to the third floor. The stairs were filthy and stank of urine.

"That means you want to leave tomorrow." And he added, "Send me your address and I'll come to see you; I've taken a liking to you."

The room was clean and neatly furnished. She looked at the white iron bed on which lay a pair of men's pajamas with cherry-red stripes.

If I throw up, she thought, he'll chase me out of here and it will all be for nothing.

"Please give me the documents, sir, I'll get the money out right away," she said.

"Sir? When you go to bed with someone, he's not a sir! Put your money away, we have time."

It probably doesn't take long, she thought. I'm not afraid of anything. Mama will be happy when I bring the papers. I should have done it a week ago. We would already be in Warsaw. I was stupid. He's even nice, he was always nice to me at work, and he could have informed.

"Don't just stand there, little one."

He sat down on the bed and took off his shoes. When he took off his trousers and carefully folded them along the crease, she turned her head away.

"I'll turn off the light," she said.

She heard his laughter and she felt flushed.

An hour later there was a knock at the door.

"Who's there?" he shouted from the bed.

"It's me, I've got business for you, open up!"

"The hell with you, what a time for business! What's up?"

"I'm not going to talk through the door. Do you have someone in there?"

"Yes."

"It's important and it ought to be taken care of fast. They could steal it from under our noses, and it would be too bad to lose all that good money."

"Get dressed," said the man. "You heard, someone's here on business. A man doesn't have a moment's rest! Don't put on such a mournful face, there's nothing to be sorry about! You'll be a terrific woman someday! Here you are, the birth certificates, the *Kennkarten*."

He counted skillfully, without licking his fingers. She could barely stand, and once again she felt queasy. She put the documents in her bag, the man opened the door and patted her on the shoulder. The other man, who was sitting on the stairs, turned around and looked at them with curiosity.

"Who's the girl?" he asked, entering the room.

"Oh, just a whore."

"I thought she was a virgin," he said, surprised. "Pale, teary-eyed, shaky . . ."

"Since when can't virgins be whores?"

"You're quite a philosopher," the other man said, and they both burst out laughing.

The Gray Zone

Kurt

Bernard Gotfryd

On a wet morning during the winter of 1941 a tall, lean soldier with high cheekbones and light brown eyes came into the photo studio where I worked. The lapels of his tunic were adorned with insignia of the Waffen SS; on his hat was a round black patch with a silver skull and crossbones. Around his waist he wore a black leather belt from which hung a bayonet in a green metal sheath. The sight of him sent shivers down my spine.

In a hardly audible voice he greeted me with a prolonged "*Guuten Morgen*" and asked me if I spoke German. "Somewhat," I answered. He then took off his gloves and energetically began to wipe his muddy boots on the decaying doormat until it split in two. When I asked him to have a seat he thanked me politely and walked over to inspect a display of photographs on one of the reception-room walls.

As soon as I had finished with the other customers—all of them German soldiers—I asked the SS man if I could be of help to him. "Yes," he told me, speaking softly, almost apologetically. "I would like to be photographed." His name was Kurt, he told me, and he insisted that was all the name I needed. Soon after he was photographed, realizing that we were alone in the reception room, he turned abruptly to ask, "Could you tell me the meaning of the *Kommissarische Leitung* sign displayed over this establishment?" I was surprised by his naïve question; everyone knew full well what *Kommissarische Leitung* meant.

"This used to be a Jewish-owned business," I answered dutifully. "It was taken over recently by the German state, and it's being administered by a trustee, with the former owner as an employee."

As soon as I finished my explanation he told me how impressed he was with my knowledge of the German language. "You speak much better than I expected. And you," he asked, "are you a Jew?"

"Yes, I am," I answered, somewhat frightened. Quickly he reached inside the canvas pouch he carried under his arm and pulled out a small loaf of bread. "Please take this, it's for you," he said. I was surprised and thanked him for it; as I turned to put it with my things behind the desk two German officers came in. Kurt gave them a Nazi salute and left. I didn't know what to think of such an act of generosity, especially on the part of an SS man.

I didn't stop to think that there might be something wrong with the bread; I only wondered why Kurt had given it to me. How could I turn down food under any circumstances? We were hungry.

When I took home the bread that evening and told my parents about Kurt they thought the entire incident highly suspect. They warned me to be cautious and not to ask the SS man for anything. I assured them that I hadn't, that he had given me the loaf of bread of his own volition.

A few days after Kurt was photographed he came back to the studio to place his photo order. He seemed to linger after he had done so; as soon as the reception room emptied he gave me a tightly packed canvas pouch full of food. I was reluctant to take it and wanted to reimburse him for it, but he refused to accept any money. We had a fairly long conversation about camera techniques and films, but he volunteered nothing about himself. He liked to take pictures of landscapes, he told me, but still had difficulties getting the right exposures. Then he asked me all about life in the ghetto, and about my family.

"One day when this war is over," Kurt said, "we'll have a long talk. Not now; it may be dangerous."

At the time, my grandmother was recovering from a stroke and needed a medication that wasn't available at any of the local apothecaries. Some days after, as a last resort, I asked Kurt if he might obtain some; the following day he brought a supply large enough to last for weeks. Again he refused even to discuss compensation, saying, "This is the least I could do for your sick grandmother."

Soon after Kurt brought a picture of his own grandmother into the studio and ordered a copy of it for his wallet. Many German soldiers would bring their old family photos to be copied so that they could carry them in their wallets. Looking at the picture after he had gone, I realized that there was nothing typically Germanic about his grandmother; for one reason or another I made an extra print and took it home to show it to my parents. They were astonished to see that Kurt's grandmother was dark-eyed and had Semitic features. "She looks so Jewish," my mother commented. From then on my parents speculated frequently on Kurt's origins. My mother insisted—given his irregular behavior—that there had to be a Jewish connection; thereafter Kurt became "the Jewish SS man."

Some weeks went by without a visit from Kurt. I worried that someone had seen him giving me food and had denounced him to the Gestapo. I had heard of a similar case in which a German soldier had been helping a Jewish woman and her child with food; he was betrayed, charged with *Rassenschande* (violation of the Nuremberg racial laws), court-martialed, and sentenced to a hard-labor camp. Kurt's disappearance became one more of our daily concerns. Quite often I heard my mother say, "I hope Kurt didn't get in trouble for helping Jews."

Quite unexpectedly, toward the end of May, 1942, after an absence of over a year, Kurt showed up again. He arrived early one morning, soon after I had opened the studio. I hardly recognized him. He was pale and thin, and obviously in poor health. As my eyes adjusted to the dim light of the reception-room corner where he stood I realized that the left sleeve of his jacket was tucked into his belt, and that there was no arm inside it. He greeted me in a shaky voice; pointing to his sleeve, he said, "Wars aren't much fun, but I still have my right arm."

I wanted to let him know how sorry I was about his arm, but I wasn't sure if I should. I felt awkward; being a Jew, I was hardly allowed such intimacy with a member of the *Herrenvolk*. If only he hadn't been wearing that dreadful uniform, things would have been different; my worst nightmares involved men dressed in uniforms like Kurt's. Still, afraid as I was, I was curious about how and where he had lost his arm.

Kurt started talking. "They want me to get an artificial arm," he said, "but I would rather not have one. I can live with one arm; it's probably safer that way. I won't have to go back to the Russian front," he said, smiling sadly.

I wasn't sure what he was implying. Could a man in an SS uniform possibly be against the war? I was confused; I couldn't figure him out.

Kurt inquired about my family; as usual he produced a voluminous bag of food. I begged him to accept some form of payment, but he wouldn't hear of it.

"Take it," he insisted. "Your family must be hungry, and I have too much to eat."

As soon as the reception room started to fill up Kurt took out some film, which he left for processing. As he turned toward the door he threw a Nazi salute to one of the officers in the reception room. I could see him leaving through the glass-paneled door; he wore a funny smile on his face. I wondered whether his Nazi salute wasn't a fake.

That evening I told my parents about Kurt's reappearance. They blessed him for his deeds and wished him good health. I was afraid that Kurt was perhaps overdoing things, and so as not to arouse any suspicions I decided to stop accepting food parcels from him.

August of 1942 began with an unusual heat wave. Before long rumors started circulating about deportations. Some months back we had heard dreadful accounts of deportations at the Warsaw ghetto, but very few people were willing to believe the same could happen in our own city. By the time we realized otherwise it was too late. Two consecutive deportations took place that summer, and out of twenty-eight thousand people not quite five thousand remained. We were squeezed into an area consisting of three narrow streets of two-story houses.

After the deportations Kurt returned once more to the studio. He wanted to know if I was still there and what had happened to my family. He told me how sorry he was about my mother's deportation and my grandmother's death; I was afraid to tell him that my grandmother had been shot. "The war won't last much longer," he said. He asked me to draw a diagram of the house in the ghetto where I lived. I hesitated at first, but, not wanting to make him feel as if I distrusted him, I finally drew the diagram. That night I had nightmares about being arrested by the Gestapo and shipped off to a camp.

The following week the studio itself was confiscated. I lost my job and my contact with Kurt, though soon I was hired by another studio owned by a Polish couple of German descent. They were given permission by the *Polizeiführer* to employ three Jews; I was one of them.

On a cold, rainy Sunday morning several weeks after we were moved into a smaller ghetto, a neighbor came rushing to our door to tell me a German soldier outside the ghetto fence was asking for me. "He sounds as if he knows you," my neighbor reported. It would have to be Kurt, I thought, somewhat frightened. I went out and, to my astonishment, found him on the other side of the fence. As soon as he saw me he yelled, *"Aufpassen"*— watch out—and threw a bag over the fence in my direction. Before I had a chance to pick up the bag another one landed at my feet.

It was daring of him. I wondered if he knew that not very far up the street stood a German police station and that patrols along the fence were quite frequent.

I walked closer to the fence to thank him and to urge him to leave. *"Danke sehr, vielen Dank"*—thank you, thank you very much—I kept repeating. "You shouldn't have done it. It's dangerous," I told him, a teenage boy advising an SS man.

"Auf Wiedersehen, mein Freund," I heard him say as he shrugged and turned to cross the street. As I watched him go a German police patrol appeared from around the corner; when he saw the patrol he quickly raised his good arm and yelled the Nazi salute at the top of his lungs.

I didn't see Kurt again until one day toward the end of the following year, when the ghetto was dissolved. One freezing afternoon we were marched to the train that would take us away; there was Kurt, rifle slung over his shoulder, in a long line of SS men standing guard. He had two arms; he must have gotten an artificial limb after all. Before boarding the cattle car I filed past him at a fairly close distance. I hoped he would notice me, but he wasn't looking in my direction. He was looking at the sky instead, as if trying to ignore what was happening around him.

It was snowing when the train started moving. I pushed my way closer to the door; through the crack I could see Kurt's silhouette getting smaller and smaller until it dissolved behind a thick screen of snowflakes. I was in a rage. I wanted to scream, just to let him know that this was probably the last time he would ever see me. Soon it got dark. Exhausted and hungry, I slipped to the floor of the moving car. I can still remember the monotonous knocking of the wheels against the track seams, the arguments people were having over space in the overcrowded car, but mostly I remember my own fury over whether Kurt had seen me get on that train.

Kurt

The following morning, to my surprise, I recognized Leon, a friend of my brother's. He sat on the floor at the far end of the car. When I called his name he came over to join me at the door, and for the rest of the trip we stood up talking. We hadn't seen each other for over two years, since the creation of the ghetto, and there was a lot to talk about.

Many years later, when the war was over but his image was still fresh in my memory, I tried to find Kurt. I didn't get very far. I had never known either his last name or where he came from. All I remembered was that he was tall and lean, that he wore a long green military tunic with SS insignia on his lapels, and that he was charitable and good at heart.

Helmut Reiner

Bernard Gotfryd

On a very beautiful Sunday afternoon in August of 1942 a heavyset man dressed in a Gestapo uniform, fully armed and wearing a steel helmet, left the Radom ghetto escorting a man and a woman and a sickly-looking little boy. He had a full, massive face with broad jawbones and light blue eyes; his name was Helmut Reiner. His expression was extremely serious, as if he was trying to add an air of formality to his mission. Heavy beads of perspiration rolled down his face onto his neck, dripping under the collar of his woolen tunic. Clearly he hadn't thought to loosen the collar; to do so would be against regulations.

Leaving the ghetto, Reiner turned to the right, heading north toward Zeromskiego Street. His steps—in heavy boots with reinforced soles—echoed metallically against the rows of low-lying tenements.

The couple under escort, perhaps in their thirties, were the Orensteins, the highly skilled local photographer to whom I had been apprenticed, and his wife. They appeared agitated. They were dressed lightly; on their left arms they wore white arm bands with blue Stars of David. As the boy couldn't keep up with the fast pace of the adults, his father soon stooped to carry him along.

Orenstein had strong features, and his scarred eye, the result of a childhood accident, added a certain severity to his looks. He was well built, of medium height, and his pitch-black hair was neatly combed and parted on the left side. With his free arm he carried a small suitcase; a faded green knapsack was strapped to his back. The perspiration running down his forehead nearly blinded him, but he had no way of wiping it away; he was clearly interested in getting away from the ghetto as fast as he possibly could.

The somewhat plump Mrs. Orenstein wore a flowery dress and a beige raincoat. She had on high-heeled shoes, which made it more difficult for her to walk on the cobblestone streets. There was fear in her eyes, but every now and then she would smile faintly at the boy to reassure him that all was well.

The little boy sat in the crook of his father's arm, holding tightly to his neck. He was clearly unwell; his skin seemed to have turned a yellowish green. Only when he saw a woman with a dog come out of a building did his face light up; one never saw dogs in the ghetto.

The four continued in the heat along Zeromskiego Street, away from the ghetto. Few pedestrians stopped to look; since the deportations had begun one saw Jews escorted in and out of the ghetto quite often.

Most of the day truckloads of SS and Ukrainian auxiliary detachments in battle gear arrived to take up positions around the ghetto. The diesel exhaust of the heavy trucks left dark brown trails of foul-smelling vapors behind, making it difficult to breathe. Small groups of SS officers, dressed in their best and displaying rows of ribbons and other Nazi paraphernalia on their chests, congregated at intersections outside the ghetto. They talked excitedly, passing bottles of French liqueur to one another.

As Reiner and his trio approached the last manned intersection outside the main gate of the ghetto, a group of SS officers stopped them. Reiner quickly pulled a letter from his leather pouch, unfolded it, and held it up for inspection. The officers examined it, asked some questions, and, returning Reiner's Nazi salute, told him to proceed.

As they passed a church a small wedding party with a priest was coming out. A young photographer was taking pictures. The Orensteins heard the young bride say aloud, "I wonder where he's taking them," but no one answered. Two German soldiers came out of a building and, noticing the trio under escort, stopped for a few seconds, smiling knowingly.

Moving along Zeromskiego Street, the little party soon arrived at a building marked #25, which they entered through the gate. Two little boys raced tricycles at the far end of the yard. Another fifty meters to the right was a double door leading to the photographic studio that had belonged to the Orensteins and which was now the property of the Nazis. Reiner fished a key from his pants pocket, opened the padlock, and, entering after the Orensteins, locked the door from the inside.

"Thank God we're here," he said in his heavy Viennese dialect, taking off his helmet. Orenstein's wife, hugging the boy with tears in her eyes, thanked him profusely for his deed. "I'll never forget what you did for us, Herr Reiner," she vowed, touching the sleeve of his tunic. He just looked at her and smiled.

"Now that we're here I might as well tell you about the letter. The signature on that letter that I showed to the SS at the intersection is a fake, and we were very lucky. I'm going to leave you here for the next two days," Reiner said. "You must be absolutely quiet and not let anybody in, no matter who they are. I'm taking the key with me. By Tuesday, I think, everything will be over, and I'll be back. I must get back to my station; God only knows what is awaiting me there. I beg you not to worry. The worst is over, so relax now. Let me have some water, please, and I shall take my leave."

Mrs. Orenstein went to the back of the studio and brought a tall glass of water for Reiner. He emptied it with two long gulps and wiped his mouth with the back of his hand. "By the way," he said, "I left some food for you in the closet. Nothing fancy, but it should suffice."

"We thank you wholeheartedly, Herr Reiner," Mr. Orenstein said.

"Well, then, good-bye until Tuesday," Reiner replied, and he left. He locked the double gate from the outside and pinned on it a sizable white sign that read "Confiscated by order of the Gestapo."

Among Helmut Reiner's duties was that of photographer at the Gestapo headquarters. High-ranking Gestapo officials were not to be photographed in privately owned studios; photography at Gestapo headquarters became solely Reiner's responsibility. Orenstein, a master in his art, was his negative retoucher.

As soon as Reiner had heard about the upcoming deportation in the ghetto he decided to keep Orenstein out of it. He had known him for a couple of years; he respected him for his superb craftsmanship and punctuality. Reiner knew that he was taking a chance protecting a Jew, but he was willing to do it; it wasn't in his nature to turn his back on people in need of help, particularly on an esteemed friend. The whole idea smelled of danger, but it could have been more dangerous to be shipped to the Russian front.

He certainly didn't want to fight the Russians. Reiner knew that the Nazis had no chance against them; Napoleon and others before him had tried and failed. The country was immense, the winters were severe, and partisans were everywhere, he was told. As far as he was concerned, he had had enough fighting. When in Vienna on furlough he had even told his wife what a decent couple the Orensteins were and how badly off the Polish Jews were; she had approved of his helping them.

Reiner wanted to stay in Poland as long as he possibly could. Things weren't too bad for him there. If he could only have Orenstein, his photography operation at the Gestapo might be assured, and he might not have to go to the east. He contemplated taking it up with his superior, Obersturmführer Rauscht, but decided against it. He felt that Rauscht wouldn't like the idea, especially since it involved a Jew. That was when he decided to take the responsibility upon himself.

"Just in case the tide turns. After all, this war won't go on forever. One must look further than one's own nose," he had told his wife, Trude.

After Reiner left the studio the Orensteins collapsed from near exhaustion. Their anxieties had nearly paralyzed them, especially after they had learned that the signature on the letter was a fake. If it was discovered, it could mean their lives; the thought made them even more nervous.

Orenstein's wife stretched out a blanket on the studio floor and put the boy down. He promptly fell asleep. It was time for him to eat, but he couldn't tolerate food. He was losing strength by the hour, and his parents knew that there was little hope for him. Only a miracle could save him. Quietly they sat back, staring at his little face and listening to his irregular breathing.

They heard noises from the outside; every time someone walked near the doorway their hearts would stop. They only hoped that no one had seen them coming into the studio. In the worst case they could escape by the back door, but where would they go with a sick child? Who would take them in?

They sat on the floor with their backs against the wall, conversing in a whisper. Even whispering seemed loud to them, however; they remembered seeing a Nazi poster outside the gate calling on all Germans to be silent. "The enemy is listening," the poster boasted in big, bold letters.

Their mutual desperation seemed to have brought the Orensteins closer. "At least," Mrs. Orenstein kept saying, "we are together as a family. Whatever the outcome, we must be determined to stay together." Her husband listened and, sighing heavily, shook his head in agreement. There wasn't much for him to say. He knew how helpless they were, and his helplessness only added to his anger.

The couple sat there whispering to each other late into the night when suddenly a deafening racket of rifle fire rang out, followed by loud roars of speeding vehicles. They knew that the deportation in the ghetto had begun. They feared that Reiner might show up at any minute to deliver them back to the ghetto; perhaps the rescue had been an artificial gesture on the Austrian's part. As much as they were in his debt, they still had reason to distrust him. After all, he was a member of the Gestapo.

The shooting continued throughout the night, and the boy kept twisting and turning, calling out to his parents from his disturbed sleep. The Orensteins worried about the family and friends they had left behind in the ghetto. Would they all be deported? Would anyone be left? Perhaps it would have been better to have gone with them.

It was dawn when the shooting subsided. Orenstein walked to the door and noticed a thin streak of daylight stealing through the narrow crack of the double gate. He stretched out on the floor and promptly fell asleep, the light touching his shoulder. This was as close as he came to the outside world that day.

Another night set in for the Orensteins, and more rifle shots followed, only this time not as prolonged as the night before. When it was over there was complete silence. Not even footsteps could be heard; it was as if the world had come to an end.

When Reiner returned to his station that Sunday afternoon he found orders to report for duty. Shortly a truck sped him and his unit to the ghetto. They were to search apartments and cellars for anyone in hiding; the orders were to shoot on sight. Reiner found a woman with a child in her arms hiding in a cellar. He asked her to come out. He nearly begged her, but she refused. The frightened child stared at him with huge eyes and began crying. Reiner's superior officer was with him; he ordered Reiner to shoot. It made him sick, but he could not disobey the order. He fired.

After it was over he thought about the Orenstein boy. He still couldn't understand why the woman had refused to come out of the cellar. It was suicidal, he thought. Being able to save the

Orensteins made him feel better; it gave his bad conscience a sense of equilibrium. "There was nothing I could have done about the woman and child," he told his wife Trude when he saw her some months later. "They were going to die anyway."

After all, his was not a premeditated murder, Trude assured him. He was under orders, and in the long run he might have done the woman and child a favor by killing them instantly and preventing humiliation, torture, and ultimately death by gassing. They knew where these people were being shipped. Reiner had heard his superiors talk about it at headquarters some time before.

"Not a word to anybody, not even to your own wives," they had warned. It was a secret, and they were under oath, but most of the rank and file had found out, and some of them had even had a chance to witness it.

At first Trude had difficulty believing such stories, but she knew that Helmut told her the truth. "You must do what is right and just," she told him always.

Tuesday came, and the deportation was finished. Close to noon Reiner went to the studio. His expression had hardened, and he looked as if he needed sleep. He was abrupt, had little to say; he inquired how the Orensteins were and asked them to get ready. Now that the deportation was over he was going to escort them back to the new, smaller ghetto. "Going back won't be troublesome at all," he assured them.

The bright sunlight nearly blinded the Orensteins after almost three days in darkness, but the pleasant breeze felt invigorating. They were glad not to have to hide any longer; now they could speak to each other above a whisper. The boy smiled for the first time in days. He seemed to have lost weight, however, and he kept asking for water, unable to quench his thirst.

The new ghetto looked as though a storm had hit. There wasn't enough housing to accommodate the nearly three thousand people who remained; the little housing available was deplorable. With Reiner's intervention the Orensteins were given a room they would share with another couple and their two children. Their parents, their siblings, and most of their friends had been deported.

For almost another year Orenstein was employed by Reiner, retouching the Gestapo negatives. Occasionally Reiner would visit him in the ghetto, bringing along extra food.

Late in 1943 the last of the ghetto was liquidated, and the Orensteins were shipped to camps. The orders were to finalize the Jewish question, and there was nothing Reiner could do to save them. As far as he knew, there wasn't going to be a single Jew left in the whole of occupied Poland.

Meanwhile the Russian front kept advancing, and there was talk about his unit being shipped to the front lines. Happily, his diabetes started acting up; the Gestapo doctor ordered a medical leave, and Reiner went home to Vienna. Soon after he arrived the war came to an end.

The Orensteins survived the camps, although their son did not; soon after the deportation he died. After the war was over they found each other among the survivors searching for relatives all over the European continent. Sick and worn out, ridden with guilt and anger, they settled in Sweden.

After the war ended Reiner was troubled by nightmares. The woman and child he had shot in the ghetto in Radom kept appearing in his dreams. They disturbed him more and more, though only his wife Trude knew about his anxiety.

"Pull yourself together, Helmut," she counseled him. "Forget about all the bad things that happened. You must start a new life. You did all you could, and there is no reason for you to feel the way you do. You were under orders, and that was it."

Early one morning in the summer of 1945, standing in a bread-line, Reiner was recognized by a former neighbor who denounced him as having belonged to the Gestapo. There were no other charges against him; only the Gestapo membership. Reiner was arrested.

Reiner's wife soon tired of the rumors she had to listen to every morning in the breadline. She wasn't the only one; everybody had a skeleton in his closet, and some of them were far larger than Reiner's, but it was nerve-racking all the same. She knew she should try to produce a statement from someone who had known Helmut during the occupation days in Poland. Trude couldn't think of anyone who had known him except the Orensteins, and they were probably dead. She didn't think they could have survived the camps; Helmut had told her what those places were like.

Still, she checked the camp survivor registers, published in papers and bulletins throughout Europe. Trude got hold of a newspaper that listed the Orensteins' address in Sweden. Hoping these were the right Orensteins, she quickly wrote them and told them what had happened to her husband. They were her only hope.

Before long she received an answer. Yes, they were the Orensteins she was looking for. They were happy to come to Vienna and do whatever was required of them; it was their chance to reciprocate.

"My dear Frau Reiner," Orenstein wrote, "Your husband saved us from deportation, risking his own life, and this we will never forget. You can count on us. We shall come to Vienna as soon as we get our travel permits."

Trude Reiner was touched by Orenstein's words. She was very eager to meet the couple; she hoped they would be her husband's saviors.

Within weeks the Orensteins arrived in Vienna. They brought along notarized testimony describing in detail Reiner's deeds on their behalf. Several days after the presentation of this testimony to the Allied Military Court Reiner was freed and cleared of his membership in the Gestapo and the Nazi party.

Naturally, Trude Reiner invited the Orensteins to join her family in a small celebration of Reiner's acquittal. "Just a few close relatives eager to meet you and raise a toast to Helmut's freedom," she told the Orensteins.

They gathered the following day at Reiner's apartment. There were several elderly women and a few men, mostly relatives, all dressed in their best. Reiner, in his loose-fitting suit (he had shed some weight in jail), embraced the Orensteins warmly and introduced them to those gathered.

"Now listen, everybody, I just want to say a few words," he announced in his deep, shaky voice. "I want you to meet my Jewish friends from Poland who turned out to be my saviors. I know it sounds strange, but it's true. Let's have a toast to the Orensteins; long live our friendship.

"But I want to say something else as well," he continued. "There is something that pains me a lot and disturbs my peace of mind. The eyes of a child follow me everywhere I go. . . . Maybe I shouldn't talk about it now, but it would be wrong not to. . . . Here I am celebrating my liberation, but my conscience will never be free. I don't think I can spell it out, but I would like you to know that terrible things were happening in Poland, and it pains me that I was a part of it, that I didn't do enough to stop it."

He started sobbing. His wife led him out of the room; a dead silence followed. The Orensteins couldn't understand the meaning of Reiner's speech and his reaction to his newfound freedom. Did he mean their little boy's eyes followed him? They would have liked to tell him again how much they appreciated what he had done for them and their son, but they were at a loss for words. Instead they sat at the table with total strangers, yesterday's enemies, now suddenly friends. It was all very confusing. Reiner's sudden breakdown further puzzled and dismayed them.

Trude Reiner returned to her guests. "I'm very sorry about what happened," she began, and, turning to the Orensteins, she continued, "I can't understand what upset him. He was in such high spirits and was so happy to hear that you survived the war. Perhaps the jail experience upset him. After all the things he has done for others, risking his own life, and then to be imprisoned—that must have been too much for him. Don't you think so?"

"Of course, we understand," Orenstein answered. "We have nothing but great respect and admiration for your husband, and we are ready to stand by him. That much we owe him."

There was nothing more the Orensteins could do in Vienna, where they felt uneasy and out of place; they planned to return to Sweden the following day. The war was over, and the Nazis were defeated; still, they felt surrounded by them, and they were uncomfortable.

"Why do you think Reiner risked his life to save us?" Orenstein asked his wife as soon as they were back at their hotel room that evening. "I can't believe he could have done it for selfish reasons. One really has to be decent and courageous at heart, don't you think?"

After a moment Mrs. Orenstein answered, "Whatever his reason was, were the roles reversed, I still wonder if any of us could equal him in his deed. The only thing that puzzles me is his speech; I still don't know whose eyes follow him and why. But I have no right to ask. That's his business."

The Orensteins sat up most of the night reminiscing about their time in hiding in the dark studio, only three years earlier; it seemed much further away somehow. They continued to wonder about the fates of their deported relatives and friends, whom they still felt they had betrayed.

"There are no words to express the guilt," Mrs. Orenstein said after some discussion, and she began to cry. Her husband comforted her and urged her to sleep.

It was still early when the telephone woke them. Trude Reiner asked them to stay on in Vienna. A terrible tragedy had taken place, she told them. Helmut was dead. He had accidentally shot himself that morning while dismantling a gun.

By the Railway Track

Zofia Nalkowska

Translated from the Polish by Diana Kuprel

Yet another person now belongs to the dead: the young woman by the railway track whose escape attempt failed. One can make her acquaintance only through the tale of a man who had witnessed the incident but is unable to understand it. She lives on only in his memory.

Those who were being transported to extermination camps in the lead-sealed boxcars of the long trains would sometimes escape en route. Not many dared such a feat. The courage required was even greater than that needed to go hopelessly, unresisting and meek, to a certain death.

Sometimes the escape would succeed. The deafening clatter of the rushing boxcars prevented those on the outside from hearing what went on inside.

The only means of escape was by ripping up the floorboards. In the cramp of jammed-in, starved, foul-smelling, filthy people, it seemed an improbable gambit. Even to move was impossible. The beaten human mass, wriggling with the rushing rhythm of the train, reeled and rocked in the suffocating stench and gloom. Nevertheless, even those who, weak and fearful, would never dream of escaping themselves understood their obligation to help others. They'd lean back, pressing against one another, and lift their shit-covered legs in order to open a way to freedom for others.

Successfully prying open one end of the floorboard raised a glimmer of hope. A collective effort was required to tear it up. It took hours. Then there remained still the second and the third boards.

Those closest would lean over the narrow aperture, then back away fearfully. Courage was called for to crawl hand and foot through the chink into the din and crash of iron, into the gale of the smoking wind below, above the gliding bases, to reach the axle and, in this catch-hold, to crawl to the spot from which jumping would guarantee the best chance at salvation. To drop somehow, some way, in between the rails or through the wheels. Then, to recover one's senses, roll down unseen from the mound, and escape into the strange, temptingly dark forest.

People would often fall under the wheels and be killed on the spot, struck by a protruding beam, the edge of a bar, thrown forcefully against a signal pole or roadside rock. Or they'd break their arms and legs, and be delivered thus unto the greater cruelty of the enemy.

Those who dared to step into the roaring, crashing, yawning mouth were aware of what they risked. Just as those who remained behind were, even though there was no possibility of looking out through the sealed doors or high-set windows.

The woman lying by the track belonged to those who dared. She was the third to step through the opening in the floor. A few others rolled down after her. At that moment a volley of shots rang out over the travelers' heads—an explosion on the roof of the boxcar. Suddenly the shots fell silent. The travelers could now regard the dark place left by the ripped-up boards as though it were the opening to a grave. And they could ride on calmly, ever closer to their own death, which awaited them at the crossroads.

The smoke and rattle of the train had long since disappeared into the darkness.

All that remained was the world.

The man, who can neither understand nor forget, relates his story once again.

When the new day broke, the woman was sitting on the dew-soaked grass by the side of the track. She was wounded in the knee. Some had succeeded in escaping. Further from the track, another lay motionless in the forest. A few had escaped. Two had died. She was the only one left like this, neither alive nor dead.

She was alone when he found her. But slowly people started to appear in that empty space, emerging from the brick kiln and village. Workers, women, and a boy stood fearful, watching her from a distance.

Every once in a while, a small chain of people would form. They'd cast their eyes about nervously and quickly depart. Others would approach, but wouldn't linger for long. They would whisper among themselves, sigh, and walk away.

The situation was clear. Her curly, raven hair was obviously disheveled, her too-dark eyes overflowed the lowered lids. No one uttered a word to her. It was she who asked if the ones in the forest were alive. She learned they weren't.

The day was white. The space open onto everything as far as the eye could see. People had already learned of the incident. It was a time of terror. Those who offered assistance or shelter were marked for death.

She begged one young man, who was standing for a while longer, then started to walk away, only to turn back, to bring her some Veronal from the pharmacy. She offered him money. He refused.

She lay back for a while, her eyes shut. Then she sat up again, shifted her leg, clasped it with both hands, and brushed her skirt from her knee. Her hands were bloodied. Her shattered knee a death sentence. She lay quietly for a long time, shutting her too-black eyes against the world.

When she finally opened them again, she noticed new faces hovering around her. The young man still lingered. So she asked him to buy her some vodka and cigarettes. He rendered her this service.

The gathering beside the mound attracted attention. Someone new would latch on. She lay among people but didn't count on anyone for help. She lay like an animal that had been wounded during a hunt but which the hunters had forgotten to kill off. She proceeded to get drunk. She dozed. The power that cut her off from all the others by forming a ring of fear was unbeatable.

Time passed. An old village woman, gasping for breath, returned and, drawing near, stole a tin cup of milk and some bread from beneath her kerchief. She bent over, furtively placed them in the wounded woman's hand, and left immediately, only to look on from a distance to check whether she would drink the milk. It was only when she noticed two policemen approaching from the village that she disappeared, drawing her scarf across her face.

The others dispersed, too. Only the slick, small-town guy who had brought her the vodka and cigarettes continued to keep her company. But she no longer wanted anything from him.

The police came to see what was going on. They quickly sized up the situation and deliberated on to how to handle it. She begged them to shoot her. In a low voice, she tried to negotiate with them, provided they keep the whole thing quiet. They were undecided.

They, too, left, conferred, stopped, and walked on further. What they would finally decide was not certain. In the end, however, they did not care to carry out her request. She noticed that the kind young man, who had lit her cigarettes with a lighter that didn't want to light, followed after. She had told him that one of the two dead in the forest was her husband. That piece of news seemed to have caused him some unpleasantness.

She tried to swallow the milk but, preoccupied, set the cup down on the grass. A heavy, windy, spring day rolled over. It was cool. Beyond the empty field stood a couple of huts; at the other end, a few short, scrawny pines swept the sky with their branches. The forest, their destination, sprang up further from the railway. This emptiness was the whole of the world she saw.

The young man returned. She swallowed some more vodka and he lit her cigarette. A light dusk brushed across the sky from the east. To the west, skeins and smudges of clouds branched up sharply.

More people, on their way home from work, turned up and were told what had happened. They spoke as though she couldn't hear them, as though she were no longer there.

"The dead one there's her husband," a woman's voice spoke up.

"They tried to escape from the train into the forest. But they shot at them with a rifle. They killed her husband, and she was left alone. Shot in the knee. She couldn't get any further.

"From the forest she could easily have been taken somewhere. But here, with everyone watching, there's no way."

The old lady who had returned for her tin cup said those words. Silently she watched as the milk soaked into the grass.

So no one would intercede by removing her before nightfall, or by calling a doctor, or by taking her to the station so she could get to a hospital. Nothing of the kind would happen. She could only die, one way or another.

When she opened her eyes at dusk, there was no one around except for the two policemen who had come back and the one who would no longer go away. Again she pleaded with them to kill her, but without any expectation that they would do so. She covered her eyes with her hands so as not to see anymore.

The policemen still hesitated about what to do. One tried to talk the other into doing it. The latter retorted, "You do it yourself."

Then she heard the young man's voice saying, "Well then give it to me."

Again they debated, quarreled. From beneath her lowered eyelids she watched the policeman take out his revolver and hand it to the stranger.

A small group of people standing further back watched as he bent over her. They heard the shot and turned away in disgust.

"They could at least have called in someone. Not do it like that. Like she was a dog."

When it grew dark, two people emerged from the forest to get her. They located the spot with a bit of difficulty. They assumed she was sleeping. But when one of them took her by the shoulder, he understood at once that he was dealing with a corpse.

She lay there all that night and into the morning, until just before noon, when a bailiff arrived and ordered her buried together with the other two who had died by the railway tracks.

"Why he shot her isn't clear," the narrator said. "I couldn't understand it. Maybe he felt sorry for her. . ."

The Abyss

Yom Kippur:
The Day Without Forgiveness

Elie Wiesel

Translated from the French by Steven Donadio
    With a lifeless look, a painful smile on his face, while digging a hole in the ground, Pinhas moved his lips in silence. He appeared to be arguing with someone within himself and, judging from his expression, seemed close to admitting defeat.

    I had never seen him so downhearted. I knew that his body would not hold out much longer. His strength was already abandoning him, his movements were becoming more heavy, more chaotic. No doubt he knew it too. But death figured only rarely in our conversations. We preferred to deny its presence, to reduce it, as in the past, to a simple allusion, something abstract, inoffensive, a word like any other.

    "What are you thinking about? What's wrong?"

    Pinhas lowered his head, as if to conceal his embarrassment, or his sadness, or both, and let a long time go by before he answered, in a voice scarcely audible: "Tomorrow is Yom Kippur."

    Then I too felt depressed. My first Yom Kippur in the camp. Perhaps my last. The day of judgment, of atonement. Tomorrow the heavenly tribunal would sit and pass sentence: "And like unto a flock, the creatures of this world shall pass before thee." Once upon a time—last year—the approach of this day of tears, of penitence and fear, had made me tremble. Tomorrow, we would present ourselves before God, who sees everything and who knows everything, and we would say: "Father, have pity on your children." Would I be capable of praying with fervor again? Pinhas shook himself abruptly. His glance plunged into mine.

"Tomorrow is the Day of Atonement and I have just made a decision: I am not going to fast. Do you hear? I am not going to fast."

I asked for no explanation. I knew he was going to die and suddenly I was afraid that by way of justification he might declare: "It is simple, I have decided not to comply with the law anymore and not to fast because in the eyes of man and of God I am already dead, and the dead can disobey the commandments of the Torah." I lowered my head and made believe I was not thinking about anything but the earth I was digging up under a sky more dark than the earth itself.

We belonged to the same Kommando. We always managed to work side by side. Our age difference did not stop him from treating me like a friend. He must have been past forty. I was fifteen. Before the war, he had been *Rosh-Yeshiva*, director of a rabbinical school somewhere in Galicia. Often, to outwit our hunger or to forget our reasons for despair, we would study a page of the Talmud from memory. I relived my childhood by forcing myself not to think about those who were gone. If one of my arguments pleased Pinhas, if I quoted a commentary without distorting its meaning, he would smile at me and say: "I should have liked to have you among my disciples."

And I would answer: "But I am your disciple, where we are matters little."

That was false, the place was of capital importance. According to the law of the camp I was his equal; I used the familiar form when I addressed him. Any other form of address was inconceivable.

"Do you hear?" Pinhas shouted defiantly. "I will not fast."

"I understand. You are right. One must not fast. Not at Auschwitz. Here we live outside time, outside sin. Yom Kippur does not apply to Auschwitz."

Ever since Rosh Hashana, the New Year, the question had been bitterly debated all over camp. Fasting meant a quicker death. Here everybody fasted all year round. Every day was Yom

Kippur. And the book of life and death was no longer in God's hands, but in the hands of the executioner. The words *mi yichye umi yamut*, "who shall live and who shall die," had a terrible real meaning here, an immediate bearing. And all the prayers in the world could not alter the *Gzar-din*, the inexorable movement of fate. Here, in order to live, one had to eat, not pray.

"You are right, Pinhas," I said, forcing myself to withstand his gaze. "You *must* eat tomorrow. You've been here longer than I have, longer than many of us. You need your strength. You have to save your strength, watch over it, protect it. You should not go beyond your limits. Or tempt misfortune. That would be a sin."

Me, his disciple? I gave him lessons, I gave him advice, as if I were his elder, his guide.

"That is not it," said Pinhas, getting irritated. "I could hold out for one day without food. It would not be the first time."

"Then what is it?"

"A decision. Until now, I've accepted everything. Without bitterness, without reservation. I have told myself: 'God knows what he is doing.' I have submitted to his will. Now I have had enough, I have reached my limit. If he knows what he is doing, then it is serious; and it is not any less serious if he does not. Therefore, I have decided to tell him: 'It is enough.' "

I said nothing. How could I argue with him? I was going through the same crisis. Every day I was moving a little further away from the God of my childhood. He had become a stranger to me; sometimes, I even thought he was my enemy.

The appearance of Edek put an end to our conversation. He was our master, our king. The Kapo. This young Pole with rosy cheeks, with the movements of a wild animal, enjoyed catching his slaves by surprise and making them shout with fear. Still an adolescent, he enjoyed possessing such power over so many adults. We dreaded his changeable moods, his sudden fits of anger: without unclenching his teeth, his eyes half-closed, he would beat his victims long after they had lost consciousness and had ceased to moan.

"Well?" he said, planting himself in front of us, his arms folded. "Taking a little nap? Talking over old times? You think you are at a resort? Or in the synagogue?"

A cruel flame lit his blue eyes, but it went out just as quickly. An aborted rage. We began to shovel furiously, not thinking about anything but the ground which opened up menacingly before us. Edek insulted us a few more times and then walked off.

Pinhas did not feel like talking anymore, neither did I. For him the die had been cast. The break with God appeared complete.

Meanwhile, the pit under our legs was becoming wider and deeper. Soon our heads would hardly be visible above the ground. I had the weird sensation that I was digging a grave. For whom? For Pinhas? For myself? Perhaps for our memories.

On my return to camp, I found it plunged in feverish anticipation: they were preparing to welcome the holiest and longest day of the year. My barracks neighbors, a father and son, were talking in low voices. One was saying: "Let us hope the roll-call does not last too long." The other added: "Let us hope that the soup is distributed before the sun sets, otherwise we will not have the right to touch it."

Their prayers were answered. The roll-call unfolded without incident, without delay, without public hanging. The section-chief hurriedly distributed the soup; I hurriedly gulped it down. I ran to wash, to purify myself. By the time the day was drawing to a close, I was ready.

Some days before, on the eve of Rosh Hashana, all the Jews in camp—Kapos included—had congregated at the square where roll was taken, and we had implored the God of Abraham, Isaac, and Jacob to end our humiliation, to change sides, to break his pact with the enemy. In unison we had said *Kaddish* for the dead and for the living as well. Officers and soldiers, machine guns in hand, had stood by, amused spectators, on the other side of the barbed wire.

Now, we did not go back there for *Kol Nidre*. We were afraid of a selection: in preceding years, the Day of Atonement had been turned into a day of mourning. Yom Kippur had become *Tisha b'Av*, the day the Temple was destroyed.

Thus, each barracks housed its own synagogue. It was more prudent. I was sorry, because Pinhas was in another block.

A Hungarian rabbi officiated as our cantor. His voice stirred my memories and evoked that legend according to which, on the night of Yom Kippur, the dead rise from their graves and come to pray with the living. I thought: "Then it is true; that is what really happens. The legend is confirmed at Auschwitz."

For weeks, several learned Jews had gathered every night in our block to transcribe from memory—by hand, on toilet paper—the prayers for the High Holy Days. Each cantor received a copy. Ours read in a loud voice and we repeated each verse after him. The *Kol Nidre*, which releases us from all vows made under constraint, now seemed to me anachronistic, absurd, even though it had been composed in similar circumstances, in Spain, right near the Inquisition stakes. Once a year the converts would assemble and cry out to God: "Know this, all that we have said is unsaid, all that we have done is undone." *Kol Nidre*? A sad joke. Here and now we no longer had any secret vows to make or to deny: everything was clear, irrevocable.

Then came the *Vidui*, the great confession. There again, everything rang false, none of it concerned us anymore. *Ashamnu*, we have sinned. *Bagadnu*, we have betrayed. *Gazalnu*, we have stolen. What? Us? We have sinned? Against whom? by doing what? We have betrayed? Whom? Undoubtedly this was the first time since God judged his creation that victims beat their breasts accusing themselves of the crimes of their executioners.

Why did we take responsibility for sins and offenses which not one of us could ever have had the desire or the possibility of committing? Perhaps we felt guilty despite everything. Things were simpler that way. It was better to believe our punishments had meaning, that we had deserved them; to believe in a cruel but just God was better than not to believe at all. It was in order not to provoke an open war between God and his people that we had chosen to spare him, and we cried out: "You are our God, blessed be your name. You smite us without pity, you shed our blood, we give thanks to you for it, O Eternal One, for you are determined to show us that you are just and that your name is justice!"

I admit having joined my voice to the others and implored the heavens to grant me mercy and forgiveness. At variance with everything my lips were saying, I indicted myself only to turn everything into derision, into farce. At any moment I expected the Master of the universe to strike me dumb and to say: "That is enough—you have gone too far." And I like to think I would have replied: "You, also, blessed be your name, you also."

Our services were dispersed by the camp bell. The section-chiefs began to yell: "Okay, go to sleep! If God hasn't heard you, it's because he is incapable of hearing."

The next day, at work, Pinhas joined another group. I thought: "He wants to eat without being embarrassed by my presence." A day later, he returned. His face even more pale, even more gaunt than before. Death was gnawing at him. I caught myself thinking: "He will die because he did not observe Yom Kippur."

We dug for several hours without looking at each other. From far off, the shouting of the Kapo reached us. He walked around hitting people relentlessly.

Toward the end of the afternoon, Pinhas spoke to me: "I have a confession to make."

I shuddered, but went on digging. A strange, almost child-like smile appeared on his lips when he spoke again: "You know, I fasted."

I remained motionless. My stupor amused him.

"Yes, I fasted. Like the others. But not for the same reasons. Not out of obedience, but out of defiance. Before the war, you see, some Jews rebelled against the divine will by going to restaurants on the Day of Atonement; here, it is by observing the fast that we can make our indignation heard. Yes, my disciple and teacher, know that I fasted. Not for love of God, but against God."

He left me a few weeks later, victim of the first selection.

He shook my hand: "I would have liked to die some other way and elsewhere. I had always hoped to make of my death, as of my life, an act of faith. It is a pity. God prevents me from realizing my dream. He no longer likes dreams."

Nonetheless, he asked me to say *Kaddish* for him after his death, which, according to his calculations, would take place three days after his departure from camp.

"But why?" I asked, "since you are no longer a believer?"

He took the tone he always used when he explained a passage in the Talmud to me: "You do not see the heart of the matter. Here and now, the only way to accuse him is by praising him."

And he went, laughing, to his death.

The Shawl

Cynthia Ozick

Stella, cold, cold, the coldness of hell. How they walked on the
roads together, Rosa with Magda curled up between sore breasts,
Magda wound up in the shawl. Sometimes Stella carried Magda.
But she was jealous of Magda. A thin girl of fourteen, too small,
with thin breasts of her own, Stella wanted to be wrapped in a
shawl, hidden away, asleep, rocked by the march, a baby, a round
infant in arms. Magda took Rosa's nipple, and Rosa never stopped
walking, a walking cradle.

There was not enough milk; sometimes Magda sucked air;
then she screamed. Stella was ravenous. Her knees were tumors
on sticks, her elbows chicken bones.

Rosa did not feel hunger; she felt light, not like someone walking but like someone in a faint, in trance, arrested in a fit, someone who is already a floating angel, alert and seeing everything,
but in the air, not there, not touching the road. As if teetering on
the tips of her fingernails. She looked into Magda's face through
a gap in the shawl: a squirrel in a nest, safe, no one could reach
her inside the little house of the shawl's windings. The face, very
round, a pocket mirror of a face: but it was not Rosa's bleak com-
plexion, dark like cholera, it was another kind of face altogether,
eyes blue as air, smooth feathers of hair nearly as yellow as the
Star sewn into Rosa's coat. You could think she was one of *their*
babies.

Rosa, floating, dreamed of giving Magda away in one of the
villages. She could leave the line for a minute and push Magda
into the hands of any woman on the side of the road. But if she
moved out of line they might shoot. And even if she fled the

The Call of Memory

line for half a second and pushed the shawl-bundle at a stranger, would the woman take it? She might be surprised, or afraid; she might drop the shawl, and Magda would fall out and strike her head and die. The little round head. Such a good child, she gave up screaming, and sucked now only for the taste of the drying nipple itself. The neat grip of the tiny gums. One mite of a tooth tip sticking up in the bottom gum, how shining, an elfin tombstone of white marble gleaming there. Without complaining, Magda relinquished Rosa's teats, first the left, then the right; both were cracked, not a sniff of milk. The duct-crevice extinct, a dead volcano, blind eye, chill hole, so Magda took the corner of the shawl and milked it instead. She sucked and sucked, flooding the threads with wetness. The shawl's good flavor, milk of linen.

It was a magic shawl, it could nourish an infant for three days and three nights. Magda did not die, she stayed alive, although very quiet. A peculiar smell, of cinnamon and almonds, lifted out of her mouth. She held her eyes open every moment, forgetting how to blink or nap, and Rosa and sometimes Stella studied their blueness. On the road they raised one burden of a leg after another and studied Magda's face. "Aryan," Stella said, in a voice grown as thin as a string; and Rosa thought how Stella gazed at Magda like a young cannibal. And the time that Stella said "Aryan," it sounded to Rosa as if Stella had really said, "Let us devour her."

But Magda lived to walk. She lived that long, but she did not walk very well, partly because she was only fifteen months old, and partly because the spindles of her legs could not hold up her fat belly. It was fat with air, full and round. Rosa gave almost all her food to Magda, Stella gave nothing; Stella was ravenous, a growing child herself, but not growing much. Stella did not menstruate. Rosa did not menstruate. Rosa was ravenous, but also not; she learned from Magda how to drink the taste of a finger in one's mouth. They were in a place without pity, all pity was annihilated in Rosa, she looked at Stella's bones without pity. She was sure that Stella was waiting for Magda to die so she could put her teeth into the little thighs.

Rosa knew Magda was going to die very soon; she should have been dead already, but she had been buried away deep inside the magic shawl, mistaken there for the shivering mound of Rosa's breasts; Rosa clung to the shawl as if it covered only herself. No one took it away from her. Magda was mute. She never cried. Rosa hid her in the barracks, under the shawl, but she knew that one day someone would inform; or one day someone, not even Stella, would steal Magda to eat her. When Magda began to walk Rosa knew that Magda was going to die very soon, something would happen. She was afraid to fall asleep; she slept with the weight of her thigh on Magda's body; she was afraid she would smother Magda under her thigh. The weight of Rosa was becoming less and less; Rosa and Stella were slowly turning into air.

Magda was quiet, but her eyes were horribly alive, like blue tigers. She watched. Sometimes she laughed—it seemed a laugh, but how could it be? Magda had never seen anyone laugh. Still, Magda laughed at her shawl when the wind blew its corners, the bad wind with pieces of black in it, that made Stella's and Rosa's eyes tear. Magda's eyes were always clear and tearless. She watched like a tiger. She guarded her shawl. No one could touch it; only Rosa could touch it. Stella was not allowed. The shawl was Magda's own baby, her pet, her little sister. She tangled herself up in it and sucked on one of the corners when she wanted to be very still.

Then Stella took the shawl away and made Magda die.

Afterward Stella said: "I was cold."

And afterward she was always cold, always. The cold went into her heart: Rosa saw that Stella's heart was cold. Magda flopped onward with her little pencil legs scribbling this way and that, in search of the shawl; the pencils faltered at the barracks opening, where the light began. Rosa saw and pursued. But already Magda was in the square outside the barracks, in the jolly light. It was the roll-call arena. Every morning Rosa had to conceal Magda under the shawl against a wall of the barracks and go out and stand in the arena with Stella and hundreds of others, sometimes for hours, and Magda, deserted, was quiet under the shawl, sucking on her corner. Every day Magda was silent, and so she did not die. Rosa saw that today Magda was going to die, and at the same time a fearful joy ran in Rosa's two palms, her fingers were on fire, she was astonished, febrile: Magda, in the sunlight, swaying on her pencil legs, was howling. Ever since the drying up of Rosa's nipples, ever since Magda's last scream on the road, Magda had been devoid of any syllable; Magda was a mute. Rosa believed that something had gone wrong with her vocal cords, with her windpipe, with the cave of her larynx; Magda was defective, without a voice; perhaps she was deaf; there might be something amiss with her intelligence; Magda was dumb. Even the laugh that came when the ash-stippled wind made a clown out of Magda's shawl was only the air-blown showing of her teeth. Even when the lice, head lice and body lice, crazed her so that she became as wild as one of the big rats that plundered the barracks at daybreak looking for carrion, she rubbed and scratched and kicked and bit and rolled without a whimper. But now Magda's mouth was spilling a long viscous rope of clamor.

"Maaaa—"

It was the first noise Magda had ever sent out from her throat since the drying up of Rosa's nipples. "Maaaa . . . aaa!"

Again! Magda was wavering in the perilous sunlight of the arena, scribbling on such pitiful little bent shins. Rosa saw. She saw that Magda was grieving for the loss of her shawl, she saw that Magda was going to die. A tide of commands hammered in Rosa's nipples: Fetch, get, bring! But she did not know which to go after first, Magda or the shawl. If she jumped out into the arena to snatch Magda up, the howling would not stop, because Magda would still not have the shawl; but if she ran back into the barracks to find the shawl, and if she found it, and if she came after Magda holding it and shaking it, then she would get Magda back, Magda would put the shawl in her mouth and turn dumb again.

Rosa entered the dark. It was easy to discover the shawl. Stella was heaped under it, asleep in her thin bones. Rosa tore the shawl free and flew—she could fly, she was only air—into the arena. The sunheat murmured of another life, of butterflies in summer. The light was placid, mellow. On the other side of the steel fence, far away, there were green meadows speckled with dandelions and deep-colored violets; beyond them, even farther, innocent tiger lilies, tall, lifting their orange bonnets. In the barracks they spoke of "flowers," of "rain": excrement, thick turd-braids, and the slow stinking maroon waterfall that slunk down from the upper bunks, the stink mixed with a bitter fatty floating smoke that greased Rosa's skin. She stood for an instant at the margin of the arena. Sometimes the electricity inside the fence would seem to hum; even Stella said it was only an imagining, but Rosa heard real sounds in the wire: grainy sad voices. The farther she was from the fence, the more clearly the voices crowded at her. The lamenting voices strummed so convincingly, so passionately, it was impossible to suspect them of being phantoms. The voices told her to hold up the shawl, high; the voices told her to shake it, to whip with it, to unfurl it like a flag. Rosa lifted, shook, whipped, unfurled. Far off, very far, Magda leaned across her air-fed belly, reaching out with the rods of her arms. She was high up, elevated, riding someone's shoulder. But the shoulder that carried Magda was not coming toward Rosa and the shawl, it was drifting away, the speck of Magda was moving more and more into the smoky distance. Above the shoulder a helmet glinted. The light tapped the helmet and sparkled it into a goblet. Below the helmet a black body like a domino and a pair of black boots hurled themselves in the direction of the electrified fence. The electric voices began to chatter wildly. "Maamaa, maaa-maaa," they all hummed together. How far Magda was from Rosa now, across the whole square, past a dozen barracks, all the way on the other side! She was no bigger than a moth.

All at once Magda was swimming through the air. The whole of Magda traveled through loftiness. She looked like a butterfly touching a silver vine. And the moment Magda's feathered round head and her pencil legs and balloonish belly and zigzag arms splashed against the fence, the steel voices went mad in their growling, urging Rosa to run and run to the spot where Magda had fallen from her flight against the electrified fence; but of course Rosa did not obey them. She only stood, because if she ran they would shoot, and if she tried to pick up the sticks of Magda's body they would shoot, and if she let the wolf's screech ascending now through the ladder of her skeleton break out, they would shoot; so she took Magda's shawl and filled her own mouth with it, stuffed it in and stuffed it in, until she was swallowing up the wolf's screech and tasting the cinnamon and almond depth of Magda's saliva; and Rosa drank Magda's shawl until it dried.

Sparks of Humanity

The Camp Blanket

Sara Nomberg-Przytyk

Translated from the Polish by Roslyn Hirsch

We dragged ourselves along the highways for a few more days, until we reached a side station where flatcars were waiting for us, the kind that you ship lumber in. It is difficult for me to say how long the terrible walk lasted. I could no longer tell the difference between day and night. There was no food, and we quenched our thirst with snow, which was plentiful. At one point, someone in the escort brought the news that the Bolsheviks were getting closer. From that time on, the tempo of our wandering speeded up. Everybody mustered the last remaining ounce of strength; none of us wanted to fall behind just when freedom seemed so close.

As usually happens in situations of this kind, news traveled from mouth to mouth, which caused wings to grow on our shoulders.

"Listen," Zenia whispered into my ear while walking, "the Russian command sent out a special company of soldiers just to liberate the transport from Auschwitz. They will be here soon."

I believed what she was saying. I did not even ask where she heard the news. I listened for the echo of shots, and I waited for freedom.

Next to me two girls were talking about something very quietly. By their sad faces you could tell that the news was not very good.

"What happened?" I asked.

"Not far from here, on the side of the road," one of them explained, "is a little forest. The machine guns are already set up there. They will take care of us quickly."

"Don't babble nonsense," I said sharply. "There are too many of us. They wouldn't have time to cover their tracks. The escorts are afraid of the Russian army. They won't do it."

But anxiety remained. It was already dark when we found ourselves standing in front of the open railway cars. They started loading us onto the flatcars, which were slippery with ice. There was a chaos of squeezing, shrieking, beating, and shooting. I became separated from my friends. Someone pushed me from behind, and I found myself in the car. The first women to be herded into the car tried to sit down, but they had to get up quickly in order not to be trampled by the women who were being pushed in after them. We were squeezed into the car so tightly that we could not even move an arm or a leg. I thought to myself that if we had to travel this way for any distance nobody would survive. Standing motionless we would all freeze. I even imagined that we would all become one stony mass with many heads.

Before the train left, two older soldiers got into the cars. They were our escort. They set a little bench in the back of the wagon, sat down, and did not even look at us. They spoke quietly to each other in Hungarian. The train pulled out and picked up speed quickly. The wind almost tore our heads off. Our legs were burning, as if exposed to real fire. No one spoke, because it would have been impossible to hear. The pervasive death-like silence was broken only by the roar of the wheels and the whistle of the wind.

Not far from me stood two young Polish girls.

"Zosiu," one said to the other, "I am going to jump off the train. What about you?"

"I will jump after you," answered the other.

Slowly they moved to the wall of the wagon. My heart stopped beating out of fear. I wished they would succeed. In fact, it was possible to try to escape. The car was open, and the escort consisted of two Hungarians who had their own problems. I did not turn my head in their direction. I just listened carefully.

"Where are you crawling, you louse?" I heard the German *kapo* call out. There followed a terrible beating with a stick. The girl fell on the floor. That was the end of her. She was trampled to death by the German functionaries.

"Hey, there!" one of them yelled to the escorts. "A woman died here. Can we get rid of the body? There is no room for it in the wagon."

"Throw her out," one of them answered.

"Hey, hop, hey, hop." The body of the young girl went flying out of the car. None of us said anything. No one could be found who reacted like a human being to this monstrous crime. Why did we keep quiet? After all, it was not fear that closed our mouths. They numbered about ten to fifteen, and we were more than a hundred. It was all part of the routine. In camp they were the ones who did the hitting, while we were the ones who got the beatings and who did not even have the right to defend ourselves or shield ourselves from the blows. That is what the camp had done to us. It had stripped us of the capacity to make a human gesture or to react normally when confronted by an enemy.

Once again the thumping of the wheels made the time go by. We passed by large estates and small towns. Everything was so dark that it was difficult to orient ourselves and figure out where we were. A noise reached my ears, some sort of whining explanation. A woman had seated herself because she could no longer stand. The criminals pounced on her.

"Hey, there. Escort!" shouted one of the *kapos*. "A woman died. Can we throw her out?"

Once again there was the thump of a body cast out of the car. Now this sound started to repeat itself often. I came to the realization that the *kapos* were killing the women and getting rid of the bodies so that they would have more comfortable accommodations. Maybe, I thought, they will kill us all. They would be by themselves, and then they would be able to lie down comfortably on the floor. I was standing far enough from the German *kapos*, separated from them by a crowd of women. My legs hurt terribly, and I dreamt of only one thing, to sit down. I wanted to sit just for a moment, a short moment. But to sit in this car was impossible.

My attention was drawn to a booth located between the cars; inside the booth was a bench. I was seized with a desire to get to the booth. I thought that I would sit down and leave behind this car where the criminals were killing women before our very eyes, instead of standing here silent and scared. This nagging idea even killed my fear; the soldier escorting us might think that I was trying to run away and he might gun me down. Slowly I moved to the back of the car, and without thinking I put one leg over and then the other. I was in the booth. I sat down. I was sweating like a church mouse. I had succeeded! I sat down on the bench. I stretched my legs out in front of me. No one told me to return; I could travel here quietly. I felt so good, so comfortable. I dozed off. The cold awakened me. Now I felt cold. I had nothing to cover myself with. The wind and frost were tearing my head off. I was freezing. In the car the bodies were packed tightly together and were warming each other. Here I was alone and there was no place to move. I was afraid that the Hungarian soldiers or the German *kapos* might notice me.

I blew into my hands. I rubbed my feet together, but that did not help much. Sleep, which I could not shake off, overcame me. I fell asleep. Then a knocking on the wall of the booth woke me up, and I heard a feeble whisper:

"Please, ma'am, don't sleep! It's dangerous. You will freeze."

At first I was sure that I must be dreaming, that I must be talking to myself. With all my might I tried to open my eyes and lift my wobbly head. But I could not. It was beyond my strength. I fell asleep again.

"Please, ma'am," a loud whisper and a knocking on the wall reached me as if through a fog. "Please stretch out your hand and take the blanket. Quick," the urging voice insisted from the other world. "Please don't think about it. Just stretch out your hand."

I stretched out my arm and someone from the car really handed me a gray blanket from the camp. It was not a dream after all. "There is somebody in the car," I thought, "who wants to help me. Somebody wants me to live." I threw the blanket over my head. I wrapped my back and chest and hid my hands.

Now I knocked on the wall of the booth. "Please, ma'am, you saved my life. I feel warm now. Do you need the blanket?"

"No," a whisper came back. "We had two blankets, my daughter and I. We covered ourselves with one, and we are warm."

How is this possible? I pondered. On one side such bestiality, and on the other unselfish love toward another creature. Then I realized that I did not even know my savior's name and that I would never be able to repay her for the gray blanket that, for me, meant the difference between life and death.

"Ma'am." I knocked again. "Please give me your name. I really must know your name." Silence. "Can you hear me?" I called out loud. "Please. Your name." "Your name, your name, your name," was repeated in the echo of the wheels.

"Stretch out your hand." I heard a whisper from behind the wall. I stretched out my hand. In my hand I found a dry crust of bread from the camp. I chewed it up and then let the dry crumbs dissolve in my mouth. "Your name, your name," I insisted.

"Your name, your name, name." The wind was blowing in my ears.

Trying to Start Anew

An Encounter in Linz

Bernard Gotfryd

On May 6, 1945, twenty-four hours after I was liberated from Gusen, I was exploring the streets of the very foreign-feeling city of Linz. As I had walked out of that hell I had promised myself to forget everything I remembered; later I found it difficult to believe that I was even alive. I wanted a new identity and a new lease on life; I felt at a loss, totally detached from everything I had once known. Faint images and strange faces moved before my eyes. I could make no sense of them and simply kept moving. After hours of walking I wound up in a residential area; everywhere I looked I saw small, well-kept homes with fenced-in gardens. Hardly anyone was in sight. An elderly couple walked by, their eyes focused intently on the sidewalk, as if they were looking for something they had lost. I felt as if I had known this neighborhood, that just around the corner would be a house I recognized, but every time I turned a corner everything was the same, strange and foreign. It was so peaceful I felt as if I were in a dream, that all this wasn't real.

The sun shone brilliantly; the sky was dotted with small, puffy clouds. Around the next corner I saw an elderly couple sitting side by side in worn armchairs on the front porch of their house. They could have been my grandparents vacationing, they could have been any old couple in my home town. I walked over to the fence and—for some reason—stopped. Much to my surprise, the couple greeted me and invited me to join them on the porch, which I did.

The man rose and introduced himself. "Herr Gartner and Frau Gartner, my wife," he said, pointing at the woman sitting next to him. He pulled over a heavy metal garden chair and asked me to sit down. Herr Gartner was a bit on the pudgy side and had a round, unshaven face with several days' growth of stubble. He wore a gray felt hat turning to green around the band, a pair of faded corduroy pants, a green cardigan sweater worn at the elbows, and a pair of felt slippers. The sour smell of perspiration emanated from him. Frau Gartner was thin and bony, almost sickly-looking. She had dark eyes with long lashes and held her hands clasped as if in prayer. She wore an old flowery housedress with a dark woolen blazer over it; she had wound a scarf around her neck. Before I had a chance to introduce myself Frau Gartner spoke up. "Please have some tea with us," she said in a low voice.

"Thank you very much, I hope I am not imposing," I responded, stunned by the invitation.

"No, not at all," she assured me. "It will be nice to have someone to talk to. My husband and I have been alone for quite some time." She stood up and went into the house; soon she returned carrying a tray with three cups of tea and a basket of cookies.

I quickly introduced myself and told the Gartners about my time in the camps. Herr Gartner told me the public had been assured that such camps were only for criminals, communists, and antistate elements, but they hadn't believed it. I assured him that my only crime was that I happened to be Jewish. The Gartners were understanding and very apologetic. Herr Gartner told me that he was a friend of the Jews; during World War I he was stationed in Poland with the Austrian Imperial Army, and he had become friendly with a number of Jewish families. He was very fond of Jews, he said. He and his wife had also suffered a loss, he recalled sadly, since two of their sons and a nephew who had served in the Wehrmacht never came back from the war.

Frau Gartner urged me to eat. I didn't have to be asked twice; I hadn't tasted a cookie since I was in Maidanek with Leon, a little over a year before. I was hungry, but I tried to control my appetite. I didn't want them to know how starved I really was. We sat on the porch talking for a long time; before I knew it, it was past curfew. Herr Gartner said I couldn't walk back to the city and suggested that I spend the night. The Gartners had ample room; there was an empty bedroom on the second floor that hadn't been used for some time. It had belonged to Horst, one of their sons who hadn't come back from the war. I was asked to make myself at home. I was very grateful for their hospitality and immediately got to like the Gartners.

Frau Gartner served a vegetable broth with beans and potatoes; it was the best meal I had tasted in a long time. I washed it down with ersatz coffee and felt better than I had in ages. Frau Gartner told me at length about how difficult the war had been and how happy they were that it was finally over. Everything had been rationed, and there had been long lines in front of shops. I heard her out, marveling over how little the Gartners knew about what had happened to us in Poland and in the rest of Nazi-occupied Europe. I decided not to get into this. I thanked Frau Gartner for her good supper, and her husband showed me upstairs to my room.

The smallish room was square in shape and furnished with antiques. It had an old mahogany bed with a tall bedstead; next to it stood a night table. Across the room was a matching chest of drawers. At the foot of the bed stood an old trunk adorned with lots of metal. The floor was covered with a bright Oriental rug. Herr Gartner showed me to the bathroom and made sure that I had everything I needed; he then turned on the lamp on the night table and left.

The first thing I noticed after Herr Gartner had gone was the mirror on the wall; I had not seen myself since before the camps. Reflected was the face of a perfect stranger—gaunt, gray, wholly unfamiliar. I was shocked. I tried to smile and do imitations; pulling my lower lip down over my chin, I made myself into my uncle in Warsaw. I found a pair of old glasses in the bathroom and tried them on; my magnified eyes reminded me of my grandfather. I stood in front of the mirror making faces until I ran out of characters to imitate and finally gave up. This was how I remembered my relatives. They became real; the mirror brought them back.

Next I noticed something I had not seen before because of my fascination with the mirror. On the wall hung a framed certificate of achievement from the Hitler Youth. Next to it was another certificate issued in the name of Horst Gartner, congratulating him upon his acceptance into the Waffen SS. Between and above the two certificates hung a picture of a young man in a black uniform with skull-and-crossbones insignia in his lapels and on his cap. I stood there, a cold sweat running down my back, studying the photograph. The young man's sunken eyes reminded me of the skull insignia on his cap and lapels; they were equally expressionless. On his left cheek below his eye was a scar.

Didn't his parents know what the SS was about? Why did Herr Gartner tell me that his sons had served in the Wehrmacht? I kept thinking, how ignorant does he think I am? And I have to sleep in this murderer's bed? There wasn't much I could do about it. The curfew was on, confining me to the house; I decided to go to bed.

As I was about to stretch out, on impulse I pulled out the night table drawer and saw a packet of mail inside it tied with a worn white ribbon. There were several letters from a Scharenführer Horst Gartner of the Einsatzkommando with the return address of Feld Post at the Ostfront. That was in Russia. They dated back to 1942 and 1943. Unable to resist, I pulled out one letter. I knew what the Einsatzkommando was all about; they were the butchers and the killers in Europe. I unfolded the letter and with difficulty began to decode Horst Gartner's not very neat Gothic handwriting. I always had difficulties reading the Gothic alphabet.

Horst Gartner told his parents how proud he was to be a part of this modern crusade and how honorably he was serving the Reich and the New Order of Europe. He hoped that they were proud of him, too. I nearly fainted. How could Herr Gartner pretend not to know any of this about his own son? I couldn't believe it. He must have known what the SS was about; he couldn't be that gullible. Such a sweet, hospitable couple. I was shaking with rage. I deposited the letters in the drawer and went to bed; I was too exhausted to stay up any longer. As I was about to fall asleep a thought occurred to me. Suppose their son Horst was back here in hiding? He might come at any moment to his parents' house: it was a possibility. What then? I decided to try not to fall asleep. I dozed off but woke up several times, disturbed by someone's snoring. Later on it got quiet again; I could hear an insect buzzing at the window. I was a nervous wreck. The slightest sound made me jump. I imagined all kinds of things; I couldn't forgive myself for having been so truthful. Finally it started to get light. I looked out the window to see the rising sun and decided to leave the Gartners as soon as I possibly could.

Suddenly I heard a gentle knocking at my door. I went over to open it, and there was Herr Gartner, entirely dressed, excusing himself for waking me up. It was not quite seven o'clock, and he and his wife were going out to get in the breadline, he told me. They would be back within the hour, he hoped. He just wanted to let me know that I would be left in the house alone; would I mind? I assured him that it would be all right. "I'm a big fellow," I remember having said. As soon as they left I washed up and prepared to leave. I watched them through the window to make sure that the two of them had gone; I didn't think I could face them again after the discoveries of the evening. I was sorry to leave so rudely, but I had no alternative; to me they were part of a conspiracy, parents of a murderer. I found a pencil and some paper on the kitchen table and decided to write them a thank-you note. I concocted a lie about a toothache, saying I had to find a dentist in a hurry; I excused myself for leaving without saying good-bye in person and thanked them for their hospitality. I never gave them the slightest hint that I knew anything about their son.

Somewhere in the house a clock struck nine times. It sounded like the clock in my grandparents' house. I looked into the next room and saw a silver candle holder—exactly the kind of a candle holder I used to see every Friday night on our dining room table—atop a dresser. There was no doubt in my mind that it had come from a Jewish home. It had a massive square base and was etched with a pattern of grape leaves. Obviously it was part of a pair. Why only one? I kept wondering. As I turned to leave I saw a little alcove with a small mahogany table inside it; on top of the table was the other candle holder. Next to it stood a silver Passover wine cup with the Star of David engraved on it. I was incensed. Herr Gartner must have known that these were items of Jewish origin. How could he pretend to such ignorance? It was unforgivable.

A gray and white cat on the porch watched me leave. He tried to come closer, but I chased him away. I made sure to memorize the address.

It was still chilly outside, but the air was invigorating. I wasn't sure which streets to take back to the city and started out rather blindly, hoping not to bump into my hosts. I stopped a youngster and asked him for directions. As it turned out, I was on the right track, and soon enough I was back in Linz. The city was alive with people. Groups of liberated prisoners of various nationalities congregated at street corners and in the squares, trying to communicate with American soldiers. Most of them were still dressed in their striped camp uniforms; some wore civilian clothes they must have found in abandoned homes or had received from charities. None of the garments fit by a long shot. Emaciated faces attempted smiles, creating deep lines around the former prisoners' cheeks. All sorts of questions were being asked in every imaginable tongue.

Austrian women rushed by with little children in strollers, overloaded with personal belongings. There were few young men to be seen. Most of the shops were still barricaded; others had been broken into and were totally empty. Only bakeries were open; long lines of elderly people formed in front of them, waiting for their bread rations. Everything was being rationed, even milk. The Austrians seemed to be used to this system, and they waited patiently, with blank expressions on their faces, for their turn.

None of them smiled or spoke. I felt sorry for them and hated them at the same time. These were the parents of our killers and executioners. Didn't they know what had happened to most of Europe? How could they not have known what their sons and husbands had been up to?

I continued on aimlessly, thinking about the Gartners. I imagined Horst everywhere, watching me, following me, waiting for the right moment to kill me. I was almost sure I had seen his face before, perhaps in one of the camps, in transit, or maybe in the ghetto. I couldn't be certain any longer, but I knew those eyes I had seen in the photograph: eyes that sized up the victim while they waited for the kill. I was getting paranoid and hungry; I was obsessed with the idea that Horst was after me. I decided to get out of Linz.

Two years later, after I had emigrated to America, I wrote to the Gartners. I still remembered their address. Almost immediately I received an answer. Herr Gartner informed me that Frau Gartner had died. Evidently she had suffered a heart attack when she had found out that their son Horst was tried by a Polish court and subsequently executed. Herr Gartner didn't elaborate about Horst's trial or about his crimes. He himself had diabetes and said he would be very grateful if I could mail some insulin to him, as there was a shortage of it in Austria. He also told me that of the six Gartner relatives who had fought in the German army a single nephew had come back. He was a paraplegic, confined to a wheelchair. War wasn't good for anybody, he concluded, not even for the people at the top who started it.

I sent insulin regularly for some time until one day I received a letter from his nephew announcing that Herr Gartner had died. In his will he had left me a silver wine cup and two silver candlesticks.

The Watch
Elie Wiesel

Translated from the French by Elie Wiesel

For my bar mitzvah, I remember, I had received a magnificent gold watch. It was the customary gift for the occasion, and was meant to remind each boy that henceforth he would be held responsible for his acts before the Torah and its timeless laws.

But I could not keep my gift. I had to part with it the very day my native town became the pride of the Hungarian nation by chasing from its confines every single one of its Jews. The glorious masters of our municipality were jubilant: they were rid of us, there would be no more kaftans on the streets. The local newspaper was brief and to the point: from now on, it would be possible to state one's place of residence without feeling shame.

The time was late April, 1944.

In the early morning hours of that particular day, after a sleepless night, the ghetto was changed into a cemetery and its residents into gravediggers. We were digging feverishly in the courtyard, the garden, the cellar, consigning to the earth, temporarily we thought, whatever remained of the belongings accumulated by several generations, the sorrow and reward of long years of toil.

My father took charge of the jewelry and valuable papers. His head bowed, he was silently digging near the barn. Not far away, my mother, crouched on the damp ground, was burying the silver candelabra she used only on Shabbat eve; she was moaning softly, and I avoided her eyes. My sisters burrowed near the cellar. The youngest, Tziporah, had chosen the garden, like myself. Solemnly shoveling, she declined my help. What did she have to hide? Her toys? Her school notebooks? As for me, my only possession was my watch. It meant a lot to me. And so I decided to bury it in a dark, deep hole, three paces away from the fence, under a poplar tree whose thick, strong foliage seemed to provide a reasonably secure shelter.

All of us expected to recover our treasures. On our return, the earth would give them back to us. Until then, until the end of the storm, they would be safe.

Yes, we were naïve. We could not foresee that the very same evening, before the last train had time to leave the station, an excited mob of well-informed friendly neighbors would be rushing through the ghetto's wide-open houses and courtyards, leaving not a stone or beam unturned, throwing themselves upon the loot.

Twenty years later, standing in our garden, in the middle of the night, I remember the first gift, also the last, I ever received from my parents. I am seized by an irrational, irresistible desire to see it, to see if it is still there in the same spot, and if defying all laws of probability, it has survived—like me—by accident, not knowing how or why. My curiosity becomes obsession. I think neither of my father's money nor of my mother's candlesticks. All that matters in this town is my gold watch and the sound of its ticking.

Despite the darkness, I easily find my way in the garden. Once more I am the bar mitzvah child; here is the barn, the fence, the tree. Nothing has changed. To my left, the path leading to the Slotvino Rebbe's house. The Rebbe, though, had changed: the burning bush burned itself out and there is nothing left, not even smoke. What could he possibly have hidden the day we went away? His phylacteries? His prayer shawl? The holy scrolls inherited from his famous ancestor Rebbe Meirl of Premishlan? No, probably not even that kind of treasure. He had taken everything along, convinced that he was thus protecting not only himself but his disciples as well. He was proved wrong, the wonder rabbi.

But I mustn't think of him, not now. The watch, I must think of the watch. Maybe it was spared. Let's see, three steps to the right. Stop. Two forward. I recognize the place. Instinctively, I get ready to re-enact the scene my memory recalls. I fall on my knees. What can I use to dig? There is a shovel in the barn; its door is never locked. But by groping around in the dark I risk stumbling and waking the people sleeping in the house. They would take me for a marauder, a thief, and hand me over to the police. They might even kill me. Never mind, I'll have to manage without a shovel. Or any other tool. I'll use my hands, my nails. But it is difficult; the soil is hard, frozen, it resists as if determined to keep its secret. Too bad, I'll punish it by being the stronger.

Feverishly, furiously, my hands claw the earth, impervious to cold, fatigue and pain. One scratch, then another. No matter. Continue. My nails inch ahead, my fingers dig in, I bear down, my every fiber participates in the task. Little by little the hole deepens. I must hurry. My forehead touches the ground. Almost. I break out in a cold sweat, I am drenched, delirious. Faster, faster. I shall rip the earth from end to end, but I must know. Nothing can stop or frighten me. I'll go to the bottom of my fear, to the bottom of night, but I will know.

What time is it? How long have I been here? Five minutes, five hours? Twenty years. This night was defying time. I was laboring to exhume not an object but time itself, the soul and memory of that time. Nothing could be more urgent, more vital.

Suddenly a shiver goes through me. A sharp sensation, like a bite. My fingers touch something hard, metallic, rectangular. So I have not been digging in vain. The garden is spinning around me, over me. I stand up to catch my breath. A moment later, I'm on my knees again. Cautiously, gently I take the box from its tomb. Here it is, in the palm of my hand: the last relic, the only remaining symbol of everything I had loved, of everything I had been. A voice inside me warns: Don't open it, it contains nothing but emptiness, throw it away and run. I cannot heed the warning; it is too late to turn back. I need to know, either way. A slight pressure of my thumb and the box opens. I stifle the cry rising in my throat: the watch is there. Quick, a match. And another. Fleetingly, I catch a glimpse of it. The pain is blinding: could this thing, this object, be my gift, my pride? My past? Covered with dirt and rust, crawling with worms, it is unrecognizable, revolting. Unable to move, wondering what to do, I remain staring at it with the disgust one feels for love betrayed or a body debased. I am angry with myself for having yielded to curiosity. But disappointment gives way to profound pity: the watch too lived through war and holocaust, the kind reserved for watches perhaps. In its way, it too is a survivor, a ghost infested with humiliating sores and obsolete memories. Suddenly I feel the urge to carry it to my lips, dirty as it is, to kiss and console it with my tears, as one might console a living being, a sick friend returning from far away and requiring much kindness and rest, especially rest.

I touch it, I caress it. What I feel, besides compassion, is a strange kind of gratitude. You see, the men I had believed to be immortal had vanished into fiery clouds. My teachers, my friends, my guides had all deserted me. While this thing, this nameless, lifeless thing had survived for the sole purpose of welcoming me on my return and providing an epilogue to my childhood. And there awakens in me a desire to confide in it, to tell it my adventures, and in exchange, listen to its own. What had happened in my absence: who had first taken possession of my house, my bed? Or rather, no; our confidences could wait for another time, another place: Paris, New York, Jerusalem. But first I would entrust it to the best jeweler in the world, so that the watch might recover its luster, its memory of the past.

It is growing late. The horizon is turning a deep red. I must go. The tenants will soon be waking, they will come down to the well for water. No time to lose. I stuff the watch into my pocket and cross the garden. I enter the courtyard. From under the porch a dog barks. And stops at once: he knows I am not a thief, anything but a thief. I open the gate. Halfway down the street I am overcome by violent remorse: I have just committed my first theft.

I turn around, retrace my steps through courtyard and garden. Again I find myself kneeling, as at Yom Kippur services, beneath the poplar. Holding my breath, my eyes refusing to cry, I place the watch back into its box, close the cover, and my first gift once more takes refuge deep inside the hole. Using both hands, I smoothly fill in the earth to remove all traces.

Breathless and with pounding heart, I reach the still deserted street. I stop and question the meaning of what I have just done. And find it inexplicable.

In retrospect, I tell myself that probably I simply wanted to leave behind me, underneath the silent soil, a reflection of my presence. Or that somehow I wanted to transform my watch into an instrument of delayed vengeance: one day, a child would play in the garden, dig near the tree and stumble upon a metal box. He would thus learn that his parents were usurpers, and that among the inhabitants of his town, once upon a time, there had been Jews and Jewish children, children robbed of their future.

The sun was rising and I was still walking through the empty streets and alleys. For a moment I thought I heard the chanting of schoolboys studying Talmud; I also thought I heard the invocations of Hasidim reciting morning prayers in thirty-three places at once. Yet above all these incantations, I heard distinctly, but as though coming from far away, the tick-tock of the watch I had just buried in accordance with Jewish custom. It was, after all, the very first gift that a Jewish child had once been given for his very first celebration.

Since that day, the town of my childhood has ceased being just another town. It has become the face of a watch.

An Old Acquaintance

Elie Wiesel

Translated from the French by Steven Donadio

In a bus, one summer evening, in Tel Aviv. The sultriness of the day, instead of lessening, leaves behind a heavy stagnant heat which insinuates itself into every pore, weighs on every gesture and breath, blurs every image. People doze on their feet, about to drop into the void. Breathing, even looking, requires immense effort.

We are hardly moving. As we make our way up the principal thoroughfare, Allenby Boulevard, toward the center of town, traffic moves slower and slower and soon it will come to a standstill. Used to this kind of adversity, the passengers demonstrate their wisdom. Some read the newspaper, others chat or scan the advertisements for wines, shaving creams, cigarettes. The driver whistles the latest hit tune. Too bad, I will have to get off at the next stop. I have an appointment. I shall make it faster on foot.

But it is a long way to the next stop. We do not seem to be moving. One bottleneck after another. As if three lanes of cars had broken down. I want to get off: the doors do not open until the bus comes to a complete stop. Useless to argue: the driver's nerves are up to anything. Not mine. Irritated, I curse myself for not having foreseen this. I made a mistake to take the bus. And to think we are in the land of the prophets!

To pass the time I play my favorite game. I pick someone at random and, without his knowing it, establish a mute exchange. Seated across from me is a middle-aged man with a lost look. I examine him thoroughly from head to toe. Easy to classify. Office worker, government clerk, foreman. The anonymous type. Avoiding extremes, responsibilities. He takes orders only to transmit them. Neat, punctual, efficient. He is not at the top of the ladder nor is he at the bottom. Neither rich nor poor, happy or unhappy. He just makes a living. He holds his own. Against everybody.

I put myself in his place: I think and dream like him. I am the one his wife will greet with love or rancor; the one who will drown my resentment in sleep or in solitary drinking; the one my friends betray and my subordinates detest; the one who has wasted my life and now it is too late to begin again.

Caught up in the game, I suddenly realize the passenger looks familiar. I have seen before that bald head, that hard chin, that thin nose. I have seen before that wrinkled forehead, those drooping ears. He turns around to glance outside, I see his neck: red, naked, enormous. I have seen that neck before. A shudder runs through me. It is no longer a matter of curiosity or game. The time changes pace, country. The present is in the grip of all the years black and buried. Now I am glad I accepted the engagement for this evening, and that I decided against going by taxi.

The passenger does not suspect a thing. He has just lost his anonymity, returned to his prison, but he does not know it yet. Now that I have him, I will not let him get away again. What is he thinking about? Probably nothing. Thinking frightens him. Talking frightens him. Memories, words frighten him: that can be read on his lifeless face. This passenger, I am trying to place him, I know him; I used to practice that same defense myself. The best way to keep from attracting the executioner's attention was not to see him. In order not to be noticed, you must murder imagination: dissolve, blend into the frightened mass, reduce yourself to an object. Go under in order to survive. But the man still does not realize my growing interest in him. Were a hundred of us looking him over, he would not notice any the more.

I leave my seat and stand up directly in front of him. I brush up against him, my knees touch his, but his eyes keep their distance. In a very low voice I say: "I think I know you."

He does not hear. He is playing deaf, blind, dead. Just the way I used to do. He is taking refuge in absence, but tenaciously I track him. I repeat my sentence. Slowly, warily, he comes to life. He raises his tired eyes toward me.

"Were you speaking to me?"

"To you."

"You were saying?"

"I think I have met you somewhere before."

He shrugs his shoulders. "You're mistaken, I don't know you."

The bus starts up, then stops again. I lean over the passenger, who is pretending to ignore me, as if the incident were closed. I admire him: he acts well, he does not even blink. We are so close to one another that our breaths mingle, a drop of my sweat falls onto his shirt. He still does not react. If I were to slap him, he would say nothing. A matter of habit, of discipline. The lesson: conceal pain, because it excites the executioner much more than it appeases him. With me, this technique will not be of any help to him: I know the routine.

"You're not from around here," I say.

"Leave me alone."

"You're from somewhere else. From Europe."

"You're disturbing me. I'd appreciate it if you would stop pestering me."

"But you interest me."

"Too bad. You don't interest me at all. I haven't the slightest desire to talk or listen to you. Go back to your seat before I get angry. You hear me? Beat it!"

The tone of his voice startles me. For an instant, our glances meet. Nothing more is needed: I see myself twenty years ago, a tin plate in my hand, before this all-powerful master who was distributing the evening soup to a pack of starved corpses. My humiliation gives way to a somber joy which I can scarcely contain. According to the Talmud, only the mountains never meet: for the men who climb them, no circle is closed, no experience unique, no loss of memory definitive.

"I have some questions to ask you," I say.

"I don't give a damn about you or your questions."

"Where were you during the war?"

"That's none of your business."

"In Europe—right?"

"Leave me alone."

"In an occupied country, right?"

"Stop annoying me."

"In Germany perhaps?"

The bus stops at last at a station and the man takes advantage of the opportunity: he leaps up and rushes toward the exit; I follow him. "How odd, we're getting off at the same place."

He steps back quickly to let me pass. "I made a mistake, my stop is further on."

I too pretend to step down and immediately turn back. "How odd, so is mine."

We remain standing near the door. Two women have already taken our places.

"May I go on with our conversation?"

"I don't know who you are or what you could want of me," he says, his teeth clenched. "Your questions are uncalled for, your manners disagreeable and out of place. I don't know what game you're playing, but I refuse any part of it. You do not amuse me."

"You don't remember me. It is understandable. I've changed, I've grown up, I've gained weight, I'm better dressed, I feel well, I walk without fear of collapsing, I lack neither food nor friendship. What about you? How do you feel? Answer me, it interests me. Well, what do you say? No insomnia at night, no pangs of anxiety in the morning?"

Once again he takes shelter behind a mask of indifference, a state of non-being. He thinks himself secure, unattackable. But I pursue him relentlessly:

"Let's start again, shall we? We've established your place of residence during the war: somewhere in Germany. Where, ex-

actly? In a camp. Naturally. With other Jews. You are Jewish,
aren't you?"

He answers me with lips so thin they are almost nonexistent,
in a tone which still has lost nothing of its assurance:

"Go to hell, I tell you. Shut up. There's a limit to my patience. I
would not like to cause a scene, but if you force me. . ."

I pay no attention to his threat. I know he will do nothing, he
will not complain, he will not use his fists, not he, not here, not
in public: he is more afraid than I of the police. So I proceed:

"What camp were you in? Come on, help me, it's important.
Let's see: Buchenwald? No, Maidanek? No, not there either.
Bergen-Belsen? Treblinka? Ponar? No, no. Auschwitz? Yes? Yes,
Auschwitz. More precisely, in a camp which was part of Aus-
chwitz, Javischowitz? Gleivitz? Monovitz? Yes, that's it—there
we are—Monovitz-Buna. Or am I mistaken?"

He performs well, he knows his lesson thoroughly. Not a shiver,
not the slightest reaction. As if I weren't speaking to him, as if my
questions were addressed to someone else, dead a long time. Still,
his efforts not to betray himself are becoming visible now. He
controls his hands poorly, clasping and unclasping them; clench-
ing his fingers which he hides behind his back.

"Let's get down to specifics. What did you do there? You weren't
just a simple inmate? Not you. You are one of those who knew
neither hunger nor weariness nor sickness. You are not one of
those who lived in expectation of death, hoping it would nor be
too long in coming so that they could still die like men and not
like unwanted beasts—unwanted even by death itself. Not you,
you were head of a barracks, you had jurisdiction over the life and
death of hundreds of human beings who never dared watch as
you ate the dishes prepared specially for you. It was a sin, a crime
of high treason, to catch you unawares during one of your meals.
And what about now? Tell me, do you eat well? With appetite?"

He moistens his lips with his tongue. An almost imperceptible
sigh escapes him. He has to redouble his efforts not to answer,
not to take up the challenge. His muscles stiffen, he will not hold

out much longer. The trap is closing on him, he is beginning to understand that.

"What about the barracks number? The seat of your kingdom? Do you remember it? Fifty-seven. Barracks fifty-seven. It was right in the center of the camp, two steps away from the gallows. I've a good memory, haven't I? And you? Is your memory still alive? Or did it bury us all a second time?"

The conductor announces a stop; the barracks-chief does not move: it seems all the same to him. The door opens, a couple gets off, a young mother gets on pushing her little boy in front of her. The driver calls out, "Hey, lady, you owe me a *groosh* or a smile!" She gives him both. We start off again. My prisoner no longer notices: he has lost touch with reality. Outside is the city, so close, so unreal, the city with its lights and its sounds, its joys, its laughter, its hates, its furies, its futile intrigues; outside is freedom, forgetfulness if not forgiveness. At the next stop the prisoner could take flight. He will not, I am sure. He prefers to let me act, decide for him. I know what he is feeling: a mixture of fear, resignation, and also relief. He too has returned to the world of barbed wire: as in the past, he prefers anything whatsoever to the unknown. Here, in the bus, he knows what places him in jeopardy and that reassures him: he knows my face, my voice. To provoke a break would be to choose a danger the nature of which escapes him. In the camp, we settled into a situation this way and for as long as possible did anything to keep from changing it. We dreaded disturbances, surprises. Thus, with me, the accused knows where he stands: I speak to him without hate, almost without anger. In the street, the throng might not be so understanding. The country is bursting with former deportees who refuse to reason.

"Look at me. Do you remember me?"

He does not answer. Impassive, unyielding, he continues to look into the emptiness above the heads of the passengers, but I know his eyes and mine are seeing the same emaciated, exhausted bodies, the same lighted yard, the same scaffold.

"I was in your barracks. I used to tremble before you. You were the ally of evil, of hunger, of cruelty. I used to curse you."

He still does not flinch. The law of the camp: make yourself invisible behind your own death mask. I whisper: "My father was also in your barracks. But he didn't curse you."

Outside, the traffic starts to move, the driver picks up speed. Soon he will shout, "Last stop, everybody off!" I have passed my stop, no matter. The appointment no longer seems important. What am I going to do with my prisoner? Hand him over to the police? "Collaboration" is a crime punishable by law. Let someone else finish the interrogation. I shall appear as a witness for the prosecution. I have already attended several trials of this kind: a former Kapo, a former member of the *Judenrat*, a former ghetto policeman—all accused of having survived by choosing cowardice.

PROSECUTION: "You have rejected your people, betrayed your brothers, given aid to the enemy."

DEFENSE: "We didn't know, we couldn't foresee what would happen. We thought we were doing the right thing, especially at the beginning; we hoped to alleviate the suffering of the community, especially during the first weeks. But then it was too late, we no longer had a choice, we couldn't simply go back and declare ourselves victim among victims."

PROSECUTION: "In the Ghetto of Krilov, the Germans named a certain Ephraim to the post of president of the Jewish council. One day they demanded he submit a list of thirty persons for slave labor. He presented it to them with the same name written thirty times: his own. But you, to save your skin, you sold your soul."

DEFENSE: "Neither was worth very much. In the end, suffering shrinks them and obliterates them, not together but separately: there is a split on every level. Body and mind, heart and soul, take different directions; in this way, people die a dozen deaths even before resigning themselves or accepting a bargain with the devil, which is also a way of dying. I beg of you, therefore: do not judge the dead."

PROSECUTION: "You are forgetting the others, the innocent, those who refused the bargain. Not to condemn the cowards is to wrong those whom they abandoned and sometimes sacrificed."

DEFENSE: "To judge without understanding is a power, not a virtue. You must understand that the accused, more alone and therefore more unhappy than the others, are also victims; more than the others, they need your indulgence, your generosity."

I often left the courtroom depressed, disheartened, wavering between pity and shame. The prosecutor told the truth, so did the defense. Whether for the prosecution or for the defense, all witnesses were right. The verdict sounded just and yet a flagrant injustice emerged from these confused and painful trials; one had the impression that no one had told the truth, that the truth lay somewhere else—with the dead. And who knows if the truth did not die with them. I often used to think: "Luckily, I am witness and not judge: I would condemn myself." Now I have become judge. Without wanting it, without expecting it. That is the trap: I am at the point where I cannot go back. I must pass sentence. From now on, whatever my attitude may be, it will have the weight of a verdict.

The smell of the sea rises to my nostrils, I hear the whisper of the waves, we are leaving the center of the city and its lights. We are coming to the end of the line. I must hurry and make a decision, try my former barracks-chief. I will take on all the roles: first, the witnesses, then the judge, then the attorney for the defense. Will the prisoner play only one role, the accused—the victim? Full powers will be conferred upon me, my sentence will be without appeal. Facing the accused, I will be God.

Let us begin at the beginning. With the customary questions. Last name, first name, occupation, age, address. The accused does not recognize the legitimacy of this procedure, or of the court; he refuses to take part in the trial. It is noted. His crimes are what interest us, not his identity. Let us open the dossier, examine the charges leveled against him. Once again I see the scene of the crime, the uniform face of suffering; I hear the sound of the whip on emaciated bodies. At night, surrounded by his sturdy proteges, the accused shows he is skilled in doing two things at once: with one hand he distributes the soup, with the other he beats the inmates to impose silence. Whether the tears and moaning touch him or irritate him does not matter. He hits harder to make them stop. The sight of the sick enrages him: he senses in them a bad omen for himself. He is particularly cruel with the aged: "Why are you hanging on to this disgusting, filthy life? Hurry up and die, you won't suffer anymore! Give your bread to the young, at least do one good deed before you croak!"

One day he saw my father and me near the barracks. As he always did, my father was handing me his half-full bowl and ordering me to eat. "I'm not hungry anymore," he explained and I knew he was lying. I refused: "Me neither, Father, really, I'm not hungry anymore." I was lying and he knew it, too. This same discussion went on day after day. This time the barracks-chief came over and turned to my father: "This your son?" —Yes.— "And you aren't ashamed to take away his soup?"—But . . . — "Shut up! Give him back that bowl or I'll teach you a lesson you won't soon forget!"

To keep him from carrying out that threat, I grabbed the bowl and started eating. At first I wanted to vomit but soon I felt an immense well-being spread through my limbs. I ate slowly to make this pleasure, stronger than my shame, last longer. Finally, the barracks-chief moved on. I hated him, and yet, down deep, I was glad that he had intervened. My father murmured, "He's a good man, charitable." He was lying, and I lied too: "Yes, Father, charitable."

How do you plead: guilty or not guilty?

My father did not conceal his pride: his son had obeyed him. As in the past. Even better than in the past. So there was, in the camp, in the midst of this organized insanity, someone who depended on him and in whose eyes he was not a servile rag. He did not realize that it had not been his will I had been performing, but yours. I was aware of that, and so were you, but I refused to think of it; you did not. I also knew that by obeying you both as your slave and your accomplice, I was cutting short my father's life by one breath, by one awakening. I buried my remorse in the yellowish soup. But you were wiser and certainly shrewder than my father; you were not deceived. As you moved away, you had an air of assurance, as if to say: "That's the way it is, that's life, the boy will learn, he'll find his way and who knows? someday maybe he'll succeed me." And I did not give the soup back to my father. I did nor hurl myself at you and tear from you your eyes and your tongue and your victory. Yes, I was afraid, I was a coward. And hunger was gnawing at me: that's what you had counted on. And you won.

Has the accused anything to say in his defense?

You always won, and sometimes, at night, I thought that maybe you were the one who was right. For us, you were not just the whip or the ax in the murderer's hand: you were the prince who played the game of death, you were its prophet, its spokesman. You alone knew how to interpret the rages of the executioner, the silences of the earth; you were the guide to follow; whoever imitated you, lived; the others would perish. Your truth was the only valid truth, the only truth possible, the only truth that conformed to the wishes and designs of the gods.

Guilty or not guilty?

Instead of rejoining the ranks of the victims, of suffering like us and with us, instead of weeping without tears and trembling before the incandescent clouds, instead of dying like us and with us, perhaps even for us, you chose to reign over the work of darkness, proclaiming to whomever wanted to hear that pity was criminal, generosity fruitless, senseless, inhumane. One day after the roll-call you gave us a long lecture on the philosophy of the concentration camp: every man for himself, every man the enemy of the next man, for each lived at the other's expense. And you concluded: "What I am telling you is true and immutable. For know that God has descended from heaven and decided to make himself visible: I am God."

How do you plead?

The judge hears the stifled moans of the witnesses, living and dead; he sees the accused heat up one old man who was too slow in taking off his cap, and another because he did not like his face. "You, you look healthy to me," says the accused, and punches him in the stomach. "And you, you look sick to me, you're pale," and he slaps his face. Itzik has a heavy shirt: the accused takes it away from him. Itzik protests and he is already writhing in pain. Izso has held onto his old shoes: the accused claims them. Izso, clever, hands them over without saying a word. The accused takes them with a contemptuous smile: look at this imbecile, he does not even resist, he does not deserve to live.

Well, then? Guilty or not guilty?

And what if everything could be done over again? What are you now compared to what you were then? Tell us about your repentance, your expiation. What do you tell your wife when she offers you her pride, when she speaks of the future of your children? What do you see in the eyes of the passerby who says to you "good morning," "good evening," and "*shalom*," "peace be with you"?

"Well?" yells the driver. "How many times do I have to tell you we're here?"

He looks at us in his rear-view mirror, shouts louder. Our inertia is too much for him. He turns around in his seat and shouts again: "Boy, you must be deaf! Don't you understand Hebrew?"

My prisoner pretends not to understand any language. He sleeps, he dreams, transported somewhere else, in another time, the end of another line. He is waiting for me to make the first move, to break the curse that separates us from other men. As in the past with his masters, he will follow, he will obey.

The driver is getting angry. These two speechless and immobile phantoms apparently want to spend the night in his bus. Do they think they are in a hotel? He gets up, grumbling, "I'll show you,

you'll see." He moves toward us, looking furious. My prisoner waits for him without flinching, indifferent to whatever may happen. I touch his arm.

"Come on, let's go."

He complies mechanically. Once down, he stands stationary, and wisely waits for me on the sidewalk. He could make a dash for the dark little streets that lead to the ocean. He does not. His will has defaulted. He is not about to upset the order of things, to speculate on an uncertain future. Above all, no initiative, that was the golden rule at camp.

The bus starts up and leaves: here we are alone. I have nothing more to say to him. A vague feeling of embarrassment comes over me, as if I had just done something foolish. All of a sudden, I become timid again. And in a weak voice I ask him: "You really don't remember me?"

In the darkness I can no longer make out his face. I no longer recognize him. Doubt chokes me: and what if it was not he?

"No," he says, after a long silence, "I don't remember you."

I no longer recognize the sound of his voice. It used to be gruff, cutting. It has become clear, humane.

"And yourself? Do you remember who you were?"

"That is my business."

"No. It is my business, too."

I suddenly think I must put an end to this: but how? If he whimpers and justifies himself and begs my forgiveness, I will have him arrested. And if he keeps on denying everything? What would he have to say for me to let him go? I do not know. It is up to him to know.

Abruptly he stiffens. I know his eyes have regained their coldness, theft hardness. He is going to speak. At last. In defending himself he is going to throw all the light on this mystery to which we remain chained forever. I know he will speak without altering the thin line of his lips. At last he is speaking. No: he is shouting. No! he is yelling! Without preparation, without warning. He insults me, he is offensive. Not in Hebrew—in German. We are no longer in Israel but somewhere in the universe of hate. He is the barracks-chief who, his hands clasped behind his back, "advises" one of his slaves to leave at once or he will regret the day he was born. Will he hit me, break my bones, make me eat dirt, as he is threatening to do? No one would come to my aid: in camp it is the strongest and most brutal who is in the right. Is he going to crush me in his claws, murder me? If he does, I will carry his secret with me. Can one die in Auschwitz, after Auschwitz?

The barracks-chief is lecturing me the way he used to and I do not hear what he is saying. His voice engulfs me, I let myself drown in it. I am no longer afraid. Not of dying nor even of killing. It is something else, something worse. I am suddenly aware of my impotence, of my defeat. I know I am going to let him go free, but I will never know if I am doing this out of courage or out of cowardice. I will never know if, face to face with the executioner, I behaved like a judge or a victim. But I will have acquired the certitude that the man who measures himself against the reality of evil always emerges beaten and humiliated. If someday I encounter the Angel of Death himself in my path, I will not kill him, I will not torture him. On the contrary. I will speak to him politely, as humanely as possible. I will try to understand him, to divine his evil; even at the risk of being contaminated.

The barracks-chief is shouting obscenities and threats; I do not listen. I stare at him one last time without managing to distinguish his features in the night. My hands in my pockets, I turn around and begin to walk, slowly at first, then faster and faster, until I am running. Is he following me?

He let me go. He granted me freedom.

The Second Generation and Beyond

Adam

Kurt Vonnegut, Jr.

It was midnight in a Chicago lying-in hospital.

"Mr. Sousa," said the nurse, "your wife had a girl. You can see the baby in about twenty minutes."

"I know, I know, I know," said Mr. Sousa, a sullen gorilla, plainly impatient with having a tiresome and familiar routine explained to him. He snapped his fingers. "Girl! Seven, now. Seven girls I got now. A houseful of women. I can beat the stuffings out of ten men my own size. But, what do I get? Girls."

"Mr. Knechtmann," said the nurse to the other man in the room. She pronounced the name, as almost all Americans did, a colorless Netman. "I'm sorry. Still no word on your wife. She is keeping us waiting, isn't she?" She grinned glassily and left.

Sousa turned on Knechtmann. "Some little son of a gun like you, Netman, you want a boy, bing! You got one. Want a football team, bing, bing, bing, eleven, you got it." He stomped out of the room.

The man he left behind, all alone now, was Heinz Knechtmann, a presser in a dry-cleaning plant, a small man with thin wrists and a bad spine that kept him slightly hunched, as though forever weary. His face was long and big-nosed and thin-lipped, but was so overcast with good-humored humility as to be beautiful. His eyes were large and brown, and deep-set and long-lashed. He was only twenty-two, but seemed and felt much older. He had died a little as each member of his family had been led away and killed by the Nazis, until only in him, at the age of ten, had life and the name of Knechtmann shared a soul. He and his wife, Avchen, had grown up behind barbed wire.

He had been staring at the walls of the waiting room for twelve hours now, since noon, when his wife's labor pains had become regular, the surges of slow rollers coming in from the sea a mile apart, from far, far away. This would be his second child. The last time he had waited, he had waited on a straw tick in a displaced-persons camp in Germany. The child, Karl Knechtmann, named after Heinz's father, had died, and with it, once more, had died the name of one of the finest cellists ever to have lived.

When the numbness of weary wishing lifted momentarily during this second vigil, Heinz's mind was a medley of proud family names, gone, all gone, that could be brought to life again in this new being—if it lived. Peter Knechtmann, the surgeon; Kroll Knechtmann, the botanist; Friederich Knechtmann, the playwright. Dimly recalled uncles. Or if it was a girl, and if it lived, it would be Helga Knechtmann, Heinz's mother, and she would learn to play the harp as Heinz's mother had, and for all Heinz's ugliness, she would be beautiful. The Knechtmann men were all ugly, the Knechtmann women were all lovely as angels, though not all angels. It had always been so—for hundreds and hundreds of years.

"Mr. Netman," said the nurse, "it's a boy, and your wife is fine. She's resting now. You can see her in the morning. You can see the baby in twenty minutes."

Heinz looked up dumbly.

"It weighs five pounds nine ounces." She was gone again, with the same prim smile and officious, squeaking footsteps.

"Knechtmann," murmured Heinz, standing and bowing slightly to the wall. "The name is Knechtmann." He bowed again and gave a smile that was courtly and triumphant. He spoke the name with an exaggerated Old World pronunciation, like a foppish footman announcing the arrival of nobility, a guttural drum roll, unsoftened for American ears. "*KhhhhhhhhhhhhhhhhNECHT! mannnnnnnnnnnnn.*"

"Mr. Netman?" A very young doctor with a pink face and close-cropped red hair stood in the waiting-room door. There were circles under his eyes, and he spoke through a yawn.

"Dr. Powers!" cried Heinz, clasping the man's right hand between both of his. "Thank God, thank God, thank God, and thank you."

"Um," said Dr. Powers, and he managed to smile wanly.

"There isn't anything wrong, is there?"

"Wrong?" said Powers. "No, no. Everything's fine. If I look down in the mouth, it's because I've been up for thirty-six hours straight." He closed his eyes, and leaned against the doorframe. "No, no trouble with your wife," he said in a faraway voice. "She's made for having babies. Regular pop-up toaster. Like rolling off a log. Schnip-schnap."

"She is?" said Heinz incredulously.

Dr. Powers shook his head, bringing himself back to consciousness. "My mind—conked out completely. Sousa—I got your wife confused with Mrs. Sousa. They finished in a dead heat. Netman, you're Netman. Sorry. Your wife's the one with pelvis trouble."

"Malnutrition as a child," said Heinz.

"Yeah. Well, the baby came normally, but, if you're going to have another one, it'd better be a Caesarean. Just to be on the safe side."

"I can't thank you enough," said Heinz passionately.

Dr. Powers licked his lips, and fought to keep his eyes open. "Uh huh. 'S O.K.," he said thickly. " 'Night. Luck." He shambled out into the corridor.

The nurse stuck her head into the waiting room. "You can see your baby, Mr. Netman."

"Doctor—" said Heinz, hurrying out into the corridor, wanting to shake Powers' hand again so that Powers would know what a magnificent thing he'd done. "It's the most wonderful thing that ever happened." The elevator doors slithered shut between them before Dr. Powers could show a glimmer of response.

"This way," said the nurse. "Turn left at the end of the hall, and you'll find the nursery window there. Write your name on a piece of paper and hold it against the glass."

Heinz made the trip by himself, without seeing another human being until he reached the end. There, on the other side of a large glass panel, he saw a hundred of them cupped in shallow canvas buckets and arranged in a square block of straight ranks and files.

Heinz wrote his name on the back of a laundry slip and pressed it to the window. A fat and placid nurse looked at the paper, not at Heinz's face, and missed seeing his wide smile, missed an urgent invitation to share for a moment his ecstasy.

She grasped one of the buckets and wheeled it before the window. She turned away again, once more missing the smile.

"Hello, hello, hello, little Knechtmann," said Heinz to the red prune on the other side of the glass. His voice echoed down the hard, bare corridor, and came back to him with embarrassing loudness. He blushed and lowered his voice. "Little Peter, little Kroll," he said softly, "little Friedrich—and there's Helga in you, too. Little spark of Knechtmann, you little treasure house. Everything is saved in you."

"I'm afraid you'll have to be more quiet," said a nurse, sticking her head out from one of the rooms.

"Sorry," said Heinz. "I'm very sorry." He fell silent, and contented himself with tapping lightly on the window with a fingernail, trying to get the child to look at him. Young Knechtmann would not look, wouldn't share the moment, and after a few minutes the nurse took him away again.

Heinz beamed as he rode on the elevator and as he crossed the hospital lobby, but no one gave him more than a cursory glance. He passed a row of telephone booths and there, in one of the booths with the door open, he saw a soldier with whom he'd shared the waiting room an hour before.

"Yeah, Ma—seven pounds six ounces. Got hair like Buffalo Bill. No, we haven't had time to make up a name for her yet . . . .

That you, Pa? Yup, mother and daughter doin' fine, just fine. Seven pounds six ounces. Nope, no name. . . . That you, Sis? Pretty late for you to be up, ain't it? Doesn't look like anybody yet. Let me talk to Ma again. . . . That you, Ma? Well, I guess that's all the news from Chicago. Now, Mom, Mom, take it easy—don't worry. It's a swell-looking baby, Mom. Just the hair looks like Buffalo Bill, and I said it as a joke, Mom. That's right, seven pounds six ounces. . . ."

There were five other booths, all empty, all open for calls to anyplace on earth. Heinz longed to hurry into one of them breathlessly, and tell the marvelous news. But there was no one to call, no one waiting for the news.

But Heinz still beamed, and he strode across the street and into a quiet tavern there. In the dank twilight there were only two men, tete-a-tete, the bartender and Mr. Sousa.

"Yes sir, what'll it be?"

"I'd like to buy you and Mr. Sousa a drink," said Heinz with a heartiness strange to him. "I'd like the best brandy you've got. My wife just had a baby!"

"That so?" said the bartender with polite interest. "Five pounds nine ounces," said Heinz.

"Huh," said the bartender. "What do you know."

"Netman," said Sousa, "wha'dja get?"

"Boy," said Heinz proudly.

"Never knew it to fail," said Sousa bitterly. "It's the little guys, all the time the little guys."

"Boy, girl," said Heinz, "it's all the same, just as long as it lives. Over there in the hospital, they're too close to it to see the wonder of it. A miracle over and over again—the world made new."

"Wait'll you've racked up seven, Netman," said Sousa. "*Then* you come back and tell me about the miracle."

"You got seven?" said the bartender. "I'm one up on you. I got eight." He poured three drinks.

"Far as I'm concerned," said Sousa, "you can have the championship."

Heinz lifted his glass. "Here's long life and great skill and much happiness to—to Peter Karl Knechtmann." He breathed quickly, excited by the decision.

"*There's* a handle to take ahold of," said Sousa. "You'd think the kid weighed two hundred pounds."

"Peter is the name of a famous surgeon," said Heinz, "the boy's great-uncle, dead now. Karl was my father's name."

"Here's to Pete K. Netman," said Sousa, with a cursory salute.

"Pete," said the bartender, drinking.

"And here's to *your* little girl—the new one," said Heinz. Sousa sighed and smiled wearily. "Here's to her. God bless her."

"And now, *I'll* propose a toast," said the bartender, hammering on the bar with his fist. "On your feet, gentlemen. Up, up, everybody up."

Heinz stood, and held his glass high, ready for the next step in camaraderie, a toast to the whole human race, of which the Knechtmanns were still a part.

"Here's to the White Sox!" roared the bartender. "Minoso, Fox, Mele," said Sousa.

"Fain, Lollar, Rivera!" said the bartender. He turned to Heinz. "Drink up, boy! The White Sox! Don't tell me you're a Cub fan."

"No," said Heinz, disappointed. "No—I don't follow baseball, I'm afraid." The other two men seemed to be sinking away from him. "I haven't been able to think about much but the baby."

The bartender at once turned his full attention to Sousa. "Look," he said intensely, "they take Fain off of first, and put him at third, and give Pierce first. Then move Minoso in from left field to shortstop. See what I'm doing?"

"Yep, yep," said Sousa eagerly.

"And then we take that no-good Carrasquel and . . ."

Heinz was all alone again, with twenty feet of bar between him and the other two men. It might as well have been a continent.

He finished his drink without pleasure, and left quietly.

At the railroad station, where he waited for a local train to take him home to the South Side, Heinz's glow returned again as he saw a co-worker at the dry-cleaning plant walk in with a girl. They were laughing and had their arms around each other's waist.

"Harry," said Heinz, hurrying toward them. "Guess what, Harry. Guess what just happened." He grinned broadly.

Harry, a tall, dapper, snub-nosed young man, looked down at Heinz with mild surprise. "Oh—hello, Heinz. What's up, boy?"

The girl looked on in perplexity, as though asking why they should be accosted at such an odd hour by such an odd person. Heinz avoided her slightly derisive eyes.

"A baby, Harry. My wife just had a boy."

"Oh," said Harry. He extended his hand. "Well, congratulations." The hand was limp. "I think that's swell, Heinz, perfectly swell." He withdrew his hand and waited for Heinz to say something else.

"Yes, yes—just about an hour ago," said Heinz. "Five pounds nine ounces. I've never been happier in my life."

"Well, I think it's perfectly swell, Heinz. You should be happy."

"Yes, indeed," said the girl.

There was a long silence, with all three shifting from one foot to the other.

"Really good news," said Harry at last.

"Yes, well," said Heinz quickly, "well, that's all I had to tell you."

"Thanks," said Harry. "Glad to hear about it." There was another uneasy silence.

"See you at work," said Heinz, and strode jauntily back to his bench, but with his reddened neck betraying how foolish he felt.

The girl giggled.

Back home in his small apartment, at two in the morning, Heinz talked to himself, to the empty bassinet, and to the bed.

He talked in German, a language he had sworn never to use again.

"They don't care," said Heinz. "They're all too busy, busy, busy to notice life, to feel anything about it. A baby is born." He shrugged. "What could be duller? Who would be so stupid as to talk about it, to think there was anything important or interesting about it?"

He opened a window on the summer night, and looked out at the moonlit canyon of gray wooden porches and garbage cans. "There are too many of us, and we are all too far apart," said Heinz. "Another Knechtmann is born, another O'Leary, another Sousa. Who cares? Why should anyone care? What difference does it make? None."

He lay down in his clothes on the unmade bed, and, with a rattling sigh, went to sleep.

He awoke at six, as always. He drank a cup of coffee, and with a wry sense of anonymity, he jostled and was jostled aboard the downtown train. His face showed no emotion. It was like all the other faces, seemingly incapable of surprise or wonder, joy or anger.

He walked across town to the hospital with the same detachment, a gray, uninteresting man, a part of the city.

In the hospital, he was as purposeful and calm as the doctors and nurses bustling about him. When he was led into the ward where Avchen slept behind white screens, he felt only what he had always felt in her presence—love and aching awe and gratitude for her.

"You go ahead and wake her gently, Mr. Netman," said the nurse.

"Avchen—" He touched her on her white-gowned shoulder. "Avchen. Are you all right, Avchen?"

"Mmmmmmmmmmm?" murmured Avchen. Her eyes opened to narrow slits. "Heinz. Hello, Heinz."

"Sweetheart, are you all right?"

"Yes, yes," she whispered. "I'm fine. How is the baby, Heinz?"

"Perfect. Perfect, Avchen."

"They couldn't kill us, could they, Heinz?"

"No."

"And here we are, alive as we can be."

"Yes."

"The baby, Heinz—" She opened her dark eyes wide. "It's the most wonderful thing that ever happened, isn't it?"

"Yes," said Heinz.

The Name

Aharon Megged

Translated from the Hebrew by Minna Givton
Grandfather Zisskind lived in a little house in a southern sub-
urb of the town. About once a month, on a Saturday afternoon,
his granddaughter Raya and her young husband Yehuda would
go and pay him a visit.

Raya would give three cautious knocks on the door (an agreed
signal between herself and her grandfather ever since her childhood, when he had lived in their house together with the whole
family) and they would wait for the door to be opened. "Now
he's getting up," Raya would whisper to Yehuda, her face glowing, when the sound of her grandfather's slippers was heard from
within, shuffling across the room. Another moment, and the key
would be turned and the door opened.

"Come in," he would say somewhat absently, still buttoning
up his trousers, with the rheum of sleep in his eyes. Although it
was very hot he wore a yellow winter vest with long sleeves, from
which his wrists stuck out—white, thin, delicate as a girl's, as was
his bare neck with its taut skin.

After Raya and Yehuda had sat down at the table, which was
covered with a white cloth showing signs of the meal he had
eaten alone—crumbs from the Sabbath loaf, a plate with meat
leavings, a glass containing some grape pips, a number of jars
and so on—he would smooth the crumpled pillows, spread a
cover over the narrow bed and tidy up. It was a small room, and
its obvious disorder aroused pity for the old man's helplessness
in running his home. In the corner was a shelf with two sooty
kerosene burners, a kettle and two or three saucepans, and next

to it a basin containing plates, knives and forks. In another corner was a stand holding books with thick leather bindings, leaning and lying on each other. Some of his clothes hung over the backs of the chairs. An ancient walnut cupboard with an empty buffet stood exactly opposite the door. On the wall hung a clock which had long since stopped.

"We ought to make Grandfather a present of a clock," Raya would say to Yehuda as she surveyed the room and her glance lighted on the clock; but every time the matter slipped her memory. She loved her grandfather, with his pointed white silky beard, his tranquil face from which a kind of holy radiance emanated, his quiet, soft voice which seemed to have been made only for uttering words of sublime wisdom. She also respected him for his pride, which had led him to move out of her mother's house and live by himself, accepting the hardship and trouble and the affliction of loneliness in his old age. There had been a bitter quarrel between him and his daughter. After Raya's father had died, the house had lost its grandeur and shed the trappings of wealth. Some of the antique furniture which they had retained—along with some crystalware and jewels, the dim lustre of memories from the days of plenty in their native city—had been sold, and Rachel, Raya's mother, had been compelled to support the home by working as a dentist's nurse. Grandfather Zisskind, who had been supported by the family ever since he came to the country, wished to hand over to his daughter his small capital, which was deposited in a bank. She was not willing to accept it. She was stubborn and proud like him. Then, after a prolonged quarrel and several weeks of not speaking to each other, he took some of the things in his room and the broken clock and went to live alone. That had been about four years ago. Now Rachel would come to him once or twice a week, bringing with her a bag full of provisions, to clean the room and cook some meals for him. He was no longer interested in expenses and did not even ask about them, as though they were of no more concern to him.

"And now . . . what can I offer you?" Grandfather Zisskind

would ask when he considered the room ready to receive guests.

"There's no need to offer us anything, Grandfather; we didn't come for that," Raya would answer crossly.

But protests were of no avail. Her grandfather would take out a jar of fermenting preserves and put it on the table, then grapes and plums, biscuits and two glasses of strong tea, forcing them to eat. Raya would taste a little of this and that just to please the old man, while Yehuda, for whom all these visits were unavoidable torment, the very sight of the dishes arousing his disgust, would secretly indicate to her by pulling a sour face that he just couldn't touch the preserves. She would smile at him placatingly, stroking his knee. But Grandfather insisted, so he would have to taste at least a teaspoonful of the sweet and nauseating stuff.

Afterwards Grandfather would ask about all kinds of things. Raya did her best to make the conversation pleasant, in order to relieve Yehuda's boredom. Finally would come what Yehuda dreaded most of all and on account of which he had resolved more than once to refrain from these visits. Grandfather Zisskind would rise, take his chair and place it next to the wall, get up on it carefully, holding on to the back so as not to fall, open the clock and take out a cloth bag with a black cord tied around it. Then he would shut the clock, get off the chair, put it back in its place, sit down on it, undo the cord, take out of the cloth wrapping a bundle of sheets of paper, lay them in front of Yehuda and say:

"I would like you to read this."

"Grandfather," Raya would rush to Yehuda's rescue, "but he's already read it at least ten times. . . ."

But Grandfather Zisskind would pretend not to hear and would not reply, so Yehuda was compelled each time to read there and then that same essay, spread over eight, long sheets in a large, somewhat shaky handwriting, which he almost knew by heart. It was a lament for Grandfather's native town in the Ukraine which had been destroyed by the Germans, and all its Jews slaughtered. When he had finished, Grandfather would take the sheets out of his hand, fold them, sigh and say:

"And nothing of all this is left. Dust and ashes. Not even a tombstone to bear witness. Imagine, of a community of twenty thousand Jews not even one survived to tell how it happened. . . . Not a trace."

Then out of the same cloth bag, which contained various letters and envelopes, he would draw a photograph of his grandson Mendele, who had been twelve years old when he was killed; the only son of his son Ossip, chief engineer in a large chemical factory. He would show it to Yehuda and say:

"He was a genius. Just imagine, when he was only eleven he had already finished his studies at the Conservatory, won a scholarship from the Government and was considered an outstanding violinist. A genius! Look at that forehead . . ." And after he had put the photograph back he would sigh and repeat "Not a trace."

A strained silence of commiseration would descend on Raya and Yehuda, who had already heard these same things many times over and no longer felt anything when they were repeated. And as he wound the cord round the bag the old man would muse: "And Ossip was also a prodigy. As a boy he knew Hebrew well, and could recite Bialik's poems by heart. He studied by himself. He read endlessly, Gnessin, Frug, Bershadsky . . . You didn't know Bershadsky; he was a good writer . . . . He had a warm heart, Ossip had. He didn't mix in politics, he wasn't even a Zionist, but even when they promoted him there he didn't forget that he was a Jew. . . . He called his son Mendele, of all names, after his dead brother, even though it was surely not easy to have a name like that among the Russians. . . . Yes, he had a warm Jewish heart. . . ."

He would turn to Yehuda as he spoke, since in Raya he always saw the child who used to sit on his knee listening to his stories, and for him she had never grown up, while he regarded Yehuda as an educated man who could understand someone else, especially inasmuch as Yehuda held a government job.

Raya remembered how the change had come about in her grandfather. When the war was over he was still sustained by uncertainty and hoped for some news of his son, for it was known that very many had succeeded in escaping eastwards. Wearily he would visit all those who had once lived in his town, but none of them had received any sign of life from relatives. Nevertheless he continued to hope, for Ossip's important position might have helped to save him. Then Raya came home one evening and saw him sitting on the floor with a rent in his jacket. In the house they spoke in whispers, and her mother's eyes were red with weeping. She, too, had wept at Grandfather's sorrow, at the sight of his stricken face, at the oppressive quiet in the rooms. For many weeks afterwards it was as if he had imposed silence on himself. He would sit at his table from morning to night, reading and re-reading old letters, studying family photographs by the hour as he brought them close to his shortsighted eyes, or leaning backwards on his chair, motionless, his hand touching the edge of the table and his eyes staring through the window in front of him, into the distance, as if he had turned to stone. He was no longer the same talkative, wise and humorous grandfather who interested himself in the house, asked what his granddaughter was doing, instructed her, tested her knowledge, proving boastfully like a child that he knew more than her teachers. Now he seemed to cut himself off from the world and entrench himself in his thoughts and his memories, which none of the household could penetrate. Later, a strange perversity had taken hold of him which was hard to tolerate. He would insist that his meals be served at his table, apart, that no one should enter his room without knocking at the door, or close the shutters of his window against the sun. When any one disobeyed these prohibitions he would flare up and quarrel violently with his daughter. At times it seemed that he hated her.

When Raya's father died, Grandfather Zisskind did not show any signs of grief, and did not even console his daughter. But when the days of mourning were past it was as if he had been restored to new life, and he emerged from his silence. Yet he did not speak of his son-in-law, nor of his son Ossip, but only of his grandson Mendele. Often during the day he would mention the boy by name as if he were alive, and speak of him familiarly, although he had seen him only in photographs—as though deliberating aloud and turning the matter over, he would talk of how Mendele ought to be brought up. It was hardest of all when he started criticizing his son and his son's wife for not having foreseen the impending disaster, for not having rushed the boy away to a safe place, not having hidden him with non-Jews, not having tried to get him to the Land of Israel in good time. There was no logic in what he said; this would so infuriate Rachel that she would burst out with, "Oh, do stop! Stop it! I'll go out of my mind with your foolish nonsense!" She would rise from her seat in anger, withdraw to her room, and afterwards, when she had calmed down, would say to Raya, "Sclerosis, apparently. Loss of memory. He no longer knows what he's talking about."

One day—Raya would never forget this—she and her mother saw that Grandfather was wearing his best suit, the black one, and under it a gleaming white shirt; his shoes were polished, and he had a hat on. He had not worn these clothes for many months, and the family was dismayed to see him. They thought that he had lost his mind. "What holiday is it today?" her mother asked. "Really, don't you know?" asked her grandfather. "Today is Mendele's birthday!" Her mother burst out crying. She too began to cry and ran out of the house.

After that, Grandfather Zisskind went to live alone. His mind, apparently, had become settled, except that he would frequently forget things which had occurred a day or two before, though he clearly remembered, down to the smallest detail, things which had happened in his town and to his family more than thirty years ago. Raya would go and visit him, at first with her mother and, after her marriage, with Yehuda. What bothered them was that they were compelled to listen to his talk about Mendele his grandson, and to read that same lament for his native town which had been destroyed.

Whenever Rachel happened to come there during their visit,

she would scold Grandfather rudely. "Stop bothering them with your masterpiece," she would say, and herself remove the papers from the table and put them back in their bag. "If you want them to keep on visiting you, don't talk to them about the dead. Talk about the living. They're young people and they have no mind for such things." And as they left his room together she would say, turning to Yehuda in order to placate him, "Don't be surprised at him. Grandfather's already old. Over seventy. Loss of memory."

When Raya was seven months pregnant, Grandfather Zisskind had in his absent-mindedness not yet noticed it. But Rachel could no longer refrain from letting him share her joy and hope, and told him that a great-grandchild would soon be born to him. One evening the door of Raya and Yehuda's flat opened, and Grandfather himself stood on the threshold in his holiday clothes, just as on the day of Mendele's birthday. This was the first time he had visited them at home, and Raya was so surprised that she hugged and kissed him as she had not done since she was a child. His face shone, his eyes sparkled with the same intelligent and mischievous light they had in those far-off days before the calamity. When he entered he walked briskly through the rooms, giving his opinion on the furniture and its arrangement, and joking about everything around him. He was so pleasant that Raya and Yehuda could not stop laughing all the time he was speaking. He gave no indication that he knew what was about to take place, and for the first time in many months he did not mention Mendele.

"Ah, you naughty children," he said, "is this how you treat Grandfather? Why didn't you tell me you had such a nice place?"

"How many times have I invited you here, Grandfather?" asked Raya.

"Invited me? You ought to have *brought* me here, dragged me by force!"

"I wanted to do that too, but you refused."

"Well, I thought that you lived in some dark den, and I have a den of my own. Never mind, I forgive you."

And when he took leave of them he said:

"Don't bother to come to me. Now that I know where you're to be found and what a palace you have, I'll come to you . . . if you don't throw me out, that is."

Some days later, when Rachel came to their home and they told her about Grandfather's amazing visit, she was not surprised:

"Ah, you don't know what he's been contemplating during all these days, ever since I told him that you're about to have a child . . . He has one wish—that if it's a son, it should be named . . . after his grandson."

"Mendele?" exclaimed Raya, and involuntarily burst into laughter. Yehuda smiled as one smiles at the fond fancies of the old.

"Of course, I told him to put that out of his head," said Rachel, "but you know how obstinate he is. It's some obsession and he won't think of giving it up. Not only that, but he's sure that you'll willingly agree to it, and especially you, Yehuda."

Yehuda shrugged his shoulders. "Crazy. The child would be unhappy all his life."

"But he's not capable of understanding that," said Rachel, and a note of apprehension crept into her voice.

Raya's face grew solemn. "We have already decided on the name," she said. "If it's a girl she'll be called Osnath, and if it's a boy—Ehud." Rachel did not like either.

The matter of the name became almost the sole topic of conversation between Rachel and the young couple when she visited them, and it infused gloom into the air of expectancy which filled the house.

Rachel, midway between the generations, was of two minds about the matter. When she spoke to her father she would scold and contradict him, flinging at him all the arguments she had heard from Raya and Yehuda as though they were her own, but when she spoke to the children she sought to induce them to meet his wishes, and would bring down their anger on herself. As time went on, the question of a name, to which in the beginning she had attached little importance, became a kind of mystery, concealing something preordained, fearful, and pregnant with life and death. The fate of the child itself seemed in doubt. In her innermost heart she prayed that Raya would give birth to a daughter.

"Actually, what's so bad about the name Mendele?" she asked her daughter. "It's a Jewish name like any other."

"What are you talking about, Mother"—Raya rebelled against the thought—"a Ghetto name, ugly, horrible! I wouldn't even be capable of letting it cross my lips. Do you want me to hate my child?"

"Oh, you won't hate your child. At any rate, not because of the name. . . ."

"I should hate him. It's as if you'd told me that my child would be born with a hump! And anyway—why should I? What for?"

"You have to do it for Grandfather's sake," Rachel said quietly, although she knew that she was not speaking the whole truth.

"You know, Mother, that I am ready to do anything for Grandfather," said Raya. "I love him, but I am not ready to sacrifice my child's happiness on account of some superstition of his. What sense is there in it?"

Rachel could not explain the "sense in it" rationally, but in her heart she rebelled against her daughter's logic which had always been hers too and now seemed very superficial, a symptom of the frivolity afflicting the younger generation. Her old father now appeared to her like an ancient tree whose deep roots suck up the mysterious essence of existence, of which neither her daughter nor she herself knew anything. Had it nor been for this argument about the name, she would certainly never have got to meditating on the transmigration of souls and the eternity of life. At night she would wake up covered in cold sweat. Hazily, she recalled frightful scenes of bodies of naked children, beaten and trampled under the jackboots of soldiers, and an awful sense of guilt oppressed her spirit.

Then Rachel came with a proposal for a compromise: that the child should be named Menachem. A Hebrew name, she said;

an Israeli one, by all standards. Many children bore it, and it occurred to nobody to make fun of them. Even Grandfather had
agreed to it after much urging.

Raya refused to listen.

"We have chosen a name, Mother," she said, "which we both
like, and we won't change it for another. Menachem is a name
which reeks of old age, a name which for me is connected with
sad memories and people I don't like. Menachem you could call
only a boy who is short, weak and not good-looking. Let's not
talk about it any more, Mother."

Rachel was silent. She almost despaired of convincing them.
At last she said:

"And are you ready to take the responsibility of going against
Grandfather's wishes?"

Raya's eyes opened wide, and fear was reflected in them:

"Why do you make such a fateful thing of it? You frighten me!"
she said, and burst into tears. She began to fear for her offspring
as one fears the evil eye.

"And perhaps there *is* something fateful in it. . . ." whispered
Rachel without raising her eyes. She flinched at her own words.

"What is it?" insisted Raya, with a frightened look at her mother.

"I don't know . . ." she said. "Perhaps all the same we are bound
to retain the names of the dead . . . in order to leave a remembrance of them. . . ." She was not sure herself whether there was
any truth in what she said or whether it was merely a stupid belief,
but her father's faith was before her, stronger than her own doubts
and her daughter's simple and understandable opposition.

"But I don't always want to remember all those dreadful things,
Mother. It's impossible that this memory should always hang
about this house and that the poor child should bear it!"

Rachel understood. She, too, heard such a cry within her as
she listened to her father talking, sunk in memories of the past.
As if to herself, she said in a whisper:

"I don't know . . . at times it seems to me that it's not Grandfather who's suffering from loss of memory, but ourselves. All of us."

About two weeks before the birth was due, Grandfather Zisskind appeared in Raya and Yehuda's home for the second time. His face was yellow, angry, and the light had faded from his eyes. He greeted them, but did not favor Raya with so much as a glance, as if he had pronounced a ban upon the sinner. Turning to Yehuda he said, "I wish to speak to you."

They went into the inner room. Grandfather sat down on the chair and placed the palm of his hand on the edge of the table, as was his wont, and Yehuda sat, lower than he, on the bed.

"Rachel has told me that you don't want to call the child by my grandchild's name," he said.

"Yes. . . ." said Yehuda diffidently.

"Perhaps you'll explain to me why?" he asked.

"We. . . ." stammered Yehuda, who found it difficult to face the piercing gaze of the old man. "The name simply doesn't appeal to us."

Grandfather was silent. Then he said, "I understand that Mendele doesn't appeal to you. Not a Hebrew name. Granted! But Menachem—what's wrong with Menachem?" It was obvious that he was controlling his feelings with difficulty.

"It's not. . . ." Yehuda knew that there was no use explaining; they were two generations apart in their ideas. "It's not an Israeli name . . . it's from the *Golah*."

"*Golah*," repeated Grandfather. He shook with rage, but somehow he maintained his self-control. Quietly he added, "We all come from the *Golah*. I, and Raya's father and mother. Your father and mother. All of us."

"Yes . . . ." said Yehuda. He resented the fact that he was being dragged into an argument which was distasteful to him, particularly with this old man whose mind was already not quite clear. Only out of respect did he restrain himself from shouting: That's that, and it's done with! . . . "Yes, but we were born in this country," he said aloud; "that's different."

Grandfather Zisskind looked at him contemptuously. Before him he saw a wretched boor, an empty vessel.

"You, that is to say, think that there's something new here," he said, "that everything that was there is past and gone. Dead, without sequel. That you are starting everything anew."

"I didn't say that. I only said that we were born in this country . . ."

"You were born here. Very nice . . ." said Grandfather Zisskind with rising emotion. "So what of it? What's so remarkable about that? In what way are you superior to those who were born *there*? Are you cleverer than they? More cultured? Are you greater than they in Torah or good deeds? Is your blood redder than theirs?" Grandfather Zisskind looked as if he could wring Yehuda's neck.

"I didn't say that either. I said that here it's different . . . ."

Grandfather Zisskind's patience with idle words was exhausted.

"You good-for-nothing!" he burst out in his rage. "What do you know about what was there? What do you know of the *people* that were there? The communities? The cities? What do you know of the *life* they had there?"

"Yes," said Yehuda, his spirit crushed, "but we no longer have any ties with it."

"You have no ties with it?" Grandfather Zisskind bent towards him. His lips quivered in fury. "With what . . . with what *do* you have ties?"

"We have . . . with this country," said Yehuda and gave an involuntary smile.

"Fool!" Grandfather Zisskind shot at him. "Do you think that people come to a desert and make themselves a nation, eh? That you are the first of some new race? That you're not the son of your father? Not the grandson of your grandfather? Do you want to forget them? Are you ashamed of them for having had a hundred times more culture and education than you have? Why . . . why, everything here"—he included everything around him in the sweep of his arm—"is no more than a puddle of tapwater against the big sea that was there! What have you here? A mixed

multitude! Seventy languages! Seventy distinct groups! Customs?
A way of life? Why, every home here is a nation in itself, with
its own customs and its own names! And with this you have ties,
you say. . . ."

Yehuda lowered his eyes and was silent.

"I'll tell you what ties are," said Grandfather Zisskind "Ties
are remembrance! Do you understand? The Russian is linked
to his people because he remembers his ancestors. He is called
Ivan, his father was called Ivan and his grandfather was called
Ivan, back to the first generation. And no Russian has said: From
today onwards I shall not be called Ivan because my fathers and
my fathers' fathers were called that; I am the first of a new Russian nation which has nothing at all to do with the Ivan. Do you
understand?"

"But what has that got to do with it?" Yehuda protested impatiently. Grandfather Zisskind shook his head at him.

"And you—you're ashamed to give your son the name Mendele
lest it remind you that there were Jews who were called by that
name. You believe that his name should be wiped off the face of
the earth. That not a trace of it should remain. . . ."

He paused, heaved a deep sigh and said:

"O children, children, you don't know what you're doing. . . .
You're finishing off the work which the enemies of Israel began.
They took the bodies away from the world, and you—the name
and the memory. . . . No continuation, no evidence, no memorial
and no name. Not a trace. . . ."

And with that he rose, took his stick and with long strides went
towards the door and left.

The new-born child was a boy and he was named Ehud, and
when he was about a month old, Raya and Yehuda took him in
the carriage to Grandfather's house.

Raya gave three cautious knocks on the door, and when she
heard a rustle inside she could also hear the beating of her anxious
heart. Since the birth of the child Grandfather had not visited
them even once. "I'm terribly excited," she whispered to Yehuda

with tears in her eyes. Yehuda rocked the carriage and did not reply. He was now indifferent to what the old man might say or do.

The door opened, and on the threshold stood Grandfather Zisskind, his face weary and wrinkled. He seemed to have aged. His eyes were sticky with sleep, and for a moment it seemed as if he did not see the callers.

"Good Sabbath, Grandfather," said Raya with great feeling. It seemed to her now that she loved him more than ever.

Grandfather looked at them as if surprised, and then said absently, "Come in, come in."

"We've brought the baby with us!" said Raya, her face shining, and her glance traveled from Grandfather to the infant sleeping in the carriage.

"Come in, come in," repeated Grandfather Zisskind in a tired voice. "Sit down," he said as he removed his clothes from the chair and turned to tidy the disordered bedclothes.

Yehuda stood the carriage by the wall and whispered to Raya, "It's stifling for him here." Raya opened the window wide.

"You haven't seen our baby yet, Grandfather!" she said with a sad smile.

"Sit down, sit down," said Grandfather, shuffling over to the shelf, from which he took the jar of preserves and the biscuit tin, putting them on the table.

"There's no need, Grandfather, really there's no need for it. We didn't come for that," said Raya.

"Only a little something. I have nothing to offer you today. . . ." said Grandfather in a dull, broken voice. He took the kettle off the kerosene burner and poured out two glasses of tea which he placed before them. Then he too sat down, said "Drink, drink," and softly tapped his fingers on the table.

"I haven't seen Mother for several days now," he said at last.

"She's busy . . ." said Raya in a low voice, without raising her eyes to him. "She helps me a lot with the baby. . . ."

Grandfather Zisskind looked at his pale, knotted and veined

hands lying helplessly on the table; then he stretched out one of them and said to Raya, "Why don't you drink? The tea will get cold."

Raya drew up to the table and sipped the tea.

"And you—what are you doing now?" he asked Yehuda.

"Working as usual," said Yehuda, and added with a laugh, "I play with the baby when there's time."

Grandfather again looked down at his hands, the long thin fingers of which shook with the palsy of old age.

"Take some of the preserves," he said to Yehuda, indicating the jar with a shaking finger. "It's very good." Yehuda dipped the spoon in the jar and put it to his mouth.

There was a deep silence. It seemed to last a very long time. Grandfather Zisskind's fingers gave little quivers on the white tablecloth. It was hot in the room, and the buzzing of a fly could be heard.

Suddenly the baby burst out crying, and Raya started from her seat and hastened to quiet him. She rocked the carriage and crooned, "Quiet, child, quiet, quiet. . . ." Even after he had quieted down she went on rocking the carriage back and forth.

Grandfather Zisskind raised his head and said to Yehuda in a whisper:

"You think it was impossible to save him . . . it was possible. They had many friends. Ossip himself wrote to me about it. The manager of the factory had a high opinion of him. The whole town knew them and loved them. . . . How is it they didn't think of it . . . ?" he said, touching his forehead with the palm of his hand. "After all, they knew that the Germans were approaching. . . . It was still possible to do something. . . ." He stopped a moment and then added, "Imagine that a boy of eleven had already finished his studies at the Conservatory—wild beasts!" He suddenly opened eyes filled with terror. "Wild beasts! To take little children and put them into wagons and deport them. . . ."

When Raya returned and sat down at the table, he stopped and became silent, and only a heavy sigh escaped from deep within him.

Again there was a prolonged silence, and as it grew heavier Raya felt the oppressive weight on her bosom increasing till it could no longer be contained. Grandfather sat at the table tapping his thin fingers, and alongside the wall the infant lay in his carriage; it was as if a chasm gaped between a world which was passing and a world that was born. It was no longer a single line to the fourth generation. The aged father did not recognize the great-grandchild whose life would be no memorial.

Grandfather Zisskind got up, took his chair and pulled it up to the clock. He climbed on to it to take out his documents.

Raya could no longer stand the oppressive atmosphere.

"Let's go," she said to Yehuda in a choked voice.

"Yes, we must go," said Yehuda, and rose from his seat. "We have to go," he said loudly as he turned to the old man.

Grandfather Zisskind held the key of the clock for a moment more, then he let his hand fall, grasped the back of the chair and got down.

"You have to go. . . ." he said with a tortured grimace. He spread his arms out helplessly and accompanied them to the doorway.

When the door had closed behind them the tears flowed from Raya's eyes. She bent over the carriage and pressed her lips to the baby's chest. At that moment it seemed to her that he was in need of pity and of great love, as though he were alone, an orphan in the world.

About the Authors

Ilse Aichinger was born to a Jewish mother and a non-Jewish father in Vienna in 1921. Her parents were divorced in 1926, and at first glance her novel, *Herod's Children*, originally published in 1948 as *Die größere Hoffnung* and awarded the Austrian State Prize for Literature, seems to be an autobiographical memoir; however, the novel inverts Aichinger's actual experience. Ilse deliberately stayed in Austria to protect her mother, and the two survived the war together, although many family members were murdered. Aichinger was the recipient of the Georg Trakl Prize in 1979, the Franz Kafka Prize in 1983, and the *Großen Öster-reichischen Staatspreis für Literature* in 1995. She lives in Bavaria.

Aharon Appelfeld was born in 1932 in Czernowitz, Romania, and at the age of eight, he witnessed the murder of his mother by the Nazis; his father was sent to a labor camp. Appelfeld escaped from the camp and wandered alone in the forests for three years, until he was discovered by the liberating forces of the Soviet Army and worked for them as a kitchen boy. In 1946, at the age of 14, he immigrated to Palestine and later fought in Israel's War of Independence. In 1960, he discovered that his father had survived and was also living in Israel. His more than 20 books, including internationally acclaimed novels, short stories, and essays, have been translated into 27 languages and explore the psychological, moral, and spiritual dimensions of the Holocaust. "I don't like to use too many words. For me, the unsaid is far more important than the said," Appelfeld told *Publishers Weekly* in a 1998 interview.

Clara Asscher-Pinkhof was born in Amsterdam in 1896 and married Avraham Asscher, the chief rabbi of Groningen, in 1919. She gave birth to six children before his death in 1926. After he died, in order to support her large family she gave readings, taught university-level courses, and wrote children's books. After the German occupation of Holland in 1940 she moved to Amsterdam, where she worked as a teacher in the schools that had been set up for Jewish children and as a volunteer assistant in the *Hollandse Schouwburg*, a Dutch theater used as a deportation center, until her deportation in May 1943. Sent first to Westerbork, she continued to work by helping in the girls' dormitory and in the nursery in the children's barrack until she was sent to Bergen-Belsen. There, in 1944, she was exchanged for German prisoners and sent to Palestine, where her daughter had lived since 1939. She resumed her writing, and *Star Children*, her collection of 68 short stories about Dutch children during the Holocaust, was published in 1946. Clara Asscher-Pinkhof died in Israel in 1984.

Rachmil Bryks was born in Skarżysko Kamienna (central Poland) in 1912. As a child he moved with his parents to Lodz. Following the outbreak of the war, Bryks tried to get to Warsaw but could not, and so he returned to Lodz. There he was arrested and sent to a prisoner-of-war camp near Kraków. After being released, he returned to Lodz, where he lived until the liquidation of the ghetto during the last days of August 1944, when he was deported to Auschwitz. From there he was sent to various labor camps in Germany; he was released on May 2, 1945. To improve his health, he was sent to Stockholm, where he worked with survivors and resumed his writing. Until his immigration to the United States in March 1949, he served as the YIVO (*Yiddisher visnshaftlekher institute*, The Institute for Jewish Research) representative in Sweden. Bryks's last book, published in his lifetime, was *Di vos zaynen nisht geblibn* [Those who didn't survive] (1972, New York and Tel Aviv), in which he described Jewish life in his home town of Skarżysko, from where his parents and other family members were sent to their death. Rachmil Bryks died in New York on October 2, 1974.

Ida Fink was born in Zbaraz, Poland, in 1921. She studied music in Lvov, but the war ended her studies. She escaped from the Zbaraz Ghetto in 1942 and lived on false papers, masquerading as a farm laborer until the war ended. In 1957 she made *aliyah* with her husband and daughter and lives in Tel Aviv. Her works, all written in Polish, include *A Scrap of Time and Other Stories* (1987), *The Journey* (1990), and *Traces* (1996). Her haunting, shattering stories earned her the Anne Frank Prize in 1985 and the Yad Vashem Prize in 1995.

Bernard Gotfryd, a native of Radom, Poland, was a teenager when the Nazis occupied Poland. Before his mother was deported, she sent her two sons into hiding with the mandate to survive and bear witness. Though his father and brother were later deported to the Szkolna labor camp, young Gotfryd found protection through his employment in a series of German-owned photography shops. He remained in Radom, working with the Polish underground, until the ghetto was liquidated in 1943. Deported to Maidanek, and the following year to Mauthausen, he spent time in six concentration camps. He was liberated from Gusen II on May 5, 1945, by Americans and was soon reunited with his brother and sister. Two years later, he immigrated to the United States, where he served in the U.S. Army Signal Corps. In 1957, he joined the staff of *Newsweek* magazine. When a *Newsweek* assignment sent him to Poland, he began to revisit the war years as a writer. Returning to his native land inspired him to write his memoirs; he realized that he had "forgotten nothing," and, indeed, he narrates his experiences with immediacy and detail, as if no time at all had elapsed. *Anton the Dove Fancier and Other Tales of the Holocaust* was published first in 1990 and in expanded form in 2000 (Johns Hopkins University Press). Bernard Gotfryd lives in Forest Hills, New York.

Albert Halper was born in Chicago in 1904. After graduating from high school and working at a number of jobs, Halper moved to New York City in 1929 with the goal of becoming a writer. His first novel, *Union Square*, was published in 1931 and became a Literary Guild selection. Halper followed this novel with a series of books based on his life in Chicago, notably a book of short stories, *On the Shore* (1934), and the novels *The Foundry*

(1934), *The Chute* (1937), *Sons of the Fathers* (1940), and *The Little People* (1942), along with two collections of essays. Concerned with class struggles, Halper's stories reflect the daily lives of everyday people during the Twenties and Thirties with sympathy and sensitivity. His stories read like social history; Halper was committed to depicting the truth of life as he saw it. Halper died in New York in 1984.

Aharon Megged was born in 1920 in Poland, and his family immigrated to Palestine in 1926. He began publishing in 1938 and is a recipient of many literary awards. In his writings, Megged creates overviews of society at large by focusing on the relationships between individuals. He was one of the first Israeli artists to examine the subject of post-Holocaust dynamics and Israel's attitude to the Holocaust. As a teenager he knew little about the Eastern European Jewish communities. Yet, in contrast to his peers, who viewed Diaspora Jews with contempt, he felt a deep kinship to his European brethren and believed that his contemporaries' attitude was superficial, that a secular Israeli culture, severed from the traditional roots of Jewish culture, including literature, folklore, and art, would lead to a shallow and ignorant society. While working in the port of Haifa, he met Holocaust refugees who spoke Yiddish and described the horrors they encountered. These survivors helped Megged understand the injustice and pain Israeli society was inflicting on those who had suffered enough. His work reflects his concern with the "new" Israelis, *sabras* (those who were born in Israel), and their attempts to discard the cultural heritage of the Diaspora.

Zofia Nalkowska was born in 1884 to avant-garde and scholarly parents. A resident of Warsaw, where she lived throughout the occupation, she was a prolific writer of novels, plays, stories, and essays, and held the distinction of being the first woman in the Polish Academy of Literature. She was also a member of the Commission for the Investigation of War Crimes in Auschwitz, established in the immediate aftermath of the war. Her collections, *Wartime Diaries* (1970) and *Medallions* (1946, 2000), detail her experiences and observations of her five years in Nazi-occupied Warsaw, give voice to her need to bear witness, and serve as both historical record and vivid testimony. Zofia Nalkowska died in Warsaw in 1954.

Sara Nomberg-Przytyk was born into a prominent Hasidic family in Lublin, Poland, in 1915. When the Germans invaded Poland in 1939, she fled east to Bialystok. She was incarcerated in the Bialystok Ghetto and deported from there in 1943 to Stutthof concentration camp; from there she was sent to Auschwitz. She survived, married in 1946, and worked as a journalist in Poland until 1968, when she immigrated to Israel where she lived for seven years before finally settling in Canada. She died in 2001.

Cynthia Ozick was born in 1928 in New York City. Her Russian immigrant parents moved the family to the Bronx, bringing with them their Lithuanian Jewish traditions, filled with skepticism, rationalism, and antimysticism. Ozick suffered the taunts and brickbats of neighborhood Christian children. However, books, particularly fairy tales, enriched her imagination. Her uncle, a respected poet, paved the way for Ozick to embark on writing as a career, and her M.A. thesis on Henry James solidified her decision to become a writer. Her stature grew quickly. Three of her stories won first prize in the O. Henry competition; five were chosen for republishing in *Best American Short Stories*. Ozick produced *The Puttermesser Papers* in 1997; in 1980, writing for the *New Yorker*, Ozick began to write about the Holocaust. In recent years, she has returned to essays and prose fiction, continuing her "task to invent civilization," opposing human nature's tendency to resort to terror.

Susan Prinz Shear is a child of Holocaust survivors and a former teacher who today teaches about the Holocaust. In 1994, quite by accident, Susan uncovered 500 letters written by her mother's family as they tried to escape from Nazi Germany. Using letters from the collection, as well as photographs and other documents, Susan developed a workshop recounting the family story and created a curriculum entitled *No Way Out: Letters and Lessons of the Holocaust* and *No Way Out: Readers' Theater.* Susan is currently working on a script of *No Way Out* for production as a full-length play.

Isaiah Spiegel was born in Lodz, Poland, in 1906. A teacher of Yiddish language and literature, he was incarcerated in the Lodz Ghetto from May 1940 until the ghetto's liquidation in 1944, when he was taken to Auschwitz and then to a slave labor camp in Saxony. While in the ghetto, Spiegel's daughter starved to death; his wife, his parents, and three sisters perished in the camps. He was only one of very few who survived the ghetto and then Auschwitz. After the war, he went back to Lodz where he resumed work as a teacher and was able to find his buried manuscripts. Reworking these, he also composed other stories as well as poems based on his Holocaust experiences, all of which earned him acclaim and a position as director of the Polish Yiddish Writers Association in 1948. He immigrated to Israel in 1951 where he continued to write in Yiddish about his imprisonments, and in 1972, he was awarded the Itsik Manger Prize. Collectively, Spiegel's stories represent one of the few existing eyewitness accounts of the Lodz Ghetto experience. He died in Israel in 1991.

Kurt Vonnegut, Jr. was born in Indianapolis, Indiana, on November 11, 1922, to third-generation German-American parents. His father and grandfather were architects, but his father lost his job during the Depression, and family finances suffered. Showing great promise as a writer, Kurt served as the editor of his high school's daily newspaper, the first of its kind published in America. Following graduation, he enrolled at Cornell University as a science major. He did not succeed in the sciences but did become a columnist and managing editor of the *Cornell Daily Sun*. However, facing poor grades and possible expulsion, he enlisted in the army in 1943. He was captured by the Germans during the Battle of the Bulge and taken to Dresden, where he was one of seven prisoners of war to survive the 1945 fire bombing of the city. Following the bombing, he was ordered by his captors to gather the victims, who had been burned beyond recognition, for burial. Both events remained seared in his memory and served as the background for *Slaughterhouse-Five*, the novel that represented his antiwar and pacifist views. After the war, he moved to Chicago and eventually to Schenectady, New York, taking a job writing publicity for General Electric. There he published his first piece of fiction, "Report on the Barnhouse Effect," for *Collier's Magazine* in 1950. His writing career flourished, and he moved to Massachusetts, where he remained for decades. He published his first novel, *Player Piano*, in 1952, and his most famous, *Slaughterhouse-Five*, in 1968. He also published extensively in magazines, including "Adam," published in April 1954 in *Cosmopolitan*. He died on April 11, 2007.

Elie Wiesel was born in Sighet, a small Hungarian (alternately Romanian) town in 1928. The third of four children, he was educated in Torah and Talmud, learning Hebrew at age three. His father, Shlomo, helped him to reason, while his mother, Sarah, taught him faith. At age 15, Wiesel was shipped by cattle car with his family to Auschwitz, Poland, and then with his father to Buchenwald, Germany, where he remained until liberation from the camps on April 11, 1945. Both his parents and his younger sister, Tzipora, were killed in the camps. His best known work, the memoir *Night*, recounts his hellish experiences there. He and two older sisters, Hilda and Bea, survived the Nazi regime. After the war, in an orphanage near Paris, he learned French, still his primary written language. He also studied philosophy at the Sorbonne but did not complete his dissertation. During these years, working for an Israeli newspaper in Paris and New York, he vowed silence about his Holocaust experiences. In 1956, however, he published *And the World Remained Silent*, which became the much condensed French and English *Night*. *Dawn* and *Day* soon completed the trilogy. Since the early Sixties, Wiesel has written, almost yearly, fiction and nonfiction books, more than 40 in all. In 1963, he became an American citizen. Forsaking journalism in 1972, the author accepted a professorship at the City College of New York, followed by his 1976 Andrew Mellon University professorship at Boston University, where he taught about the Holocaust. Wiesel now concentrates on literature and philosophy, especially ethics. Institutions of higher learning have granted him 116 honorary degrees. Some 131 awards have been awarded to him, including the humanitarian Congressional Gold Medal in 1985, the Nobel Peace Prize in 1986, the Presidential Medal of Freedom in 1992, and honorary knighthood in England in 2006 for his work in Holocaust education there. In 1980, he became the founding chairman of the United States Holocaust Memorial Council, which led to the creation of the U.S. Holocaust Memorial Museum in Washington, D.C. Today, Wiesel, the confidant of many world leaders, including United States presidents, speaks about the dangers of indifference in the face of evil. With his wife, Marion, he created the Wiesel Foundation for Humanity. Wiesel has become, for many, the chief witness of the Holocaust, a conscience for oppressed people.

About the Cover

"Transports" by Netty Vanderpol
81 hours
1985
25˝ × 22˝

Inspired by the monument in Westerbork, the track symbolizes the beginning of a journey to the frightening unknown—bent back in grief and sorrow, the journey to nowhere.

Although I had done needlepoint for many years, it was not until 1984 that I started my first piece with the Holocaust as a focus. This came when I heard Elie Wiesel urging survivors to bear witness to the evils perpetrated by the Nazis. Mine is the last generation who, by telling our stories, can help people to be more aware of the consequences of evil gone unchecked.

My memories are expressed in a language of line, tone, and texture. The unexpected pairing of thread and art was inspired by my family. In my recollections of my mother, she was always engrossed in some form of needlework, while my father was an avid collector of paintings and drawings that decorated our home. My work reveals the blending of both of their interests, combining cultural and familial influences.

I call my collected works "Every Stitch a Memory." The number of hours I spent completing this piece is listed under the title, emphasizing the endless number of stitches eliciting memories.

Scattered throughout the mostly somber tones of black, gray, and brown are bits of color, symbolizing the wish to hold on to life and hope. While the memories are there, my work helps me to move beyond.

Netty Vanderpol
Boston, MA
October 2007

CPSIA information can be obtained
at www.ICGtesting.com
Printed in the USA
LVOW08s1647240117
522002LV00003B/665/P